D1000176

The West Indian Novel
and its Background

The West Indian Novel and its Background

by

KENNETH RAMCHAND

Lecturer in English,
University of the West Indies

FABER AND FABER

London

First published in 1970
by Faber and Faber Limited
3 Queen Square London WC1
Reprinted 1971
Printed in Great Britain by
Latimer Trend & Co Ltd Plymouth

ISBN 0 571 08825 2

For
MY WIFE
MY MOTHER
and to
EDINBURGH UNIVERSITY

Contents

Contents

Author's Preface and Acknowledgements

This book is a version of a thesis presented at the University of Edinburgh. The late Professor John Butt gave his encouragement at a time when the subject of this study was not yet in fashion. I am also grateful to the University for financial assistance at a particularly difficult time; and to the Commonwealth Scholarship Commission in the United Kingdom who financed part of the research. To my colleagues and students at Edinburgh I owe much that cannot be specified. Paul Edwards has made it impossible for me to forget that life can be as interesting and enjoyable as literature.

During the period of conversion from thesis to book there was great support from colleagues in the Faculty of Humanities at the University of Kent, and financial assistance through the Dean. To Brinsley Samaroo who took time away from his own researches to comb the manuscript for errors and infelicities I am also grateful.

It is a pleasure to record my gratitude to the staff of the National Library of Scotland for their courtesy and helpfulness over a long period; thanks are due also to the British Museum and the Libraries of the University of the West Indies, the University of Guyana, and the Institute of Jamaica.

I am conscious of many deficiencies in this book. Some of these arise from the difficulty of trying to see the West Indian novel in its social and cultural context while offering a critique in more or less pure literary terms. The decision not to do a series of chapters on individual authors has led to a number of writers not being discussed as much as was perhaps due. But the greatest sin has been one of omission: there is enough relevant and interesting material left to justify the establishment of a School of Caribbean Studies at the University of the West Indies.

I can only hope that the present work will play a useful part in the years of discovery, evaluation and re-orientation ahead in the West Indies.

Introduction

Introduction

The concern in this book is with prose fiction, mainly novels, written by people who were born or who grew up in the West Indies—the formerly British islands in the Caribbean Sea and the South American mainland territory now known as Guyana. The literary works to be approached usually have a West Indian setting and contain fictional characters and situations whose social correlates are immediately recognizable as West Indian. The books have all been written in the twentieth century; and their native West Indian authors include descendants of Europeans, descendants of African slaves, descendants of indentured labourers from India, and various mixtures from these. Thus formally, to begin with, this body of fiction can be distinguished from other works written in English and drawing upon West Indian raw material.

For although there is a long and still active tradition of liberal and exotic writing in English about the Negro and about the West Indies,[1] the earliest known work of West Indian prose fiction as defined above appeared in 1903. This was Tom Redcam's *Becka's Buckra Baby* which was published in Jamaica as Number 1 of *The All Jamaica Library*. Between 1903 and June 1967, at least 162 works of prose fiction have been produced by fifty-six writers from six West Indian territories.[2] But the emphasis of a leading West Indian novelist in 1960 is just: 'The West Indian novel, by which I mean the novel written by the West Indian about the West Indian reality is hardly twenty years old.'[3] Literary criticism has to

[1] See Wylie Sypher, *Guinea's Captive Kings* (University of North Carolina Press, 1942); Eldred Jones, *Othello's Countrymen* (1965); and N. Verrle McCullough, *The Negro in English Literature* (1962).
[2] See *Appendix One* for an Author bibliography. *Appendix Two* is a Year by Year bibliography that also gives places of first publication.
[3] George Lamming, *The Pleasures of Exile* (1960), p. 68.

cope with a situation in which most of the writers are still alive, their works not yet complete.

Matters are more complicated than that. 'Living in a borrowed culture, the West Indian, more than most, needs writers to tell him who he is and where he stands.' So writes V. S. Naipaul in *The Middle Passage* (1962). It is not unique for novelists to be regarded as having something special to say to their societies. But the West Indian novelists apply themselves with unusual urgency and unanimity to an analysis and interpretation of their society's ills, including the social and economic deprivation of the majority; the pervasive consciousness of race and colour; the cynicism and uncertainty of the native bourgeoisie in power after independence; the lack of a history to be proud of; and the absence of traditional or settled values. If, however, the social consciousness of writers from the islands draws attention to itself as a peculiarly interesting matter, it is worth suggesting at once that this social consciousness is not class-consciousness. This is one point at which the West Indian writer naturally departs from the nineteenth-century English novel with which he is most familiar. Nor is the social consciousness concerned with consolidating or flattering particular groups as V. S. Naipaul declares in *The Middle Passage*.[1] Most West Indian novelists write about the whole society.

The preoccupation of West Indian writers with what some see as the chaos, others as the open possibilities of their society goes along with an interest in the previously neglected person: 'Unlike the previous governments and departments of educators, unlike the businessman importing commodities, the West Indian novelist did not look out across the sea to another source. He looked in and down at what had traditionally been ignored. For the first time, the West Indian peasant becomes other than a cheap source of labour. He became through the novelist's eye a living existence, living in silence and joy and fear, involved in riot and carnival. It is the West Indian novel that has restored the West Indian peasant to his true and original status of personality.'[2] For the first time in

---

[1] *The Middle Passage*, p. 68.
[2] George Lamming, *The Pleasures of Exile* (1960), pp. 38-9.

Introduction

writing related to the West Indies, the Black characters are not restricted to being peripheral or background figures. To this may be attributed, at least in part, the realistic exuberance with which West Indian writers of the 1930's expressed the life and surroundings of the West Indian peasant.

The challenge of articulating the hitherto obscure person has affected characterization in West Indian novels in other ways. Some writers seek ancestral inspiration in 'African traits' or an 'African personality'. Others, notably Michael Anthony[1] (Trinidad, b. 1932), ignore such imaginary but unimaginative props: Anthony's fidelity to the open consciousness of his youthful protagonists and narrators, his choice of weak characters susceptible to shock and mystery, and his portrayal of the instability of 'character' add up to a genuine exploratory attitude to 'the person'. In a more self-conscious but no less experimental manner, Wilson Harris (Guyana, b. 1921) sees the obscurity of the broken individual in the West Indies as the starting point for a creative inquiry into the question, 'What is man?'

Although West Indian novelists are aware of the main pattern of the nineteenth-century English novel—an analysis of character in relation to the manners and morals operative in a given period —it follows from the formlessness of West Indian society, and the existential position of the individual in it, that such a pattern is not one that seems relevant or comes spontaneously to the writer from the West Indies. This may well be one of the reasons for the higher reputation in Britain than in the West Indies of the Trinidadian V. S. Naipaul (b. 1932), whose deflation of characters by means associated with novels dealing with manners and morals appears to West Indians to be at least extraneous to the same author's expression of the void in colonial society. However this may be, it is worth reminding ourselves that West Indian writers in general are as much interested in society as in character, and that the interest in character is seldom one in behaviour or morals. These distinguishing emphases of West Indian writing are often in the minds of those who describe it as being involved in the

---

[1] For a chronological list of the works of authors mentioned in this section see *Author Bibliography*, *Appendix One*, pp. 293-9.

quest for national and personal identity. Literary criticism has to take account of them too.

In an area of deprivation, longing, and rootlessness, where so many people are inarticulate, the novelist may find himself tempted into passionate documentary, or criticized for not adopting pre-scribed stances. These expectations have a bearing upon the general coolness towards the novels of Michael Anthony, and may be seen in doctrinaire application in George Lamming's comments on his contemporary, John Hearne (Jamaica, b. 1926). Lamming accuses Hearne of being obsessed with 'an agricultural middle class in Jamaica', and of having 'a dread of being identified with the land at peasant level'.[1] Such a charge does little justice to Hearne's probing of the painful gap between personal allegiances and political conflict, and his exploration of love as a positive that comes to be celebrated in *The Land of the Living* (1961) where distressed Negro, displaced Jew, and disorientated female, are seen as equal subjects for love's reclaiming and responsible clasp. Nor do Lamming's remarks suggest the complexity of his own highly political novels which fulfil, at their best, a complex understanding of the artist's responsibility to himself, his society and to 'the community of Man' which is his third world: 'His responsibility to that other world, his third world, will be judged not only by the authenticity and power with which his own private world is presented, but also by the honesty with which he interprets the world of his social relations, his country, that is, for those who have no direct experience of it, but are moved by the power of his speech, his judgement and his good faith.'[2]

It is a strength of West Indian writing, with which criticism must grapple flexibly, that the attitudes of West Indian writers, their equipment as artists, and the social groups to which they give fictional prominence vary widely. If the differences between Lamming and Hearne are suggestive, the *oeuvres* of V. S. Naipaul and Wilson Harris may be used to illustrate the wide range of

[1] *The Pleasures of Exile* (1960), pp. 45–6.
[2] 'The Negro Writer and His World' in *Caribbean Quarterly*, Vol. 5, No. 2 (February 1958).

techniques and the opposite attitudes to 'reality' between which most West Indian writing lies.

Naipaul is the best known of West Indian novelists. The sense of continuity and development in his publications arises from the inventive redeployment of a repertoire of traditional novelistic skills, and a steadily darkening tone as a method of writing fiction becomes increasingly a way of seeing the world. In his first work (but the third published) *Miguel Street* (1959), a collection of stories about the characters of a fictional street, Naipaul's manner of seizing upon an essential defining trait and allowing it to express itself surprisingly (basic lack of change, and surface vitality), his precise observation of gesture and posture, and an uncanny ability to render the inflections of the speaking voice, combine with a near perfect sense of timing to produce an entertaining series of comic sketches. A performer's delight in the animation of his creatures occasionally turns into a shudder of compassion, as in 'The Maternal Instinct', or weakens into near-sentimentality as in 'B. Wordsworth', the story of a poet *manqué*. These staple features of Naipaul's fiction are added to in succeeding works: in *The Mystic Masseur* (1957) and *The Suffrage of Elvira* (1958) he replaces the flat framing of a street by the equally cohering but less easily exhaustible contours of a fictional community modelled from the East Indian presence in Trinidad. Of the three early works, *The Mystic Masseur* is the most interesting. Adopting the device of a mock-biographer quoting lavishly from the masseur's own publications, Naipaul traces the rise of Ganesh Ramsumair from country Indian to colonial politician, G. Ramsay Muir. The work satirizes the fossilized Indian community as well as the larger static Trinidad society in which Ganesh's predominantly fortuitous drift to eminence takes place. While in his first three works, however, Naipaul was, on balance, a popular but ironic entertainer and gentle satirist, his fourth, *A House for Mr. Biswas* (1961) established him as the author of a major twentieth-century novel on the increasingly rare scale of *Middlemarch*, *Anna Karenina* or *The Rainbow*. The three-generation span of the novel gives free play to Naipaul's favourite pattern of authorial stage-setting summary followed by abundantly rendered and partly illustrative epi-

Introduction

sode; and the wide cast of secondary characters allows the author's manner of swift and vivid characterization, enriched by occasional glimpses in depth, to operate with reasonable legitimacy. There are other significant developments. Instead of a vacuous character like Ganesh, the central figure is Mohun Biswas, journalist, visualized in depth as a man aware of the void of his own future and the obscurity of his origin, desperately seeking to make a dent on the world. With the creation of such a centre of interest and involvement as Mr. Biswas, the mock-biographer of *The Mystic Masseur* is replaced by the alternately ironic and caressive tones of an omniscient narrator not always able to remain on the controlling periphery. In his latest work *Mr. Stone and the Knights Companion* (1963), Naipaul's West Indian-nurtured vision of decay and ultimately illusory achievement is sombrely transplanted to an English setting and expressed in the post-retirement marriage and social work of an English bachelor terrified by the approaching end of life.

Naipaul is the most observant and the least metaphysical of West Indian novelists. His works show little sensuous awareness of the natural world. Wilson Harris's novels, on the other hand, grow out of a responsiveness to the brooding landscape and the fabulous fragmented history of his native Guyana. The declaration of the dreaming, half-blinded narrator of *Palace of the Peacock* (1960) might well serve as an epigraph: 'They were an actual stage, a presence, however mythical they seemed to the universal and the spiritual eye. They were as close to me as my ribs, the rivers and the flatland, the mountains and heartland I intimately saw. I could not help cherishing my symbolic map, and my bodily prejudice like a well-known room and house of superstition within which I dwelt. I saw this kingdom of man turned into a colony and battle-ground of spirit, a priceless tempting jewel I dreamed I possessed' (p. 20). Harris's fiction brings imperial/slave history and the aftermath into its field, but the author's way of seeing the world around him and the kind of fiction in which it expresses itself challenge us to see with new eyes.

In 'Tradition and the West Indian Novel',[1] a lecture of 1964,

---

[1] Published in a collection of critical essays by Harris, *Tradition the Writer and Society*, New Beacon Publications (1967).

Introduction

Harris used the term 'novel of persuasion' to suggest the main-stream tradition of the English nineteenth-century novel (a tradition in which Naipaul writes). 'The novel of persuasion rests on grounds of apparent common sense: a certain "selection" is made by the writer, the selection of items, manners, uniform conversation, historical situations etc., all lending themselves to build and present an individual span of life which yields self-conscious and fashionable judgements, self-conscious and fashionable moralities. The tension which emerges is the tension of individuals—great or small—on an accepted plane of society we are persuaded has an inevitable existence.' The Guyanese writer's practice in *The Far Journey of Oudin* (1961) helps us to understand these contentions better. In this novel, Harris makes use of the East Indian presence, but he does not chronicle 'an individual span of life' in the way V. S. Naipaul traces the life and death of Mohun Biswas in *A House for Mr. Biswas* (1961). And whereas Naipaul's relentless accumulation of realistic particulars from the social scene persuades us and the character that that society has 'an inevitable existence', Harris's fiction suggests a particular society only to deny its overpowering and absolute quality. Superficially, *The Far Journey of Oudin* is a witty analogy of slave history: Oudin, the landless, harbourless, jack-of-all-trades of the empty savannah is a tool used by both sides in the struggle between old (the Mohammed estate) and new economic forces (the money-lender, Ram). Since the novel opens with the death of Oudin, there is an initial temptation to think of it in terms of 'flashback'. But as the work unfolds, through apparently unrelated incidents and with arbitrary shifts in point of view, it begins to emerge that Oudin's death is only a device to remove a conventional view of the deprived character. Two versions of Oudin's life take shape: there is the socially realistic figure who suffers as a slave in an oppressive social order, and who dies having covenanted even his unborn child to the grasping Ram; and there is the god-like inheritor of the kingdom who fulfils destiny by abducting the virgin Beti, a bride and prize coveted by Ram. The two Oudins are evoked with equal credibility, both stories residing in the same events. Like Blake in the two 'Holy Thursday' poems, Harris shows and responds to the

9

coexistence of different conditions—the meek being overwhelmed by the earth, but inheriting it at the same time. Through imaginative fictions it is possible to remember that no social order is inevitable and ultimate, and that the 'individual span of life' need not be identified with the most oppressive of its possibilities. But 'the novel of persuasion', Harris might argue, with its commitment to ordinary linear time, to the creation of finite characters and to the portrayal of a self-sufficient social world with reference to which characters are valued, indulges a one-sided view of human life, a restricted vision of human capacities.

Harris's disregard for the usual conventions (time, character, social realism) in the novel arises from an almost literal-minded obsession with expressing intuitions about 'the person' and about the structure of societies men have built for themselves through the ages. He sees these intuitions, however, as being of particular and immediate concern in the West Indies. At the beginning of 'Tradition and the West Indian Novel' he finds remarkable in the West Indian 'a sense of subtle links, the series of subtle links which are latent within him, the latent ground of old and new personalities'. Harris would hardly imagine this to be an exclusive West Indian property, but such a conception of the person seems natural in the West Indies where so many cultures and peoples have interacted upon one another. Instead of creating characters whose positioning on one side or other of the region's historical conflicts consolidates those conflicts and does violence to the make-up of 'the person', the West Indian novelist should set out to 'visualise a fulfilment', a reconciliation in the person and throughout society, of the parts of a heritage of broken cultures. A vision of essential unity is pervasive in Harris's fiction, taking different forms from novel to novel. This vision and 'a conception of wider possibilities and relationships which still remains unfulfilled today in the Caribbean' are the special substance of *The Whole Armour* (1962), Harris's most obviously political novel to date.

With *The Secret Ladder* (1963) and *Heartland* (1964) Harris begins a concentrated exploration of 'the person'. The peasant types of the earlier works are replaced by central characters who are ser-

vants of modern technology—educated, articulate and introspective. In each novel there is a confrontation with an ancestral
figure (Poseidon the ancient African in *The Secret Ladder* and Petra
the pregnant promiscuous Amerindian in *Heartland*). Poseidon is
the agent through whom Fenwick becomes aware of man's frailty
and eternal endurance in an overwhelming universe; and through
Petra, Stevenson experiences the possibility of rebirth and self-
discovery. But above all it is in contact with the primeval jungle
(always a disconcerting element in Harris's novels, but coming
into its own as a prime agent here) that both Fenwick and Stevenson lose themselves as particular men in a specific social and
historical context. Both novels end in disorientation. Although it
is possible to follow Fenwick and Stevenson as we follow characters in conventional novels, Harris has no interest in his central
figures as individuals. It was necessary to begin with solid, clearly
defined and self-sufficient characters in order to dramatize their
breakdown. What Harris is trying to do in these novels is to
create a sense of man's original condition of terror and freedom
prior to the accretions of history and civilization.

The significance of this movement in Harris's oeuvre, and its
relation to his view of the possibilities in the West Indian situation
become clearer in *The Eye of the Scarecrow* (1965) and *The Waiting
Room* (1967) which open with characters in that emptied-out condition on the edge of self-discovery with which *The Secret Ladder*
and *Heartland* end. In *The Waiting Room*, a blind woman, con-
valescing after a series of operations, sits like a statue in a room
full of antiques and relics of her past. There is little authorial
direction, the language is dense and involuted, and the narrative
yields itself fragmentarily. But it is apparent that through a process
of memory of which she is not in full control, Susan Forrestal is
reliving her unfinished affair with a rapacious lover she had dismissed in the past. As the disjointed memories of her absent lover
float into the woman's consciousness, the reader becomes aware
that the statuesque person, the inanimate relics in the room and
the absent lover are bound together in the waiting-room, in the
way that the enthralled Ulysses was bound to the saving mast
while his crew moved free on the deck below, their ears, however,

Introduction

deafened to the Sirens. Such a distribution of strengths and weaknesses between animate and inanimate objects in the room allows for a relayed digestion of the whole catastrophe while offering mutual protection from its annihilating powers.

So the ground of loss or deprivation with which most West Indian writers and historians engage is not for Harris simply a ground for protest, recrimination and satire; it is visualized through the agents in his works as an ambivalent condition of helplessness and self-discovery, the starting point for new social structures. By the time that *The Waiting Room* comes to be written, Harris's exploration of this condition in the person has gone so far that the personal relationship—violent rape, irresponsible lover, involuntarily responsive mistress learning to digest catastrophe—absorbs the burden of an equally rapacious imperial relationship. Susan Forrestal, blind, helpless, and deprived, involved in the waiting-room in the development of new resources and capacities for relationships with people and things, becomes the exciting ambivalent emblem of a so-called 'hopeless', 'historyless' West Indian condition.

There can be little doubt about the richness of the West Indian literary output. Nor can its broad humane relevance and its particular significance for West Indian society be denied. The problems surrounding it, however, are enormous. The critical task cannot be properly performed without taking a larger contextual view of modern West Indian writing. For when this fiction began to appear in the early decades of the twentieth century, the underprivileged masses to whom it might speak, and whose smothered capacities its imagined worlds might have released, hardly constituted a reading public. At other levels in the society there was a combination of two main discouraging elements: a long history of indifference to the arts and sciences, and the resistance of the colonized middle class to a native literature that was not the English literature they had been brought up to consider the only literature possible. By the early 1950's the pattern was established of emigration to the Mother Country for West Indian writers

Introduction

seeking the stamp of approval and wishing to live by their pens; nearly every West Indian novel since then has been first published by London publishing houses for sale to members of the British public. So it has come about that although a distinctive body of fiction has emerged from the West Indies in the twentieth century, life in the islands is still what it has been for over three hundred years—a life without fiction.

Part I of the book deals with this condition. It ranges from the eighteenth century to the 1940's, describing the slow growth of writing in the islands in relation to the development of popular literacy and popular education, and to the rise of national feeling. The chapters on popular education in the nineteenth century, and on the lives of the Whites and Coloureds in the eighteenth and nineteenth centuries, however, show the long build-up of attitudes and conditions from which the present generation of West Indian writers felt it necessary to escape. But if the literary activity in the islands between 1903 and 1945 must be seen against such a background, it is also necessary to establish continuities between works from this period and those better-known ones that seemed to burst forth suddenly in the city of exile. H. G. de Lisser's *Jane's Career* (1914), Alfred Mendes's *Pitch Lake* (1934) and C. L. R. James's *Minty Alley* (1936) are advanced in this part of the book as West Indian novels of the earlier period which cannot be ignored by those interested in West Indian writing and a West Indian tradition.

The nostalgia of the emigré, and the professional writer's awareness of the preconceptions and the ignorance of his foreign readers affect mood, content, and expression to some extent but the novelists writing in London seldom depart from a concern with the shape and possible directions of their society, its central issues and causes, its patterns of group life, and the quality of life possible for individuals in it.

For non-West Indian critics, difficulties might well lie not so much in judging these works parochial as in becoming too engrossed in the raw material to apply critical standards. As the better metropolitan critics show little interest in the literature of underdeveloped countries it is always possible that in the hands of their colleagues, novels might become primary evidence for theories about societies. This kind of danger is encouraged by the tendency of West Indian commentators themselves to value novels according to their immediate social or political relevance. The real difficulty for a West Indian critic, nevertheless, is that in seeking to avoid a disproportionate valuation of content as against form, he might be drawn into an aestheticism that denies social function altogether.

Commentaries now growing up overseas seldom contain critical analysis, and the approaches that have been developed usually include West Indian writing only as part of a wider unit. Three such approaches take notice of some basic features—the centrality of the Negro, the aftermath of slavery and colonialism, and the use of English in a community drawn from different parts of the world. The heavy-handedness of these approaches, however, underlines the need for more particular information about the West Indian milieu, and for a less restricted view of the relationship between a literature and the society it draws upon. Part II 'Approaches' deals, therefore, with the backgrounds of Language, Race and Empire. But if one of the aims of this book is to clear the way for informed and undistracted discussion of West Indian literature, another is to perform the critical activity itself. Within the socio-historical frame adopted in Parts I and II are sections containing critical analyses of a number of works. Part I 'Life Without Fiction' takes in general a deterministic view of the effect of social factors upon the growth of a literature; the emphasis is different in Part II which drives towards a view of the autonomy of the work of art.

In Part III, 'Precursor', the study returns to a more straight-forward method. The post-1950 phenomena have tended to make the early writers from the West Indies less known. A resumé of the continuing significance of these writers is followed by an account of the life and literary career of Claude McKay (1890–1948), the first West Indian Negro novelist and the first to go into exile. The themes of McKay's fiction, the critical issues it raises, and the overall pattern of his *oeuvre* make him the type of the West Indian novelist. Earlier recognition of *Banana Bottom* (1933) as a classic of West Indian prose might have established it as a model for that imaginative fiction built around the lives of the folk towards which the present generation of West Indian writers have only just begun to move.

PART I

Life Without Fiction

I

Popular Education in the West Indies in the Nineteenth Century

The basic facts about popular (mainly Negro) education in the nineteenth century, and those broad effects of concern to the literary historian are only too well known: popular education was elementary education; it began out of public funds with the Emancipation of the slaves, but it was neither sufficiently extensive nor deep enough to create a public able to read and write —even by the least demanding criteria; the system, such as it was, produced a few distinguished Negroes for the professions (mainly Law and Medicine, with the Church a poor third), but literary Negroes in the nineteenth century were exceptions among exceptions. There are, nevertheless, good reasons for tracing what is a history of administrative incompetence, unimaginativeness, lack of purpose and conflicting interests within a social and economic depression. For one thing, the darkness that was here only yesterday persists to some extent in all the islands. More crucially, the complex of attitudes to education and the written word which have had such an adverse effect on the practical conditions for writers in the West Indies in the first half of the twentieth century, might be understood better if the different sets of attitudes making up the complex are seen in their historical context.

Included in the Act of Emancipation (1833) was a resolution to provide 'upon liberal and comprehensive principles for the religious and moral Education of the Negro population to be emancipated.'[1] The resultant Negro Education Grant was alloca-

[1] Quoted from Shirley C. Gordon, *A Century of West Indian Education* (1963), p. 20. I am greatly indebted to this source-book and to Miss Gordon's commentary.

19

ted to the different religious bodies already at work in the colonies because, it was alleged, 'the past success of these various societies in diffusing education among the Negroes, though greatly limited by a deficiency of funds, affords satisfactory grounds for anticipating the most favourable results from an increase in means'; and further, because 'the establishment of a new and distinct system would tend to interfere with their operations, without deriving any assistance from their agency.'[1]

But the missionaries were more zealous than competent: expansion was carried out without thought being given to recurrent and increasing costs of items like teachers' salaries and the maintenance of buildings; although inflated reports of success, and falsifications of the attendance books show that the sects were only too aware of one another, a duplication of facilities in select (less rural) areas occurred because there were times when each of the rival denominations preferred to believe that the others did not exist.

The different denominations did not have a system or systems, nor was there ever in the nineteenth century a coherent set of objectives for West Indian education. The Colonial Office advocated religious education, the requirements of small farmers, and a grammatical knowledge of the English language 'as the most important agent of civilisation for the coloured population of the colonies', and felt that 'the lesson books of the colonial schools should also teach the mutual interests of the mother-country and her dependencies; the rational basis of their connection, and the domestic and social duties of the coloured races'.[2] An Inspector of Schools reported in 1838, however, that the planters and employers would not support education unless it seemed to accept 'that the finger of Providence evidently points out the estate or the plantation as the natural field of industry for the majority of the rising generation of the poorer classes in these islands'.[3] The

Further quotations of source-material from it will be annotated 'Source-Book' followed by page references. Where Miss Gordon's commentary is used, however, the annotation will be 'Gordon', with page references to *A Century of West Indian Education*.

[1] Earl Grey, Prime Minister, to the Treasury, 21st July 1835. (Source-Book, p. 22.)
[2] Circular despatch . . ., 26th January 1847. (Source-Book, p. 58.)
[3] Latrobe, Inspector of Schools, Windwards and Leewards, 1838. (Source-Book, p. 30.)

recently freed population themselves were enthusiastic in the first years, then apathetic, then sceptical of 'this great Education', then suspicious of practical instruction as a planter-shaped design to restrict them to the lower stations of life. As the century wore on, however, the deprived masses were to see a more bookish education as a means of social advancement.

Twelve years after its introduction, the expensive Negro Education Grant was ended. The island legislatures were made responsible for providing to educate the people; and the labouring population were to be informed of Her Majesty's earnest desire 'that they should make every exertion in their power to obtain instruction for themselves and their children, and that they should evince their gratitude for the blessings of freedom by such present sacrifices for this object as shall make freedom most conducive in the end to their happiness and moral and spiritual well-being'.[1] From this pious and cynical moment, difficulties that were to persist into the twentieth century came clearly into view: tied to the island economies, the educational budget would vary as those economies suffered and fluctuated; conflicts between the denominations already at work and the legislatures now in financial control would further hamper development; throughout the century the freed but still depressed population would not be able to carry out the Queen's exhortations, and whenever a clash occurred between the stated need to expand or improve elementary education and the desire to produce higher forms, the legislators whose social group was more likely to benefit from secondary education would decide in their own narrow interests. It is not surprising that even as late as the 1890's, the number of pupils registered at the elementary schools was less than half of those of school age.

But if the number of school places was low, the quality of education provided was not correspondingly high. 'Existing accommodation is frequently badly planned, and in a chronic state of disrepair and insanitation. Teachers are inadequate in number and are in most Colonies not well paid. Their training is largely defective or non-existent, and far too great reliance is placed on the pupil-teacher system. . . . Curricula are on the whole ill-adapted

---

[1] Circular Despatch . . ., 1st October 1845. (Soucre-Book, p. 42.)

to the needs of the large mass of the population and adhere far too closely to models which have become out of date in the British practice from which they were blindly copied.'[1] These remarks come from the report of the Moyne Commission on education in the islands, 1938–9. In the dark days of the nineteenth century matters were even worse. The transfer of the 'payment by results' system from England entrenched memorization as a teaching method. Since there were few training colleges (4 for 44 students in Trinidad, 1900), and since their curricula were unrealistically ambitious (the failure rate was about 68 per cent), more and more pupil-teachers were recruited (the proportion of certificated teachers to pupil-teachers in Jamaica, 1899, was 411 to 533).[2] So where the underpaid and incompetent certificated teacher left off, his pupil understudy blundered on. In these conditions, irregularities in attendance (concealed by figures which cannot tell us how regularly any one pupil attended during the year, or for how many years[3] such a pupil might have carried on) were fatal.

Towards the close of the century it was becoming clear that planning popular education in the West Indies was a more formidable task than had so far been imagined:

> The difficulties attending the education of the lower classes are not fully realised: we have had to evolve our own system, and it may well be that we do not know what is most suitable for the race that we have to do with. We have had to make teachers, and that cannot be done in a generation; irregularity of attendance cripples the efforts of such teachers as we have; and their efforts are still further thwarted by the influence of the children's lives at home and the examples of their parents. A system can hardly be said to be fairly and thoroughly at work till those who have passed through the schools fill the parents' class—and it will be many

[1] West India Royal Commission Report, Cmd. 6607 (1945), p. 92.

[2] See *Special Reports on Educational Subjects*, Cmd. 2377 (1905), Vol. 12, p. 193, and Vol. 4, p. 685.

[3] The following table from *Special Reports . . .*, Vol. 4, relating to Jamaica gives an idea of the thinning-out process in all West Indian schools:

Standard	A	B	I	II	III	IV	V	VI	VII
Average Age	7	9	10	10	10	11	11	$11\frac{1}{2}$	$12\frac{1}{2}$
Number	32,917	14,308	13,101	10,278	8,917	7,040	5,084	2,580	141

years before that is true here. Finally we are apt to forget that Elementary Education is only one of the means of civilisation. While . . . the home life of most of the peasantry continues to be as uncivilised and demoralising as it is, the expenditure on elementary education must be partially wasted and disappointing.[1]

Reading, which was one of the three compulsory subjects, suffered greatly. The evidence of examination requirements and syllabuses, and what is known about teaching conditions and teaching methods support the contemporary comment: 'If you take the average schoolboy and let him read from a book in which he has been coached, he cannot explain to you at the end what he has been reading about.'[2] It is with this in mind that we can appreciate the finding of a Royal Commission on Jamaica in 1883, that of a total adult Negro population of 250,000 only 22,000 could read and write.[3] It is certain that many more than 22,000 pupils had passed through the schools in the fifty years of education before the survey. After making allowances for deaths, it is still not possible to avoid the conclusion that some of those who had parroted their way through the Reading test had lapsed easily back into their untutored states.

A certain amount of deliberate forgetting is not improbable. But even those who might have wished to, had little obvious opportunity to practise their hard-learnt skill. For what was true at the end of the century was equally depressing in the preceding years: there were no libraries, no popular newspaper, and no continuation schools or classes. There was also no possibility, so it was alleged, of instituting the latter: 'Work begins for the labouring class about six o'clock in the morning and ends about five o'clock in the afternoon, and the great majority of the people go to bed very early. A system of evening continuation schools would mean little less than a revolution in the social habits of the people, and would be difficult to introduce except to a limited extent in towns.'[4]

[1] Evidence of J. E. Williams, Inspector of Schools in *Special Reports* . . ., Vol. 4, p. 684.
[2] *Special Reports* . . ., Vol. 4, p. 678.
[3] Source-Book, p. 93.
[4] *Special Reports* . . ., Vol. 4, p. 599.

The situation is gloomier still when it is remembered that literacy for Census purposes included the merest ability to scratch out a signature: it is reasonable to suppose, in the light of what has been said about attendance at schools and teaching conditions, that many of these recorded as literate were in the lowest divisions of the literacy scale. It goes almost without saying that matters were at least as bad in the case of the incoming, and for much this century, the in-turned and not yet English-speaking East Indians in Guyana and Trinidad.

Elementary school literacy was not, of course, conceived of as a possible base condition for the reading of imaginative literature. So little was that even seen as a prospect that *Nelson's Royal Readers*, which had become established in the islands, and which contained a small enough proportion of literary material, were being seriously challenged in the 1890's by Blackie's *Tropical Readers* whose advantage was that they offered agricultural training at the same time as reading practice. So much indeed were those responsible for the curriculum committed to a strictly utilitarian principle that the Jamaica Education Commission, 1898, which cannot really be accused of advocating inter-disciplinary studies, suggested more than once in their report that 'one Reading Book including the instruction in History and Geography be specially composed'. Without suspecting the incompatibility in their aims if one Reading book were to serve in this hold-all fashion, the same Commission had prefaced their advice as follows: 'We think that Reading requires great improvement, and that greater attention and more time should be devoted to it. It would probably be improved and made more interesting, and at the same time a love of reading might be created. . . .'[1] Physical conditions in the schoolroom, the obligation to stand and deliver when the Inspector came, and the laborious memorization drills were unpleasant enough to produce poor results and to create antipathy to the very act of reading. The unrelieved factualness of approach to the Reading books prevented both pupils and teachers from even a suspicion of the pleasures and possibilities of imagination.

[1] *Special Reports . . .*, Vol. 4, pp. 647–9.

It is in the nineteenth century that we can begin to see the foundations of two characteristic twentieth-century attitudes to reading, literature and education in general. On the one hand there was the antipathy that grew up in reaction to the joyless and abortive school experience. At the same time there was the awe of the illiterate at the power of education and the written word. The illiterate's awe at the written word, and the mathematical approach to learning are turned to great comic effect in V. S. Naipaul's *The Mystic Masseur* (1957). Early in the novel, the boy-patient's amazement at the number of books in Ganesh's consulting room and rural home university leads to this set piece between the masseur and his wife:

> 'Leela', Ganesh said, 'the boy want to know how much book it have here.'
> 'Let me see,' Leela said, and hitched up the broom to her waistband. She started to count off the fingers of her left hand. 'Four hundred Everyman, two hundred Penguin—six hundred. Six hundred, and one hundred Reader's Library, make seven hundred. I think with all the other book it have about fifteen hundred good book here.'
> The taxi-driver whistled, and Ganesh smiled.
> 'They is all yours, pundit?' I asked.
> 'Is my only vice,' Ganesh said. 'Only vice. I don't smoke. I don't drink. But I must have my books. And mark you, every week I going to San Fernando to buy more, you know. How much book I buy last week, Leela?'
> 'Only three, man,' she said. 'But they was big books, big big books. Six to seven inches altogether.'
> 'Seven inches,' Ganesh said.
> 'Yes, seven inches,' Leela said.
>
> (*The Mystic Masseur*, p. 11)

The existence of these popular attitudes today lends a peculiar irony to George Lamming's claim in *The Pleasures of Exile* (1960) that 'it is the West Indian novel that has restored the West Indian peasant to his true and original status of personality' (p. 39). One is inclined to agree with Lamming that the work of most West Indian novelists 'is shot through and through with the urgency of peasant life' but the peasant (in the city slum or in the country) cannot be said to be conscious of these novels or affected by their significance.

But if the public at large were locked in illiteracy, there were some highly educated Negroes in the nineteenth century. In *The English in the West Indies* (1887), James Anthony Froude reports meeting at dinner in Barbados 'a Negro[1] of pure blood who has risen to eminence by his own talent and character. He has held the office of attorney-general. He is now chief justice of the island'. N. E. Cameron[2] lists several distinguished figures in Guyana, including the Rev. Dr. J. E. London 'a prominent and comparatively wealthy Negro' who was one of the judges at a horticultural exhibition held in the Promenade Gardens, Georgetown, in 1893. In Trinidad the exceptional J. J. Thomas had not only scored a first with *The Theory and Practice of Creole Grammar* (1869) but he published *Froudacity* (1889) a counter-blast to the English historian's anti-Negro book on the West Indies.

But the Negro's opportunities to rise were not many. Most nineteenth-century secondary schools financed from public funds were established after 1870. They were few in number: in Trinidad, for example, as late as 1902 only Queen's Royal College (120 students) was wholly maintained by the Government; St. Mary's College (200 pupils in 1902) had been affiliated since 1870 and received a small grant-in-aid. But in both these schools, fees were payable and fixed at £15 a year per pupil.[3] 'This meant that secondary education was for the middle classes who could pay for it; in fact the monied group was white and fair-skinned so that the question of colour has often been raised in connection with admission to secondary schools' (Gordon, p. 239). A Special Report of 10th October 1889 by William Miles, then principal of Queen's

---

[1] Sir William Conrad Reeves (1821–1902), chief justice of Barbados from 1836; knighted 1889. Reeves's father was in fact a White man, a Dr. Philip Reeves. Since Froude goes on to claim that Reeves's association with the West had made him an un-typical Negro (and therefore no proof of 'real' Negro capacity) it is surprising that the historian had not ferreted out the fact which would have been grist for his mill. Poor Reeves must have been hopelessly black.

[2] N. E. Cameron, *The Evolution of the Negro*, two volumes (1929) and (1934), printed by The Argosy Company Limited, Georgetown, Demerara. A rare and neglected but very useful work. The Negroes are noted in Vol. II, Bk. II, pp. 73–4: footnote to p. 49; p. 77; and footnote to pp. 123–4.

[3] *Special Reports* . . ., Vol. 12, pp. 195 and 191.

Royal College, describes the situation with peculiar authority: 'What is done therefore for secondary Education in this Colony amounts to this, that in its chief town only, professional men, Government Officers, ministers of religion and businessmen are able to get their sons a fairly good Grammar School education at a comparatively cheap rate.'[1] There was not much effective criticism of this privileged system by which one-third of the educational budget was spent on secondary education for a handful of boys whose parents were wealthy. Financial exclusiveness was reinforced by rules barring entry to the illegitimate, in practice the majority of Negro children. In the latter part of the century the authorities answered criticism by pointing to the existence of exhibition schemes by which pupils from the elementary schools could compete for two or three free places provided in the secondary establishments. But the standard of elementary education was poor, and continuity between the two levels was so little institutionalized, that only an exceptionally able and rigorously drilled pupil could qualify for an exhibition: in Trinidad in 1872 (January), twelve candidates presented themselves but only three of the six possible awards were made; in December 1872 there were sixteen candidates but, again, only three places were filled.[2] The Negro or Indian pupil who reached the required standard and got past the colour prejudice sometimes shown by the selection committees entered an exclusive arena where he could compete again for one of the few island scholarships available to British Universities.

The programme of training for the exhibitions to secondary schools was nothing short of criminal. How much the twentieth century is heir to the nineteenth in this respect becomes obvious when one sees V. S. Naipaul satirizing the system in *A House for Mr. Biswas* (1961). In a section of the novel covering the 1940's, Mr. Biswas's son Anand, placed on a special brain-food diet of milk and prunes, undergoes intense preparation:

> With the exhibition examination less than two months away, Anand lived a life of pure work. Private lessons were given in the morning for half an hour before school; private lessons were given

---

[1] Source-Book, p. 215.   [2] Source-Book, p. 244.

in the afternoon for an hour after school; private lessons were given for the whole of the Saturday morning. Then in addition to all these private lessons from his class teacher, Anand began to take private lessons from the headmaster, at the headmaster's house from five to six. He went from school to the Dairies to school again; then he went to the headmaster's where Savi waited for him with sandwiches and lukewarm Ovaltine. Leaving home at seven in the morning, he returned at half past six. He ate. Then he did his school homework; then he prepared for all his private lessons.

(*A House for Mr. Biswas*, p. 418)

Naipaul's fictional account of the 1940's is of a piece with an autobiographical recollection of an earlier period—around 1910—when C. L. R. James the distinguished historian, political theorist and commentator on the West Indian cultural scene won an exhibition (out of four available) to Queen's Royal College. James, a hot favourite, was to disappoint those who backed him for the island scholarship, but in *Beyond a Boundary* (1963) there is a very suggestive description of his trial run for the exhibition: 'On the day of the examination a hundred boys were brought from all parts of the island by their teachers like so many fighting-cocks. That day I looked at the favourites and their trainers with wide-open eyes, for I was a country bumpkin. My father, when asked about me always dismissed the enquiry with the remark, "I only brought him along to get him accustomed to the atmosphere".' Naipaul's description of the examination day in *A House for Mr. Biswas* also runs to the language of sport, but it begins in religious terms and evokes the sights and smells of the occasion first:

The exhibition candidates, prepared for years for the sacrificial day, had all dressed for the sacrifice. They all wore serge shorts, white shirts and school ties, and Anand could only guess at what charms these clothes concealed. Their pockets were stuffed with pens and pencils. In their hands they carried blotters, rulers, erasers and new pots of ink; some carried complete cases of mathematical instruments; many wore wrist-watches. The schoolyard was full of Daddies, the heroes of so many English compositions; they seemed to have dressed with as much care as their sons. The boys looked at the Daddies; and the Daddies, wrist-watchless, eyed each other, breeders of rivals.

(*A House for Mr. Biswas*, p. 425)

28

In the nineteenth century there were not as many as one hundred candidates assembled, nor was there such a concourse as Naipaul describes, but the devotion and rivalries were undoubtedly as intense.

The route through the government exhibitions was the most spectacular for the children of the poor, but it was not the only heroic one. A few parents must have scraped and sacrificed much to see their eldest or favourite or only son through secondary school. There was of course a strong element of gratuitous fulfil-ment in such enterprises, and it would be easy to satirize the would-be middle-class aspirations involved, but it is much less superficial to avoid such explanations or judgements and recognize the proportion of martyrdom poor parents had to undergo if their children were to enter the secondary schools without an exhibi-tion. Once again, novels dealing with the twentieth century illus-trate the process. In George Lamming's *Season of Adventure* (1960), Belinda, a prostitute, expels an unsatisfied black client because a more profitable American customer has appeared:

> The man stood dumb. He wanted to say something, but words were not easy to come by as he looked at Belinda.
> 'I don't know what all the new freedom mean,' she said, 'cause they all crooks the political lot, all crooks, but I see how things start to change. An' I decide to back my little boy future. I go back it, like a horse to win I go back it.'
> The man saw her turn inside, and the door closed. You could have strangled him with an infant's breath.
> Alone, sweeping the broken glass under the bed, Belinda paused and looked up at the ceiling.
> 'Jesus an' all the saints,' she cried, 'I loyal as any to my own kind. But you know, you know I didn't send him 'way for fun. You know my purpose is clean. It clean, clean.'
> And she was ready for the night: this night which was her faith in the little boy's future.
>
> (*Season of Adventure*, p. 199)

In choosing illustrations from works dealing with the twentieth century, I do not wish to give the impression that the provision of secondary education in the nineteenth century was the same as in the later period or that there were as many aspirants in the nineteenth as in the twentieth century. But it seems important to stress that the price at which secondary education was purchased for the socially depressed in the nineteenth century, and the needs to which this education was sought as an answer shaped the attitudes of the products away from the possibility of a literary culture (which would have brought neither social prestige nor financial advancement). The Cambridge Local examinations to which the secondary schools were tied provided discontented recruits for the teaching profession and self-important clerks for government and commercial offices. But there were more glittering prizes.

> Every year the two schools [Queen's Royal College and St. Mary's, the Catholic College] competed for three island scholarships worth £600 each. With one of these a boy could study law or medicine and return to the island with a profession and therefore independence. There were at that time few other roads to independence for a black man who started without means. The higher posts in the Government, in engineering and other scientific professions were monopolised by white people, and, as practically all business was also in their hands, the coloured people were, as a rule, limited to the lower posts. Thus law and medicine were the only way out. Lawyers and doctors made large fees and enjoyed great social prestige. The final achievement was when the Governor nominated one of these coloured men to the Legislative Council to represent the people. To what degree he represented them should not distract us here. We must keep our eyes on the course; exhibition, scholarship, profession, wealth, Legislative Council and the title of Honourable. Whenever someone brought it off the local people were very proud of him.
>
> *(Beyond a Boundary*, 1963, p. 31)

James's clear description relates to the first decade of the twentieth century but the patterns it distinguishes—the persistently materialistic approach to education in the West Indies in the twentieth century, and the emergence of a black middle class alienated from the people—were shaped in the nineteenth century.

Even those secondary-school graduates who only obtained office jobs or became schoolteachers held jealously on to their limited privilege. The individual blacks who had distinguished themselves were so few in number, and as a general rule so isolated from one another that a concerted leadership of the people would have been impracticable. But this question never really arose: those who had made it knew or felt that political power was held beyond their grasp, and in any case, they were too insecure in their positions of eminence to risk a backward glance at the depressed and inarticulate masses. A Dr. London smelling daffodils was always, in the nineteenth century, more likely than a J. J. Thomas trying to rouse his fellow Negroes to action and achievement.

Few Negroes in the nineteenth century cultivated the art of reading imaginative literature, and fewer attempted to write it. The period appears to have produced no novelists, only a handful of minor poets. Their poems reveal the alienation of the insecure and embryonic black middle class from the uneducated and illiterate groups to which they or their parents had belonged. It is fair to point out that the uncompromising and doctrinaire spirit in which Daly castigates four such Guyanese poets in *West Indian Freedom and West Indian Literature*[1] arises from an application of easily held twentieth-century attitudes to a less predictable nineteenth-century situation. But as we shall see, increasing literacy had to meet with the rise of nationalism before a West Indian literature could begin to emerge. For if the life without fiction of the under-privileged may be explained with reference to the deficiencies of popular education, only the absence of nationalism can account for the failures of the Whites and Coloureds.

[1] P. H. Daly, *West Indian Freedom and West Indian Literature*, The Daily Chronicle Ltd., Georgetown, 1951. The poets discussed include S. E. Wills, a humorist in dialect, and 'Leo' (Egbert Martin), whose *Poetical Works* appeared in London in 1883.

II

The Whites and Cultural Absenteeism

In 1831, a White Jamaican journalist had written in The Jamaica Petition for Representation in the British House of Commons or for Independence: 'The haughty aristocrats who have property in that Island, and who may obtain seats in the House of Commons have no community of interest, no identity of feeling with the resident inhabitants of Jamaica; to these aristocrats what may become of the people of that country is and ever must be a matter of perfect inconsequence, so long as they can retain in England what they call their station in society.'[1] The early emigration of those birds of passage who had made their West India fortunes, and the prolonged absence or non-arrival of those who came into possession of West Indian wealth and property deprived the islands of its best people[2] and gave material sanction to the idea that Britain was home and the islands a shining hunting ground. Once this idea was firmly impressed in economic terms, it began to grow in the Creole consciousness as the redeeming myth of every sordid enterprise or lack of enterprise. The native or Creole Whites were the first West Indians not because of the sour-grape or economically interested nationalism they occasionally voiced against their absentee rivals, nor so much because in adjusting to the West Indian environment they had evolved a way of life that was not quite European. Rather, it was because like all later West Indians they thought of England as home.

[1] Quoted by Philip Curtin in *Two Jamaicas*, Harvard University Press (1955), p. 51.
[2] For an account of absenteeism and its possible ill-effects on West Indian society see Orlando H. Patterson, *The Sociology of Slavery* (1967), pp. 33–51.

The Whites and Cultural Absenteeism

Both Long[1] and Bryan Edwards[2] describe the warm-heartedness, laden tables, gaiety and diversions (cards, billiards, backgammon, chess, horse-racing, hog-hunting, shooting, fishing, dancing and music) of the Creole plantocracy, defending them against charges of indolence and licentiousness. An earlier observer had been more severe: 'Learning here is at the lowest Ebb; there is no public School in the whole Island, neither do they seem fond of the Thing; several large Donations have been made for such Uses but have never taken Effect. The Office of a Teacher is look'd upon as contemptible, and no Gentleman keeps Company with one of their Character; to read, write and cast up Accounts is all the Education they desire, and these are scurvily taught. A Man of any Parts or Learning that would employ himself in that Business would be despised and starve.'[3] The White Creoles built no schools, libraries or museums. They created no works of art They constructed no roads or bridges. They left no enduring monuments.

> *Stones only, the disjecta membra of this Great House,*
> *Whose moth-like girls are mixed with candledust,*
> *Remain to file the lizard's dragonish claws;*
> *The mouths of those gate cherubs streaked with stain.*
> *Axle and coachwheel silted under the muck*
> *Of cattle droppings.*
> > *Three crows flap for the trees,*
> *And settle, creaking the eucalyptus boughs.*
> *A smell of dead limes quickens in the nose*
> *The leprosy of Empire.*
> > *'Farewell, green fields'*
> > *Farewell, ye happy groves!'*[4]

Too much can be made of the isolation of this relatively small group in precarious control of a discontented slave population as an explanation of their material excesses and spiritual aridity. Nor

[1] Edward Long, *The History of Jamaica* (1774).
[2] Bryan Edwards, *The History Civil and Commercial of the British West Indies* (1798). References are to the fifth edition of 1819.
[3] C. Leslie, *A New and Exact Account of Jamaica* (1740), pp. 36–7.
[4] Derek Walcott, 'Ruins of a Great House' from *In a Green Night* (1962).

can indolence and licentiousness and the lack of mental stamina be held as original causes. In commenting on the practice of the wealthier Creoles of sending their children to Britain to be educated,[1] Long raises the more fundamental question of orientation: 'Let me now ask, what are the mighty advantages which Britain, or the colony, has gained by the many hundreds who have received their education in the former? The answer may be, they have spent their fortunes in Britain, and learned to renounce their native place, their parents and their friends. Would it not have been better for both countries, that three fourths of them never crossed the Atlantic? Their industry is, in general, for ever lost to the place where it might have been usefully exerted.' Those who return 'regret their exile from the gay delights of London' and have a 'riveted prejudice against colony life'. Thirty years earlier, Leslie had lamented the lack of schools and patriotism in White Creole society: 'Tis a Pity, in a Place like this where the Means could be so easily afforded, something of a public Nature should not be done for the Advantage of Posterity; but when such a Spirit will appear is hard to determine.'[2] Making the same point, but with deeper insight, Long in an extended discussion,[3] views the absence of a proper seminary for the young inhabitants of the island as an unhappy defect, 'one of the principal impediments to its effectual settlement'. Protesting that 'it has too long been the custom for every father here who has acquired a little property to send his children of whatever complexion, to Britain for education' Long urges the necessity of weaning 'the inhabitants from that detrimental habit of emigration, that unhappy idea of considering this place a mere temporary abode'. Having pointed to the sharp contrast with North America where 'the lowest of their people are not left destitute for some education', the historian moves into a sentimental picture of the sufferings of parents and children separated from one another because of the need to travel to England for education. Then comes a stirring peroration in which he appeals to the patriotic instinct: 'What blessings then will await that assembly who shall patriotically resolve to prevent

[1] Long, Vol. II, pp. 248–9.   [2] Leslie, p. 37.
[3] Long Vol. II, pp. 246–260.

34

this barbarious necessity and these sorrowful events in future! They will indeed be justly styled the fathers of their country, and merit immortal honour.'

This rousing call had no effect. By the time that Long was writing, indeed, absenteeism had become a psychological pheno- menon so that for the White Creoles, England was home, the West Indies was never the loved place. Since the West Indies was not home, anything could be done there. Morals and manners de- teriorated: 'The Europeans, who at home have always been used to greater purity and strictness of manners, are too easily led aside to give a loose to every kind of sensual delight: on this account, some black or yellow *quasheba* is sought for by whom a tawny breed is produced. Many are the men of every rank, quality and degree here who would much rather riot in these goatish embraces than share the pure and lawful bliss derived from matrimonial, mutual love.'[1] Since England was the acknowledged and proud centre of art and culture, it was not necessary to renovate the sunny slum.

The stubbornly philistine state of the ruling class in West Indian society may be illustrated by an analysis of the tactics and fate of *The Jamaica Quarterly Journal and Literary Gazette/Conducted by a Society of Gentlemen*, the first issue of which appeared in July 1818. The *Journal* does not appear to have lasted more than two years,[2] although Vol. I No. I carries the names of over 450 subscribers.

In the Advertisement, the editors made the kind of appeal most likely to succeed with the planters, even indulging in a certain amount of comfortable banter: 'Although a residence in this island is too often forced and deemed an exile from the parent country; and most persons, therefore, during their stay here are anxious to glean little but golden grains, yet it admits not of a doubt but that many useful hints might be afforded, even towards the accom- plishment of that universal project.' A substantial part of the magazine catered for the interests of planters and agriculturists.

Although the editors suggested that the magazine might also carry the results of 'philosophical [scientific] inquiry which in

[1] Long, Vol. II, p. 326.
[2] I have seen only four issues, belonging to 1818 and 1819, at the British Museum.

this most fertile region has lain waste so long', the contents of available numbers show that no 'Geologist, Mineralogist or Botanist' was forthcoming.

As the failure of *Sheridan's Jamaica Monthly Magazine* between 1832 and 1834 was to demonstrate, an exclusively literary magazine was out of the question in the sugar islands. The editors of *The Jamaica Quarterly Journal* conceived of a literary section frankly as a means of conveying information about books-in-the-news at home: 'Those also who thus far removed from the sources of publication have not collections of books within their reach—to such, some notice of the literary events of the day may afford amusement and instruction.' No. II of the *Journal* (December 1818) contained a long article 'Memoirs of the Public and Private Life of the Right Hon. Richard Brinsley Sheridan' under the heading of 'Literature—Original Criticism'. And in the section for Poetry, there were six pieces: 'Lines on a beautiful Cottage'; 'To a Young Lady'; 'Hopeless Love'; 'On seeing the last rose of the season hanging on a tree'; 'Smiles'; and 'Jeu d'Esprit'. The interest in literature, judging from this magazine, was not only small; it was amateurish and trifling in practice, and turned towards England in theory.

As the myth of England as the place of values grew strong, the condition of the West Indies as a spiritual sepulchre became true. H. G. de Lisser's *The White Witch of Rosehall* (1929), set in the Jamaica of 1830's, provides a useful illustration of the contraries. The arrival of a young Englishman Robert Rutherford allows de Lisser to show the difference between the Creole White and the newly-arrived European. Rutherford's liaison with two women (the White Creole, Annie Palmer, and Millie, a coloured girl) and his taking to drink, show the loss of morals in the steamy atmosphere. In the following passage, the alcoholic ex-minister, Rider, notes his friend's deterioration and begins to take stock. His reflections provide a resumé of the England–West Indies polarities:

> Today it came into his mind that perhaps, if he could get back to England, he might be able to open another and better chapter of his life. He thought of Robert; he too if he remained in Jamaica, might become if not an outcast (for he had means), at any rate a

poor specimen of a man; he had seen such things. Robert would have a good career at home. It was better that he should return as quickly as possible. . . . In the tropics some men throve; those were the men of stern fibre or of a sort of brutal hardness. These tropics with their large servile population and small aristocracy of proprietors who lived in a world of the narrowest mental and moral horizons—what a horror they actually were. If they did not become physically the White man's grave, they formed for him as deadly a spiritual sepulchre.

(*The White Witch of Rosehall*, p. 192)

De Lisser is not a major West Indian artist, but as an illustrator, in the novel form, of the facts and issues in West Indian slave society, he is unequalled. At the end of *The White Witch of Rosehall*, the prolonged contrast between the Creole image of England as home and civilized place, and the picture of Jamaica as the place of corruption, is clinched by a short exchange between an old parson and Robert Rutherford (who is about to escape to England):

'Do you think you will ever come back to the West Indies?' asked the old parson by way of saying something.
'Never' was the reply.

In the eighteenth and nineteenth centuries, emigration, not social reform, was the way out of a corroding environment chosen by the very people whose concerted efforts might have helped to redress the evils of the past.

The absence of any tradition of artistic and scientific endeavour in White Creole society meant that when Emancipation came there were no models evolved in the islands to which the liberated slaves or their caretakers could either turn or, in revolt, turn away from. So it is that the orientation of White West Indians towards England as an educational and cultural focus came to be institutionalized in a derivative and unrealistic system of popular education imported from England; and a cultural bias, built into the colonial relationship, could never find a challenge from within West Indian society. I shall turn to some of the consequences of these elements in the colonial's structure of awareness later, when factors behind the emigration of West Indian writers to London are discussed. It is necessary to state at this point that the similarity between the intellectual and cultural states of the labouring classes in nineteenth-century England, and the liberated slaves in the West Indies is misleading. The existence of a cultured class in England from the time of Chaucer and earlier, setting a tone for the society and representing its finer aspirations meant that, however tenuously, the English working man was in contact with a tradition waiting to be democratized. In the background of the liberated slave was a cultural void.

III

The Coloureds and Class Interest

There were 30,000 Whites and 10,000 Coloureds or people of mixed blood in the Jamaica of 1798.[1] In 1844, according to the first Census, there were 69,000 Coloureds and only 15,000 Whites on the post-Emancipation scene. The Coloureds had also grown in influence: 'Let any stranger go through the shops and stores of Kingston, and see how many of them are either owned or worked by men of colour; let him go into the House of Assembly and see how large a proportion of their debates is carried on by men of colour. How large a portion of the public service is carried on by them; how well they thrive. . . .'[2] But the Coloureds did not quite manage to take political control in the nineteenth century, nor did they fill the gap left by the Whites and assume the role of cultural pace-setters. This is hardly surprising.

In the first place, there is more than an element of nonsense in speaking about a Coloured class: in complexion they ranged from near-White to Black; some were wealthy and owned property, some were well educated, and many were as poor and illiterate as Negroes. Up to the 1830's they were subject to disability laws. Few of them achieved social prominence in the eighteenth century, and when they began to gain strength, most of their energies were taken up in the fight to obtain full civil rights for their class.

In the account of popular education in the nineteenth century it was possible to omit reference to girls. About one-third of their number could expect two or three years at the elementary schools,

---

[1] Bryan Edward's estimate in *The History* . . . (1798).
[2] Anthony Trollope, *The West Indies and the Spanish Main* (1859), p. *78*.

and then life began. Coloured girls of the poorer sort were in a similar position. Most eighteenth- and nineteenth-century commentators report on the beauty, sensuality and promiscuity of Coloured women. It is known that they were in great demand as mistresses for White men. Trollope observed in 1859, however, that they did not accept this role as frequently as before, and that some of them were fashionably educated 'to know and display the little tricks and graces of English ladies'. But the size of this group and the kind of education they received abroad make it plain that the better-off Coloured woman was not in a position to help shape a civilization in the islands.

The removal of civil disabilities did not eliminate social attitudes to the man of mixed blood, nor did it settle his problems of adjustment. Bryan Edwards noted that they were 'humble, submissive and unassuming' with Whites, but 'harsh and imperious' to their own slaves. Fifty years later, symptoms had changed. The Negro was resentful: 'He thinks that the mulatto[1] is too near akin to himself to be worthy of any respect. In his passion he calls him a nigger—and protests that he is not and never will be like buckra man.' And they irritated their White neighbours by their want of meekness: 'They are always proclaiming by their voice and their look, that they are as good as the white man; but they are always showing by their voice and look also that they know that this is a false boast.' It was the Coloureds who first began to tread the weary road to Whiteness. The psychological disturbance of the mulatto was a further deterrent to their emergence as a minority group bringing sweetness and light to the society.

The Fictional Image of the Mulatto

If the Coloureds did not read or write fiction in the eighteenth and nineteenth centuries, their peculiar position of stress has made them of great interest to writers of modern West Indian fiction. Almost without exception, the literary presentations either derive from or consolidate the kind of picture outlined above, so that

[1] Strictly speaking, a mulatto is the offspring of one White and one Black parent. But it is more realistic to use the term to refer to any Coloured person who could not pass for White, and who did not consider himself a Negro.

two stereotypes of the Coloured person—the unstable mulatto (usually male) and the highly sexed and sensuous Coloured woman —appear in West Indian writing. In an area like the West Indies where many races live side by side, and where vested political interests thrive on racial divisions or misunderstandings, the common use, in works of fiction, of racial types rather than characters conceived either experimentally as by Wilson Harris or in the conventional particular-universal pattern used by V. S. Naipaul in *A House for Mr. Biswas*, is a creative failing of considerable social consequence. This discussion will be restricted to isolating the elements in the fictional image of a specific caste and considering some questions of art in a literary way, but broader issues arising from the use of stereotypes in West Indian writing in general will be very much in mind.

Examples of the unstable mulatto are to be found in Sylvia Wynter's *The Hills of Hebron* (1962), and Alvin Bennett's *God the Stonebreaker* (1964). *The Hills of Hebron* is an overloaded work by a West Indian intellectual anxious to touch upon as many themes as possible. The mulatto makes his appearance in the chapter called 'The Legend', when the Reverend Richard Brooke and his wife Cecilia appear as missionaries to the Cockpit Centre community. The usual anti-English points are made, but the main interest here is in the attitude of the mulatto deacon James Macleod to the White woman: 'Mrs. Brooke was tall, slim, with blue eyes, golden hair and a soft pink complexion; and was therefore extremely beautiful in the deacon's eyes. But she did not attract him as a woman. Only as a symbol. Conquest of her would prove that his father's white blood had cancelled out the black blood of his mother.' Having explained the character in these terms, the author moves swiftly to the point where the mulatto, who imagines on no evidence that Mrs. Brooke wants him sexually, decides to bring matters to a climax. A well-timed afternoon visit finds the Reverend's wife alone, and helpfully, taking a nap:

> When the maid woke her she dressed hastily and went into the drawing-room wondering at the deacon's coming at that hour, alarmed that some mishap might have befallen her husband. She entered the room. The deacon strode across to her and pulled her

41

to him. The smell of the coconut oil on his hair was sharply acrid in her nostrils. She was overcome by a sudden nausea and pushed him away. He swung out of the house, hurt to the quick. She was a white bitch like all the others, he told himself, and thought herself too good for him only because he was part black.

(The Hills of Hebron, p. 123)

The Hills of Hebron is clogged-up by the author's wish to handle too many West Indian issues in the one work, so that it contains a number of interesting episodes but suffers from Miss Wynter's impatient closings-in for the kill. The hurried thinness of this passage detracts from its credibility; and the urge to illustrate the mulatto yearning for whiteness and mulatto touchiness about ancestry, is fulfilled only at the price of failing to animate the fictional character. Miss Wynter does not even glimpse the comic possibility of her deacon as bungling seducer or half-hearted rapist.

Sylvia Wynter's mulatto is a symptom, not a cause of the failure of *The Hills of Hebron.* In *God the Stonebreaker,* the mulatto is the rock upon which a promising novel comes to grief. In the early part of the book, where G.B. is the undisputed centre of interest, Bennett's touch is light and his control unobtrusive. G.B., a middle-aged spinster, grandmother, and versatile trickster lives off her wits in a slum area called Swine Lane. The depressing human and social environment in which she exists is never far from the surface of the novel, but Bennett manages to keep it at a comic distance. The manipulation of different registers of English (educated authorial paraphrase of dialect, and dialect-speaking character's attempt at educated speech) establishes and maintains a comic tone; the inflated authorial commentary lends an air of mock-heroic to the middle-aged heroine's exploits. In such a context, the episode (pp. 3–7) between G.B. and Quashie, does not come over as the expulsion of a helpless tenant by a heartless landlord, but as an animated contest of tricksiness between the Anansi-like heroine and her involuntary creditor. Moreover, although G.B. is a creature ruled exclusively by self-interest, the author does not seek to persuade the reader to pass judgement upon her. Amoral and resilient, G.B. finds a thousand surprising ways of being herself, the author allowing the reader to delight in his versatile creation.

The creation of a character of such elasticity within the determining social framework is a considerable imaginative feat. But the performance is not sustained. An increasing interest in Panty, the heroine's grandson, puts G.B. in a supporting role for much of the second half of the novel. What makes this a disappointing development is that Bennett is interested in Panty only as a mulatto. Not only is Panty limited as a fictional character by the stereotype of the mulatto; his relationships with other characters are presented schematically as aspects of the mulatto's social maladjustment. Bennett's seizing upon Panty as mulatto is the signal for a more explicit concern with social issues. The comic tone begins to slip, and the authorial language starts to sound pretentious: 'The glass globe sun exploded in the sky, scattering splinters of multi-coloured light. The larger particles assembled themselves into millions of galaxies. Inside Kate's breast the sun of hope exploded and splinters of pain floated around in her head' (p. 167).

It would be difficult to establish by quotation that Panty as a fictional character is limited by the stereotypes. For the impression depends upon the accumulation of mulatto trait upon predictable mulatto trait over a number of incidents in the novel. Moreover, some of the incidents by which Bennett illustrates the mulatto characteristics are very lively when seen in isolation. Such, in a small way is the incident that illustrates the insecure mulatto insisting on his social superiority. An aged woman comes to the office where Panty works, and begs:

> 'Mi dear son, give your poor mother a penny to buy bread. Me is dying for 'ungry. You look like a very nice young massa. Me is pleased to see such a nice person working with govament.'
> Stealthily Panty threw her a quick glance to make sure that it was no one he knew and then he returned his undivided attention to his work. With her stick, the woman impatiently knocked on the counter menacingly, repeating her request a little louder than before.
> Indignantly, Panty addressed her: 'You come to beg, you should not be so rude to your superiors. I am not your son. Now go away!'
> (*God the Stonebreaker*, p. 108)

43

The episode closes with the old woman's benediction of vituperative language against mulattoes.

Panty's relationship with the Allens, an English family, and their daughter Paula, is also determined by the mulatto stereotype. Panty is the mulatto submissive before the indifferent or hostile White: 'Conscious of Mrs. Allen's dislike for him, he assumed the vain task of trying to win her esteem. His devotion to this quite unnecessary undertaking was a feat of tolerance and self-effacement' (p. 126). He is also the mulatto who wishes to be White. This is expressed in his desire to marry Paula Allen, the White girl. And it also shows itself in an aping of White ways. Connected with the mulatto desire to be White, is mulatto hypersensitivity about Black kinsfolk. The following passage economically summarizes the mulatto characteristics which determine the presentation of Panty:

> To be like his superiors became Panty's dominating obsession, so he tried in deed and word to ape Parson Allen. Panty was often jeered at, and criticised for trying to be a 'black Englishman', but he felt that he was being deliberately persecuted on account of his humble antecedents. He rapidly became socially super-sensitive, developing much intolerance for his grandmother, whom he regarded as a social stumbling-block in his way.
>
> (*God the Stonebreaker*, p. 104)

It is not very long before this stereotyped characterization and the accompanying commentary begin to bore the reader. And Bennett's compulsive interest in 'the mulatto' causes him not only to lose sight of his freely invented and more satisfactory character, but to alter unconvincingly the focus upon the earlier G.B. The resourceful and splendidly amoral trickster heroine is reduced and sentimentalized as the generous, unloved, and pathetic victim of mulatto callousness. From this violent dislocation, *God the Stonebreaker* never recovers.

The stereotypes of the Coloured woman do not appear as authorial attitudes in Christopher Nicole's *Off White* (1959), Edgar Mittelholzer's *Sylvia* (1953), or Tom Redcam's *One Brown Girl And—* (1909). Sylvia's angst-ridden sensibility is portrayed as having to do with the spirit of her time (the novel is set in the

1930's) not with the fact of her mixed blood; and Ada the shallow mulatress in Redcam's short novel derives more obviously from George Eliot's Hetty Sorrel than from an idea of mulatto sexual freedom and incapacity. But while the authors do not push their characters in the direction of the stereotype, the three heroines are portrayed as having in common a sensuous beauty which, in real life, is the basis of a continuing popular image of the Coloured woman as both sexually desirable and highly sexed. And elements deriving from the popular image appear as automatic attitudes to the heroines by other characters in the novels: men look expectantly at Sylvia or pass their hands on her thighs hoping for immediate acquiescence; and Yvonne Huntly, in *Off White*, only understands Alan Grant's confidence that she will sleep with him 'like some common whore' when he tells her she is Coloured.

It is in John Hearne's *The Faces of Love* (1957) that the type images of the Coloured person—socially insecure and sexually overcharged—are turned to impressive fictional advantage. Rachel Ascom is the daughter of a German woman by a Negro. The combination 'had given her that big, handsome body and the square-boned face that would not show age for a long time. She had been lucky too, with her skin. It was dark and taut, not sallow grey like some German and Negro mixtures, and it had a vivid texture like the surface of a thick, broad leaf' (p. 35). Rachel's heavy attraction and sensuality are testified by a line of past lovers (impulsive one-night stands studding extended 'big loves') and by her concurrent affairs with Michael Lovelace and Jojo Rygin. Switching these characteristics of the Coloured woman, we can find Rachel illustrating the insecurity and excessive regard for material possession by which the male mulatto is typed. Fabricus, the narrating character, recounts: 'The first night I had gone with her we had spent a long time talking afterwards, and she had said, "I am nothing, you see. I came from nothing and none of you people will ever forget that when I make a mistake. Everything I become I've got to show. That's why I buy such good clothes. Every time I spend ten times what I should on clothes it's like a standard I've set myself" ' (p. 59).

45

But Hearne does not present Rachel as a type. We first see her the morning after a debauch when Andrew Fabricus, the narrating character, and one of her employees, calls to remind her of an appointment she appears to have forgotten. As a past lover turned friend, Fabricus is free to enter Rachel's bedroom:

> Rachel Ascom was asleep when I went into the bedroom and switched on the green lamp on the telephone table. The stiff crinkles of her dull brown, short expensively dressed hair were still neat as they had been when she went straight to bed with hair-clips still in. The sheets were drawn up to her chin and I could see her face in a frame of white: the long, predatory curve of her flat yet arched nose; the massive cliffs of her cheek-bones, and the broad, plump, pouting firmness of her mouth. It was really a handsome face, and when awake it had a kind of fierce alertness that passed for dignity. But in the privacy and surrender of sleep there were always three worried lines grooved into the flat wide forehead, between the eyebrows.
>
> (*The Faces of Love*, p. 10)

There is a man in the bed beside Rachel, but the narrator's cool reportage of a familiar scene, and Rachel's lack of embarrassment deprive us of a cheap or moralizing response to the spectacle. The focus, initially, is on the physical heroine.

The white frame, and the past lover's close-up (magnifying nose, cheekbones and mouth) bring Rachel's face sensuously before us ('curve', 'arched', 'plump', 'pouting'), and impresses her sheer physicality ('long', 'broad', 'massive'). But the combination of suggestive physical detail with a reading of the character growing out of it is a recurrent Hearne device for establishing and interpreting his personages. The almost unobtrusive 'predatory' and the dominating features described by the narrator seem to account for the used-up man beside Rachel. Fabricus's intimate discrimination between 'the kind of fierce alertness' on her face and the dignity it passed for; and his contrast, between her waking face as he remembers it, and her sleeping face as he sees it now, shift our interest from the solidly visualized present to the waking future: for it is clearly implied by the narrator's reflections and by the 'three worried lines grooved into the flat, wide forehead' that Rachel's imposing mask and fearless sexual presence plaster over an awareness of her own vulnerability. Our knowledge that Rachel is a mulatto may speed up our recognition of the significance of the 'short *expensively* dressed hair' or seem to intensify our awareness of Rachel's insecurity, but as I have tried to demonstrate, the extract creates its complex effect without a reliance upon external knowledge.

Hearne's vivid characterization and analysis interest us in Rachel as an individual from the first appearance. This interest is concretely held as we follow Rachel through her ruthless and shady business enterprises, and as we build up a picture of her sexual relationships as emotionally parasitic or materially motivated. That these different activities do not run in separate channels is shown in her capture of Michael Lovelace, the Englishman who comes out to edit the *Newsletter*, in place of the now-retired Price—and instead of Rachel who might have been appointed:

> She had been in power so long at the *Newsletter*, and her work wa very specialised and had to do with what she and old Price could get from the paper rather than what went into it. But she knew that Michael Lovelace was there because the old man whom she had seduced, pampered, tantalised, deceived and with whom she had schemed and built, could not trust her out of his sight. To control the stranger would be something like revenge, as well as being the sealing of a point that might become vulnerable. Besides, Rachel never liked to have anyone close to her who was independent of her. It made her really uncomfortable.
>
> (*The Faces of Love*, p. 71)

Soon she begins to sleep with Lovelace, and he falls in love with her.

It is being suggested that Hearne's technique of characterization and analysis arouses and holds our interest in Rachel as an individual, so that the mulatto traits to which we make a stock response are secondary to the artistic effects; going further, if we say that Rachel is the highly sexed, immoral Coloured woman, and the socially insecure mulatto buttressing herself with material possessions, it is necessary to recognize in the same breath that Hearne has fused and metamorphosed these two images in a broader study of the psychology of power working through an extraordinarily vivid character.

Rachel's exercise of power is at its most perverse in the love triangle which is formed upon the release from prison of the ebullient Jojo Rygin, her previous lover:

> She handled the situation between Michael and Jojo in her own way. And in her own way, I suppose, she handled it very well. Jojo was not in town often enough or long enough to be a problem. He was there just enough to give her what she liked him for, and what she had nearly forgotten while he was in prison. Michael, I think, must have been in love with her even at this time. Not like he became later on, but sufficiently to be foolish and vulnerable. You could see the strain of playing the other man begin to show itself in his quick, calmly observant eyes and in his smooth, confident, pleasantly superior face. I don't know how often or how deep he had been in love before, but I don't think he had ever done this sort of thing; and from what Oliver and I could see, he hated it. He hated it and he was caught in it. Looking back, I suppose this was Rachel's shrewdest use of her power. A more stupid woman would have pretended to be in love with Michael. That would have given him some rights in the case. She didn't. She only treated him, every day, with a fond, tender comradeship and admiration, in which her magnificent sexuality came packaged and deadly, as a kind of inevitable, honest and delicious flavouring to their relationship.
>
> (*The Faces of Love*, p. 129)

This long extract is as good a pointer as any to the central place of love in Hearne's fictional world, and leads us to see how the author subjects the character to a process in the novel in relation to that value. To speak of Rachel's involvement in a process is to argue that she is not a static character (like Panty) whose predictable traits are progressively illustrated, but a developing one.

In Hearne's *Land of the Living* (1961), Stefan Mahler, the shattered refugee hero, learns to put his life together again in the warmth of Bernice's generous and exemplary love. Later, it is only when Joan recognizes that Mahler's need for her is as great as hers for him that love grows between them. Love is visualized in this novel as the very human expression of responsibility and need. Reflecting on Jojo Rygin's expectation that his coming wealth will help him to possess Rachel without rival, Fabricus the narrating character in *The Faces of Love* expresses this basic Hearne value in personal terms: 'Each of us was looking for a place to rest, and each of us had chosen his own way and the person he wanted to share that place with. There was nothing for me to say or do about Jojo or Rachel or anyone else for that matter. Only about Margaret. She was my responsibility and my love, and my worry. And she was all I needed or wanted' (p. 241). In both these novels, Hearne visualizes this principle simultaneously with a view of the vulnerability of the human person in a broken world. But 'for weeks after she dropped them [her men] they would telephone Rachel at the office or prowl forlornly on the fringes of whatever group of people she was with at a party' (p. 32). In her love affairs Rachel neither accepts responsibility for others, nor confesses her own weakness. Uncompromisingly, she sees human relationships in terms of possessing or of being possessed: ' "I told you once," she said, "nobody owns me. Jojo will take what I give him. And Michael. Nobody helped me to get where I am and nobody is going to own any part of me now" ' (p. 126). In face of her own extreme vulnerability, Rachel uses love as a compensatory exercise of power. This makes her the arch-heretic in Hearne's fictional world.

Rachel's process in the novel culminates in a martyrdom that represents a conversion to love. It is part of Hearne's rigorous approach to the character, however, that Rachel's conversion is not inevitable, and that when it takes place it is more in the nature of a spontaneous and irrevocable gesture than of an access to earthly salvation. Nevertheless, her sacrifice of her own life at the end to save Michael Lovelace, forces Fabricus to recognize the universality of Rachel's case:

> We had gone after love and attached our need to various people, and then tried to attach these people to ourselves. To use them instead of giving whatever we had to them. Which of us hadn't? Not me, certainly. . . . Not Sybil, . . . Not Jojo . . . Michael? Almost. . . . And Rachel? She had waited a long time to find the love she wanted. Maybe she had known a lot about it and had been contemptuous and terrified of what had been offered her in its place by Price, and me, and Jojo. It was hard to say. All I could see, as I went from my room, was her face, and the big, handsome

IV

New Bearings

By the 1890's the different groups in the society were drawing closer together.Froude had discounted this as a possibility in 1887: 'There are two classes in the community; their interests are opposite as they are now understood, and one cannot be trusted with control over the other' (*The English in the West Indies*, p. 286). There was a dramatic increase in emigration after Emancipation, and as Black majority rule became more and more foreseeable those who could not bear the thought of 'a black parliament and a black ministry' joined the exodus. But Froude was only part right. Many Whites moved into commerce, the civil service and private business, alongside the Coloureds; and for many Whites and would-be Whites this was the period when the West Indies began to become home. The self-seeking of particular groups was beginning to be absorbed in more inclusive national feelings. It is in this shifty context that we might consider the contrasting careers of two White West Indian writers who were contemporaries of each other.

(i) *Thomas Henry MacDermot (1870–1933): 'Tom Redcam'*
In an article of 1899 entitled 'The Present Condition of Jamaica and Jamaicans', MacDermot wrote: 'Today we lead; tomorrow we advise; and on the day following we are co-workers together with our black countrymen. It is as our actions and opinions relate to them that they will stand applauded or condemned by the future historian.'[1] As editor of the *Jamaica Times* between 1904 and 1923, his comments on public affairs, according to Roberts, pointed to

[1] Cited by W. Adolphe Roberts in *Six Great Jamaicans*, Kingston, Jamaica (1952).

an ideal of Jamaica as a recognized entity, there being 'an unhappy note in his writing when he thought that his native country was being treated as a step-child'.

Although MacDermot was not the first Creole nationalist in the West Indies, he was the first Creole who practised as a literary man.[1] In his second novel *One Brown Girl And* . . . he sets up the brown girl Liberta Passley as a likely centre of interest. She had been 'handed over to Mother England to grow and to be trained among her sturdy sons and strong-limbed health-glowing daughters'. Now that she has returned she is cut off from her people and she is heavy with the real and 'inner Liberta Passley' waiting to be released. To put it like this is to draw attention to the similarity between Redcam's opening situation, and those developed with skill and concentration by George Lamming in *Season of Adventure* (1960), and Claude McKay in *Banana Bottom* (1933).

But Redcam does not become imaginatively involved in this significant West Indian dilemma. Liberta is reduced to peripheral status as the novel turns earnestly but ineptly to other social issues. The invoking of an exceptional Negro in contrast to the mass is in the tradition of anti-slavery novelists,[2] but the White West Indian author also seems to look forward to much more recent attitudes. A physical description of Fidelia Stanton, a Negro girl employed in a Portuguese household, leads into a celebration of slave rebellions:

> The unadulterated blood of her tribe ran in her veins and she was a Coromantee, daughter that is of the bravest of all the tribes that were brought to our shores during the eighteenth century, from the West Coast of Africa. They came as slaves; but the Coromantees, brave enduring, haughty and resolute, made bad bondsmen. Men whom nature had made free in soul, their fellow men found it no easy task to fetter. Through their brief periods of quiet submission they worked wonderfully well, inspired by their pride of race to show their powers; but they sprang into rebellion as

[1] His pen name was Tom Redcam. The fiction is: *Becka's Buckra Baby* (1903) and *One Brown Girl And* . . . (1909), both published by the Times Printery, Kingston, Jamaica. Redcam's poems were collected and published as *Orange Valley and Other Poems* (1951) by the Pioneer Press, Kingston, Jamaica, with an enthusing introduction by J. E. Clare McFarlane.

[2] See Wylie Sypher, *Guinea's Captive Kings* (University of North Carolina Press, 1942).

surely as the rays of the midday sun, passed through the burning glass, kindle fire: and those rebellions which the Coromantees led. . . .

(One Brown Girl And . . ., p. 44)

This is followed by an explicitly 'corrective' view of the African past:

> It is the conventional idea that the black men brought to the West Indies as slaves came from a life wholly savage and barbarous; through which there ran not a single vein of coherent organisation; a life unredeemed by a single spark of nobility and unsustained by aught of organised government, law or order. The truth however is that in some cases these men and women came from tribes which maintained a system and code of unwritten law that embodied for the tribe at least, more thoroughly and efficiently than Christianity has yet succeeded in doing for the whole race in the West Indies, a great number of those moral obligations that are elemental and are vital to the wellbeing of a people.
>
> (One Brown Girl And . . ., p. 45)

These essays are intrusions from an artistic point of view, but they are worth noticing: they help to show how close European romantic attitudes to the African are to the sentiments of later Négritude writers from the Caribbean.

When Redcam returns to describe the master's improper advances and Fidelia's human thumping reply, there is a classic example of the difficulty of the writer who feels he must express an African personality in his Negro characters, although he himself is more familiar with another system:

> Fidelia Stanton was a full-blooded Coromantee though she knew nothing of the history of her tribe. None had ever told her of the valiant deeds of her grandfathers and of their sires; but the pure tribal blood flowing in her veins was a conducting chain along which thrilled mighty but irresistible forces that connected her in moments of emergency with that race and that past in Africa to which she belonged.
>
> (One Brown Girl And . . ., p. 44)

It is consoling to think that Fidelia's violent refusal of John Meffala was not due to the solid middle-class prudery her White West Indian author arms her with; on the other hand, it is disappointing to begin to feel that the whole thing was just a rush of the warrior blood.

Redcam's poetry and fiction are disappointing, but his activity helps to illustrate the connection between national feeling and the growth of a literature. He remains an important figure in our literary history because of the attempt he made to encourage writing and to create a book-buying public in Jamaica in the early years of this century. His *Becka's Buckra Baby* (1903) was published as No. I in an abortive project called 'The All Jamaica Library'. The publisher's foreword runs:

> In 'The All Jamaica Library' we are presenting, to a Jamaican public at a price so small as to make each publication generally purchasable, a literary embodiment of Jamaican subjects. Poetry, Fiction, History and Essays, will be included, all dealing directly with Jamaica and Jamaicans, and written by Jamaicans, many of whom are well-known to the public as successful writers. We hope to give readers something worth buying, and we hope all Jamaicans will support this attempt to develop neglected resources of mental and aesthetic wealth.

Only five volumes[1] seem to have been issued, and there were only two supporting authors.[2] Redcam's work was not of a high order, but the comic sketches of *Maroon Medicine* (1905, No. II), and the literary romanticism of *Marguerite* (1907, No. III) were even less likely to inspire a national literature. In the preface to *One Brown Girl And . . .*, moreover, a double number (IV–V) costing one shilling, the publisher-author expresses anxiety on other grounds:

> I desire to get from this novel a reasonable return in money. . . . If the public of Jamaica co-operate by the purchase of this volume, there are other stories to follow along the same channel of publication. . . . Now I would make it very clear that I ask no one, on the sentimental grounds of patronising a local writer or supporting local literature *to pay a shilling for what he or she does not want* but this I ask as the minimum of fair-play to this or to any local independent publication, whether by myself or by another, that those who want to read the book and those who read it and like it, buy it. . . . All the fine talk in the world, and all the nice expressions of enthusiasm

[1] All published by the Times Printery, Kingston, Jamaica.
[2] 'E. Snod' (E. A. Dodd), author of *Maroon Medicine*; and William Alexander Campbell, author of *Marguerite*.

and regard will avail little if the enthusiasts do not buy the local publication that they declare so well deserves support.

It was a losing battle, however, not only in the sense that the writer could not hope for an income from his fiction, but also from the point of view of prestige. Yet, when the Gleaner Company published H. G. de Lisser's *Jane: A Story of Jamaica* (1913), after newspaper serialization, it must have seemed that Redcam's example was catching. And a British edition of this novel in 1914 had the appearance of the export model of a product tested and approved first in the country of origin. But this was never to become the pattern in the literary relationship between the West Indies and Britain. Within three years de Lisser was to write in an author's note to his locally published *Triumphant Squalitone* (1917): 'There are many reasons for issuing local editions of my books. The best, from the Jamaica reader's point of view is that he obtains the work much more cheaply than he otherwise could. The Colonial Editions of my previous stories, for instance, sell at half-a-crown per copy. And that is a price which as experience has proved, very few Jamaicans can easily pay.' With the air of a man who has made good elsewhere, de Lisser went on to declare that the publishers expected no financial profit and that the reading public owed it to the advertisers (the merchants and business houses of Kingston) that they could buy his books so cheaply. The publication of *Jane's Career* (1914) and *Susan Proudleigh* (1915) in successive years by Methuen and Co. Ltd. looked forward to the West Indian writer's economic and psychological dependence upon British publishers and readers. It also signalled the end of Redcam's ideal. It is not difficult to recognize today that Redcam's efforts had been premature. But it is impossible to withhold admiration from this patriot who was in some ways too far ahead of his time.

(ii) *H. G. de Lisser (1878–1944)*

De Lisser was not a propagandist for a Jamaican literature as Redcam had been, nor did the younger man have to earn his living by writing fiction. The early death of his Portuguese father obliged the son to leave school and work for a time as clerk in a drug store and at an ironmonger's. But doors which would have been shut to an equally talented Negro were open to the white-skinned de Lisser. It was not long before he was made a library assistant at the Institute of Jamaica where he read voraciously. Roberts[1] describes the rapidity with which the talented young man rose till he became editor of the *Gleaner* (1904), a member of the Board of Governors of the Institute of Jamaica (1910), and general secretary of the Jamaica Imperial Association which was founded in 1917. As a writer, de Lisser was financially independent, and as a citizen he dominated the public life of Jamaica for almost thirty years. Claude McKay, in contrast, emigrated to the United States in 1912: the Negro's future as writer and as citizen would have been severely limited in the colony of his birth.

Each of de Lisser's novels is based upon a historical event or set in a specific period: *Jane's Career* (1913) deals with Kingston in the early decades of the twentieth century, while his last published, *The Arawak Girl* (1958), is set in the 1490's. Between these two times the other novels are systematically located. A significant pattern may be noticed. In *Jane's Career*, the central character is black, and the scene is contemporary. In *Susan Proudleigh* (1915), set topically in Panama, the central characters are still Negro, but brown-skinned. From this point, however, the novels either draw less and less upon the contemporary scene, or the central characters cease to be Black. This pattern in the *oeuvre* runs parallel with the evolution of the Fabian Socialist sympathizer and critic of colonial rule of 1913 into the arch-reactionary and conservative spokesman of later years: 'From complete self-Government for Jamaica, Good Lord deliver us. Not even Full Representative Government can be considered at a time when, to use a collo-quialism, the tail is wagging the dog, and tub-thumping is practi-cally the order of the day.' Not even the Colonial Office would hold this view propounded in a *Gleaner* editorial of 1938. De Lisser died in May 1944, a few months before what seemed to many at the time to be the new day, the proclamation in 1945 of a new Constitution and universal adult suffrage for Jamaica.

[1] Facts about de Lisser's life are taken from *Six Great Jamaicans*, Pioneer Press, Kingston, Jamaica (1951).

De Lisser's anti-nationalistic position has affected West Indian attitudes to his place in West Indian writing. Most of the novels do not encourage a favourable estimate. But it is necessary to make a claim for *Jane's Career*. It is the first West Indian novel in which the central character is Black; Jane is the first full West Indian fictional heroine; and it is in *Jane's Career* that de Lisser's attitude to his raw material and to his characters comes closest to being like that of later West Indian writers.

One element in *Jane's Career* is the process of growing up, experienced by a young country girl who comes to Kingston as a 'schoolgirl'—an apprentice domestic servant. Another element is de Lisser's wish to protest against the exploitation of domestics and to give a picture of Kingston lower-class life. The success of the novel lies in containing the protest intention within the character's process.

The work divides into five parts. In the first, Jane is the simple village girl in her father's house. In the second, she is a schoolgirl employed at a shilling per week in the home of a lower middle-class mulatto Mrs. Mason. In the third part, Jane runs away from Mrs. Mason's house and shares a room in a slum district with a virago called Sathyra. The fourth part finds Jane living by herself after a quarrel with Sathyra. Finally, Jane wins the protective affection of a young man, Vincent Broglie, who takes her to live in a respectable district called Campbell Town where they have a child and then a white wedding. To put it this way is to clear the ground for sighting the work's main weaknesses.

In the first part set in the country, de Lisser cannot help creating comic rural characters. Although the authorial voice tells of the new class of Jamaican peasants who are looking for 'some place where life would be different from what it was in the village' (p. 15), the comic presentations of Daddy Buckram the pompous village Elder, and Celestina the country girl back with city sophistication, work against the author's wish to suggest the lifelessness of the village. And when Celestina advises Jane that it is necessary to find a male friend in the big city, Jane's reply seems to be invented for comic purposes: 'But here Jane shook her head resolutely. "No", she said, "I promise me fader to keep meself up, and I gwine to do it. Perhaps I may married one of dese days; who is to tell." ' The trouble with this speech is that it is an accurate forecast of what Jane does at the end:

> In her white muslin dress, with her hair done up with ribbons, wearing high-heeled shoes and looking as though she had been born to entertaining guests, Jane is not very like the little girl we saw sitting mute and frightened as she drove into Kingston with Mrs. Mason. She is not much like the girl we saw sharing apartments with Sathyra. She looks very much tonight as if she has kept herself up; her baby is now fully developed; she has the lover she cares for, and in the other room lies 'the kid' whom all the women declare to be the 'dead image' of his father, while all the men see the mother chiefly in his lineaments. It is Jane perfectly contented at last, and dreaming of no higher fortune. It is Jane who now herself employs a schoolgirl who submissively calls her Miss Jane, and obeys her slightest command.
>
> (*Jane's Career*, p. 295)

The reader's feeling that the author is patronizing his heroine is confirmed by the ironic celebration of Jane's white wedding in the final chapter. Such a detached attitude at the end does not accord with the involvement in the longer central sections of the novel.

As Jane leaves her village, for instance, de Lisser's 'objective' narration invests the landscape with symbolic anticipations of the girl's ups and downs, moments of despair and moments of happiness in the big and tangled city:

> On either hand the forest ran, the ground often rising steeply into lofty eminences. Part of the road was in shadow, the sun not yet having climbed high enough to flood every inch of the countryside with its living light. But already the freshness of the morning was wearing away, and as she walked she saw the big green lizards chasing their prey across the ground, and amongst the trees she heard the birds piping and calling to one another. Frequently, for a little while, the entire way would be plunged in semi-darkness; this was when the great trees, bending over on either side, intermingled their branches, thus forming a leafy roof which caught and intercepted the rays of the rapidly rising sun.
>
> Sometimes the forest would end upon the right hand or the left, the roadside would break away into sheer precipice, and a great stretch of green and fertile country, flooded with warm and golden light would spread out into the distance for miles and

miles, until it merged itself into yet more distant hills and radiant sky.

Such scenes were familiar to Jane, and roused her admiration not at all. She hardly glanced to right or left as she trudged on; never once did she reflect that she was leaving all this, which had formed part of her life as far back as she could remember, and leaving it perhaps for ever.

(*Jane's Career*, pp. 34–5)

The spontaneous symbolism looks forward. The concluding authorial comment looks clumsily back and seems to lament Jane's unreflecting nature. Nevertheless, one cannot help feeling that Jane, glancing neither to right nor left, trudging on, involuntarily becomes a poignant figure in a landscape to which she is bound by a Wordsworthian 'feeling of blind love'.

The description of Jane's response to the city immediately upon arrival is equally fortunate. De Lisser's use of the omniscient novelist convention in the later novels becomes stiff. He is seldom able to move in and out of a character's consciousness as in *Jane's Career*:

... She had never seen such large houses before; in a vague sort of way she wondered how many hundreds of people lived in them, so spacious did the villas of the Kingston gentry appear to her unsophisticated eyes. Then there was the wonder of the electric-cars, things she had often heard of, but which she had never been able to imagine in any kind of way. When she came to where the road ended and the long street proper began, her amazement further increased. The numerous little shops, the houses standing close to one another, the bustle of the street, the number of people she saw moving in all directions, or lazily leaning against doors and fences, or squatting on the edges of sidewalks and wherever else they could find a seat—she had never thought that so many buildings and persons could be seen at one time; *and the farther she went the more did she become impressed with the greatness of the city in which she had come to live.*

(*Jane's Career*, p. 43)

What is truly impressive in this passage is the way in which de Lisser suggests Jane's excitement without losing a balanced view. Jane may be swept away by the new city, and the authorial voice may imitate her wonder, but the passage closes on an ironic note whose unobtrusiveness (my italics) prevents it from being a comment on the particular character. Instead it is a compassionate footnote to all our human experience.

De Lisser expresses Jane's growth in the Mason household in terms of the mastery of duties, increased familiarity with the city, and disillusion with Mrs. Mason. The author's contempt for the up-and-coming mulatto class is never out of view, but it is contained by Jane's legitimate response to her mistress:

> . . . Jane still admitted that Mrs. Mason was a lady but Jane felt that Mrs. Mason was only a lady of sorts. She lived in a street where all the houses were small and shabby, and if she did not have the merit of possessing a brown complexion, if at least one-half of her physical composition was white, there were thousands of others like her in Kingston and thousands who were lighter in colour than she could claim to be. . . . Who after all, was Mrs. Mason? Jane answered the question in her own way.
>
> (*Jane's Career*, pp. 105–6)

If one suspects at times that de Lisser is using Jane in a vendetta against the class represented by Mrs. Mason, the author's identification with the character when Jane runs away is less open to doubt.

Few of de Lisser's Negro characters are allowed to have the range of feeling of Jane. Her seduction by Mrs. Mason's nephew, Cecil, is done in terms of the confused excitement of adolescence; her recovery, and the rejection of Cecil, are presented as a triumph of youthful resilience, and as a growth in maturity. When her mother pays a visit and Mrs. Mason manages to make a good impression, de Lisser allows his heroine the complex emotion of jealousy: 'She was not so glad to see her mother now. She felt that one who should have been her friend had gone over completely to the enemy' (p. 111). Going out in a cab with Vincent Broglie, Jane is made to run from joy to shock:

> Jane felt that this was one of the treats of her life; she was proud to be driving in a cab, proud to be driving with such a person, proud that he didn't think himself too good to be seen in public with her; and her laughing face showed her pleasure. They were not far from home when, turning a corner and still chatting gaily, they had to pull up quickly to allow an electric-car to pass. Both

Jane and Vincent stared at the people in the car. Amongst the
passengers and looking full at her and her companion, was Mr.
Curden, Jane's admirer and chief.

(Jane's Career, pp. 237–8)

When Jane breaks from Mrs. Mason, quarrels with Sathyra and
goes to live in a slum yard by herself, de Lisser uses the character
as a means of exposing current evils, but the mood of the character
and the authorial comment coincide. Needless to say, the protest
itself becomes more effective for being put in this way:

> The moonlight streamed down upon the yard, throwing into relief
> every part of it, revealing the dilapidated fence, the ramshackle
> range of rooms, the little superior two-roomed cottage on the other
> side of the yard, the odds and ends of things scattered all about.
> The poverty of the place stood confessed, and Jane, seated on a
> box by the threshold of her friend's room, had before her eyes the
> material evidence of the sort of life which most of her class must
> live. Not improbably some of them had dreamt dreams such as
> hers; their fancy had been as free.
>
> *(Jane's Career,* p. 207)

And de Lisser does not allow his heroine's nostalgia to produce a
dissipating effect:

> Sometimes she thought of her home in the country; and far away
> it seemed, up there amongst the mountains, half-lost, dreaming its
> monotonous, half-idle existence away. She wondered how her
> friends were getting on, what had become of her sister, whether
> Mrs. Mason had written to tell her mother that she had run off
> without a word. All this she thought of at intervals but with no
> regrets, she did not wish to return; and she felt that, if her people
> had heard what she had done, they must have accepted the fact as
> quite natural.
>
> *(Jane's Career,* p. 212)

Jane's isolation in this long section of the novel faces de Lisser
with several alternatives. She could be presented in omniscient
narrative as a pathetic being; the comic-vulgar dialect could be
modified into a language of soliloquy and reflection as in Samuel
Selvon's later *A Brighter Sun* (1952); or the author could represent
the character's thoughts and feelings through a mixture of 'objective' narration and free reportage. As the illustrations show,

de Lisser followed the third course. The choice is significant, since it shows that de Lisser's breakthrough in the presentation of the Negro as person is still limited by a social attitude to the language of the Negro. Nevertheless, the chosen technique articulates the obscure West Indian peasant for the first time in fiction. Although the novel is marred by the writer's superior, ironic handling of the success of Jane, and although de Lisser's attitude to his West Indian raw material becomes increasingly alien and unsympathetic, *Jane's Career* belongs in art and in orientation to the West Indian canon.

V

The Drift Towards the Audience

Since 1950, most West Indian novels have been first published in the English capital, and nearly every West Indian novelist has established himself while living there. The following table gives complete figures for the period 1950–64. It is broken into five-year units to show the increase in West Indian writing and the continuing dependence upon British publishers and readers:

Five-Year Period	Number first Published	Places of Publication			
		United Kingdom	Jamaica	U.S.A.	Australia
1950–4	20	14	5	0	1
1955–9	32	28	2	1	1
1960–4	45	43	1	1	0

London is indisputably the West Indian literary capital.

The increase in West Indian writing since 1950 is clearly related to developments in popular education, and to the growth of national feeling. But the reliance upon Britain is a continuation and a consequence of a long history of economic and cultural absenteeism. The nearest thing to a chance of checking the long drift to the Mother Country occurred in Trinidad in the late 1920's and early 1930's, when there was a concentration of literary and artistic talent such as had never happened anywhere in the islands before.

Many of the names in the group who met to exchange ideas, listen to music, and to discuss the social and political condition of the island mean little today. A young librarian, Carlton Comma (now Senior Librarian of the Trinidad Public Library) kept them supplied with books and book news; a Portuguese Creole, Albert Gomes (who was to become the pre-independence equivalent of Chief Minister), lent radical fire.[1] From the beginning, the literary pace-setters were another Portuguese Creole, Alfred H. Mendes (b. 1897), and C. L. R. James (b. 1901). At Christmas 1929 and Easter 1930, Mendes and James published the two issues of a magazine called *Trinidad*, whose list of contents and contributors help to show the cosmopolitanism and the wide interests of the unofficial club.[2] But just as the group was beginning to disperse, with James and Mendes on the verge of emigration, Gomes started to edit, at his own expense, the magazine by whose name the group itself is now spoken of. Holding on to contributors in the U.S. and Britain, Gomes kept *The Beacon* alive from 1931 to 1933. Mendes writes:[3]

> *The Beacon* was, of course, the best organ of opinion in Trinidad— and nothing touching it for intelligence, wit, satire and general excellence has since appeared in Trinidad. Nothing at all. It created a furore of excitement in the island ... and it set people everywhere thinking and talking as they had never talked or thought before. *Those were the days!* ... *The Beacon* took anything into its maw, anything that was fresh, good, intelligent—stories, articles on politics, race, music—reviews of books, of music recitals, of art exhibitions—controversial letters, stimulating editorial notes writ-ten by Gomes (Gomes was essentially a polemist and not a poli-tician or writer. He tried his hand some years ago at writing novels

[1] Gomes's emotive prose address 'Black Man' in *The Beacon* of July 1931 (Vol. i, No. iv) is as fierce and relevant as any Black Power call today.

[2] The Xmas 1929 issue included stories: 'Miss Winter' and 'Booze and the Goberdaw' by R. A. C. de Boissière; 'The Thirteenth Spirit' by Joseph da Silva; 'Her Chinaman's Way' and 'Faux Pas' by Alfred H. Mendes; 'Off Shore' by F. V. S. Evans; 'Triumph' and 'Turner's Prosperity' by C. L. R. James. H. McD. Carpenter wrote on 'Pianists and Violinists on the Gramophone'. Other contributors were A. C. Farrell and Algernon Wharton. The Easter 1930 issue included poems by John Vickers, E. Adolph Carr and A. H. Mendes and stories as follows: 'The Answer' by Kathleen M. Archibald; 'On a Time' and 'The Last Lot' by F. V. S. Evans; 'A Trip to Town' by R. A. C. de Boissière; 'Rene de Malmatre' by E. C. Benson; 'The Pipe' by J. I. Da Silva; 'News' by Alfred H. Mendes and a Review by 'A.J.S.' of five novels including *Banjo* by Claude McKay, *A High Wind in Jamaica* by Richard Hughes and Hemingway's *A Farewell to Arms*.

[3] Mendes, personal communication, 10th September 1964.

The Drift Towards the Audience

and failed dismally. A lively intelligent fellow. Like myself, Portuguese) by Sidney Harland, myself, Algernon Wharton, Sonny [H. McD] Carpenter (an excellent music critic. Trinidadian of course, white) F. V. S. Evans, Nello (C. L. R.) James and so on. We had 3 rip-roaring years of tearing into every sanctity and pharisaism of the respectable folk. How hurt they were—but how much they secretly enjoyed it!

To take into account the activities of this group, while recognizing that they only happened to be the most accomplished of the literary cells that were forming in most of the islands at this time, is to modify a little the metaphor of explosion that has been used in connection with West Indian writing since 1950. In the published work of its two leading figures, Alfred H. Mendes (b. 1897) and C. L. R. James (b. 1901), we can see the decisive establishment of social realism in the West Indian novel.

James's story 'Triumph' is a good example of the realistic literature of the 'yard' which was begun in these years: 'Every street in Port of Spain proper can show you numerous examples of the type [of slum dwelling]: a narrow gateway, leading into a fairly big yard on either side of which run long low buildings, consisting of anything from four to eighteen rooms, each about twelve feet square. In these live and have always lived the porters, the prostitutes, carter-men, washer women and domestic servants of the city.'[1] The public response to the magazine in which the story appeared illustrates some of the difficulties in the social situation the *Beacon* group were contending with.

'Triumph' begins with a depressed Mamitz in depressing surroundings: 'She was shortish and fat, voluptuously developed . . . and . . . saw to it when she moved that you missed none of her charms.' In the literature of the yard, sex and an uninhibited approach by the writers are basic ingredients. So too are violence, and the uncertainty of earthly things. Mamitz's man beats her and abandons her, the kept woman sinking from prosperity to destitution. But Mamitz's fall is presented as just a little beyond the natural order of things: 'Despite her very obvious attractions, no man took notice of her.' To dispel this catastrophe, Mamitz's

[1] Quotations are from 'Triumph' in *Trinidad*, Vol. I (Xmas 1929). The story has been reprinted in Andrew Salkey (ed.), *Caribbean Stories* (1965).

friend invokes obeah, another element in this kind of literature.

When Mamitz begins to prosper again (she has two men—Popo the irresponsible man of pleasure, and Nicholas the butcher who pays the rent) Irene's attempt to cause trouble by summoning Nicholas at an unexpected hour leads to an incident in which violence and dialect come together in the characteristic manner of the literature of the yard:

> . . . Nicholas, still in his bloody butcher's apron came hot foot into the yard. He went straight up to Mamitz and seized her by the throat.
> 'Where the hell is that man you had in the room with you—the room I payin' rent for?'
> 'Don't talk dam foolishness man, le'mme go', said Mamitz.
> 'I will stick my knife into you as I will stick it in a cow. You had Popo des Vignes in that room for the whole day. Speak the truth, you dog.'
> 'You mother, you' sister, you' aunt, you' wife was the dog' shrieked Mamitz, quoting one of Celestine's most brilliant pieces of repartee.

The self-conscious introduction of episodes like this shocked the more respectable members of the Trinidad educated class, in much the same way that the Harlem writers of the late 1920's and early 1930's had shocked those Negro American conservatives anxious to be acceptable to White Americans. In the 'Editorial Notes' to the second issue of *Trinidad*, Mendes quotes *The Trinidad Guardian* of 22nd December 1929 on the impact of the Xmas 1929 number: 'Letters protesting against the obscenities of the Magazine have been pouring into the Guardian office during the past week. One is from a Boy Scout who says: "Its disagreeable implications cast unwarrantable aspersions on the fair name of our beautiful Island." Another letter describes the volume as "nasty". The writer fears that other young writers will think it smart to be the same.'

'Triumph' ends nobly, arousing pure compassion through its sordid raw material. Having foiled Irene's plan, Mamitz plasters the inside of her door with dollar notes and flings it open in full view of Irene. The ladies of the yard taunt the mischief-maker;

'Bertha, Josephine, the fat Mamitz and the rest were laughing so that they could hardly hold themselves up. Irene could find neither spirit nor voice to reply. She trembled so that her hands shook. The china bowl in which she was washing rice slipped from her fingers and broke into half a dozen pieces while the rice streamed into the dirty water of the canal.' The task of Mendes and James and their associates, however, and it is a task which remains to be done in the 1960's and 1970's, was a two-fold one: to get their countrymen to read, and at the same to teach them how to read. A brave attempt to explain how fiction works was made in 'A Commentary' by the editor of *Trinidad*, issue number 2:

> . . . [T]he creative artist is primarily concerned with the weaving of patterns: the material that he uses is so much grist to his mill, for he who is sincere about his literary work (or any other art-work for that matter) cannot stop to consider how much ugliness there is in the matter that comes his way. It would be silly to tell the architect not to build in stone because stone is rough and amorphous; to warn the sculptor to leave bronze alone because bronze is brown and blatant is like warning the priest and parson against heathens because they have no regard for *our* anthropomorphic god; even so it is futile and puerile to ask the writer of fiction to leave bodies and barrack-yards alone because they are obscene in the popular sense. It all depends on what literary treatment they receive, though it does not necessarily mean that, so treated, they shall be no longer obscenities; it simply means that they shall be obscenities presented for reasons other than raising the disgust or sexual desires of the reader.

The Trinidad audience was interested in respectability, not in questions of art.

But while the Port of Spain bourgeoisie were hostile, there were patrons' eyes in England. Stories by James and by Mendes had started appearing in English magazines since 1927.[1] Aldous Huxley, who was to do a disastrous introduction to Mendes's

---

[1] James's 'La Divina Pastora' appeared in the *Saturday Review* (15th October 1927), and in E. J. O'Brien (ed.), *Best Short Stories of 1928* (1928). 'Lai John' by Algernon Wharton and Mendes appeared in *The London Mercury* (January 1929) and in *Best Short Stories 1929* (1929), which also listed Mendes's 'Torrid Zone' as a near qualifier. O'Brien anthologized Mendes's 'Lulu Gets Married' in 1936; and John Lehmann included the same author's 'Afternoon in Trinidad' in *Penguin New Writing 6* (May 1941).

first novel *Pitch Lake* (1934), had written congratulating the
editors of *Trinidad*. Almost inevitably, both Mendes and James
emigrated, the former to the United States, the latter to Britain.
Their novels[1] were published by London publishers.

Pitch Lake is a staggering account of the deracination of a
Portuguese youth torn between the sordid shopkeeping world of
his father, and the hollow social world of second-generation
Portuguese who have made good in Port of Spain. Mendes's
craftsmanship is not as smooth or as flexible as Naipaul's, but
Pitch Lake is a fierce indictment of a colonial society which can
only offer alternative ways of death to its members. Even more
impressive is Mendes's rendering of the tortured consciousness of
his unstable central character. By narrating strictly from Joe da
Costa's point of view, Mendes allows us to experience the character's fear and insecurity, his vacillation, his disgust at others and
his self-contempt. In the final chapter he goes berserk, murders
Stella the Indian girl who is pregnant by him, and strikes out into
the night. To his tortured mind, Stella comes to represent all that
prevents him from moving smoothly into the socialite world of
his brother and sister-in-law. To the reader, the pitch lake that Joe
seeks to identify outside himself, also wells up from within.
Mendes's achievement in this novel is to allow us to measure
Joe's inadequacy and confusion, while persuading us of the value
of the human character's struggle for integrity.

There is a loss of concentration in the highly exotic *Black Fauns*
(1935), set in a yard, and constructed episodically about the lives
of a cast of man-hunting, dialect-speaking, slum-dwelling ladies.
Stimulated by Huxley's introduction, the colonial author plays the
local colour for more than it is worth. Although Mendes's capacity
for rendering states of stress is again evident in the presentation
of the brooding girl, Martha, there are long stretches of the novel
devoted to artless polemics or social advertisement. Such was the
first crude warning of the perils of the overseas audience that the
West Indian novelist was driven to woo.

[1] Alfred H. Mendes, *Pitch Lake* (1934), *Black Fauns* (1935); C. L. R. James, *Minty
Alley* (1936).

The Drift Towards the Audience

In *Beyond a Boundary* (1963), James describes his departure for England in 1932 as a necessary step in what was to be a literary career: 'I had a completed novel with me. But that was only my 'prentice hand. Contrary to accepted experience, the real *magnum opus* was to be my second novel' (p. 119). James was to distinguish himself internationally as an imaginative political theorist, and as a sensitive commentator on the West Indian social and cultural scene, but no second novel ever came to be written. The first was *Minty Alley*.

In the opening pages, James establishes the necessity for a young middle-class Negro to find cheap lodgings in a yard, No. 2 Minty Alley, where his superior social position, and his innocent tolerance make him confidant and judge to the inhabitants. As a curious outsider Haynes follows the development of the clandestine affair between Mrs. Rouse's lover, Benoit, and the nurse who is a lodger in the house; he witnesses Mrs. Rouse's suffering when the affair comes to light; and when Benoit marries the nurse, he records the obsessed Mrs. Rouse's inability to forget Benoit, and her generous love for him when he is abandoned by the nurse. At the end of the novel, the Minty Alley group break up. Haynes finds new lodgings, but often returns nostalgically to the now respectable site where so much had happened in other days.

The use of Haynes's limited perspective as the novel's point of view makes for vividness in the people of Minty Alley, since they can only reveal themselves to him in speech or in action. James's control of linguistic varieties and his ability to catch the speaking voice are crucial in this process:

> 'I am Mrs. Rouse's niece. Why she always taking up for the coolie? Everything is only Philomen, Philomen, Philomen. If I and the girl have a little disagreement, Philomen always right, I always in the wrong. Philomen is a servant. She shouldn't have more privilege than me.'
>
> 'Don't speak so loudly, Maisie. You see, Mrs. Rouse says that Philomen helps her. And you don't give much assistance.'
>
> 'But, Mr. Haynes, Philomen working. She must work. What I must help Mrs. Rouse for? For the scraps of food and clothes she give me?'
>
> 'Philomen works very hard. She is a good girl.'

'Good girl, she! Mr. Haynes, what you saying ?' Maisie laughed shortly. 'All those clothes you see her putting on on a Sunday, I could get it if I want to get it as she get them. She is the worst little prostitute in Victoria.'

'Now, Maisie——'

'But I have to speak about it, Mr. Haynes. If I don't tell you you wouldn't know. All of you only holding up Philomen as if she is a model. I'm speaking the truth. That same Philomen you praising up so much she used to live with Mr. Mill, the druggist, and Bennett, the assistant. And when old Mills find out he sack Bennett. Two of them the same time.'

(Minty Alley, pp. 124–5)

The vividness of the Minty Alley lodgers is one expression of life's triumph over narrow surroundings.

The narrative point of view restores the characters in a more fundamental sense. Since Haynes cannot know what they are thinking or doing when they are out of the range of his observation and since his protected upbringing limits his ability to guess, the characters retain autonomy as familiar but not fully known beings. Each has a mysterious life of his own. It is in this way that the comings and goings of Benoit, for instance, are fraught with possibilities. Haynes's limited perspective gives an impression of depth to the presented life of the novel in another way: because he registers, without being able to explain, the curious fixation of Mrs. Rouse upon Benoit, we are made to feel that there are hidden resources even in the hedged-in people of yard.

But *Minty Alley* is more than just a novel of the yard narrated from an unusual point of view. And Haynes is not simply a narrative device. The novel is really about the mutually impoverishing alienation of the educated West Indian from the people. James allows Haynes's economic necessity to coincide with the character's 'need to make a break' (p. 11) from the protecting world of middle-class mother and faithful family servant. The young man's growing involvement with, and appreciation of, the inhabitants of the yard are made to correspond with the degrees by which he comes to have his first sexual affair with Maisie, the yard's young fire-brand. It is a function of the author's lack of sentimentality, that Maisie should leave for the United

States by the end, rather than hang about in the hope of leading the affair with Haynes to a conventional conclusion. But Haynes has had his awakening. His returns to the respectable house that has replaced the old Minty Alley are as much an ironic comment on the rising West Indian bourgeoisie as a wistful backward glance at what is being lost.

The popular discontents that swept the West Indian islands between 1934 and 1938 mark the beginnings of modern West Indian nationalisms. The discontents owed their immediate origins to the economic depression of the 1930's but they cannot be separated from the Pan-African and Pan-Negro movements of the twentieth century; nor would they have become so articulate had the effects of popular education in the West Indies not begun to be operative. The nationalist ferment was intensified by the achievement of universal adult suffrage, and improved political constitutions in most of the territories. The new spirit showed itself in the founding of the periodicals. '*Kyk-over-al* we hope will be an instrument to help forge a Guianese people, to make them conscious of their intellectual and spiritual possibilities. There's so much we can do as a people if we can get together more, and with this magazine as an outlet, the united cultural organisations can certainly build, we believe, some achievement of common pride in the literary world, without detracting in the least from their group aims or autonomy.'[1] Even more directly connected with the national movement was *Focus*, founded in Jamaica in 1943 by the sculptress Edna Manley, wife of the labour leader, Norman Manley, who became Chief Minister of Jamaica in 1955: 'Great and irrevocable changes have swept this land of ours in the last few years, and out of these changes a new art is springing. Historically, art gives a picture of contemporary life: philosophically, it contains within it the germs of the future. This collection of short stories, essays and plays and poems fills both these roles; in them is the picture of our life today, the way we think, the acts we do; but underlying the picture of the present is the trend of the future, where new values will predominate and a new approach to

[1] A. J. Seymour's editorial in the first (December 1945) issue of *Kyk-over-al*.

things will be born.'[1] In Barbados, with less ceremony, Frank Collymore, Therold Barnes and a few other members of the Young Men's Progressive Club launched *Bim* in December 1942. 'If *Bim* has any policy other than that of fostering creative writing, it has been one of encouragement. If at times some contributions did not merit such encouragement little harm has been done. At least they did not deprive better writers of a chance.'[2] Without political affiliations like *Focus*, without a theory of literature such as that generated by Harris, Seymour and Carter in *Kyk-over-al*, but blessed with an ability to survive one financial crisis after another in the philistinism of West Indian society, *Bim* has caught on and grown almost by accident into the most West Indian periodical in the islands.[3]

If *Bim* brought West Indian writers together within the same covers for the first time, it also helped to point them towards England. In 1946, Henry Swanzy became editor of the B.B.C.'s weekly overseas broadcast, 'Caribbean Voices'. The free trade between the two institutions was of mutual advantage. *Bim* gave the permanence of print, 'Caribbean Voices' supplied cash and the promise of a literary future in England: 'You see the magic of the B.B.C. box. From Barbados, Trinidad, Jamaica and other islands, poems and short stories were sent to England; and from a London studio in Oxford Street, the curriculum for a serious all-night argument was being prepared. These writers had to argue among themselves and against the absent English critic. It was often repetitive since there were no people to talk with. The educated middle class had no time for them; and the dancing girls in the Diamond Horse Shoe simply didn't know what it was all about.'[4] The attitude of the middle class mattered because the periodicals

[1] Edna Manley in the Foreword to the 1943 *Focus*. Quoted by G. R. Coulthard in 'The West Indies' in *The Commonwealth Pen*, ed. McLeod (N.Y., 1961), p. 192.

[2] F. Collymore, 'The Story of Bim' in *Bim Vol. 10 No. 38* (Jan–June 1964), p. 68.

[3] Two recent articles on *Bim* and on *Kyk-over-al* are of special interest. In 'Kyk-over-al and the Radicals', L. E. Brathwaite gives a rough content analysis and argues that Seymour's magazine was never revolutionary in spite of editorial declarations; in 'Frank Collymore and the Miracle of Bim', Edward Baugh adds to Collymore's piece cited above. See *New World*, Guyana Independence Issue, April 1966, and Barbados Independence Issue, Vol. III, Nos. 1 and 2, 1966. Published by New World Group Ltd., Kingston, Jamaica.

[4] George Lamming, *The Pleasures of Exile* (1960), pp. 66–7.

founded in the 1940's never saw it as part of their function to raise the literacy of the public at large. Neither could the establishment of the University College of the West Indies (1948) and the founding of the journal of the Extra-Mural Department *Caribbean Quarterly* (1949) turn back the three-hundred-year-old tendency.

'Caribbean Voices' was not the only calling sound from England in the 1940's. Returning from a visit to Jamaica, Robert Herring, editor of *Life and Letters*, wrote in an editorial of January 1948:

> There is as yet in Jamaica no general means of publishing books, such as exists in most other civilised countries in the world. That may sound hard of belief but it is true. There is no firm in Jamaica which exists simply and solely to publish books. There is no branch of a British publisher. . . . It is not much more than a hundred years—one hundred and ten, to be precise—since the end of slavery, but the fight against illiteracy has made enormous strides. The latest figures are that sixty per cent of the population are now literate. . . . There are Jamaican authors and have been for long, Constance Hollar, Claude McKay and Adolphe Roberts being perhaps the most famous. But there is no Jamaican publisher. Consequently, authors such as the last two I named go to America. If a Jamaican poet wishes to produce his slim volume he has to do so at his own expense. . . . Until books can be published there can hardly be expected to be readers. A poet may write on a desert isle . . . but readers can't read or develop in reading without books.

During 1948, Herring devoted a complete issue of *Life and Letters* to Jamaican writing, and then a complete issue to West Indian writing.[1]

With so much interest in England, and so little intellectual or economic encouragement at home, the next step was inevitable. The Guyanese writer, Edgar Mittelholzer, arrived in London in 1948; in 1950, his second novel *A Morning at the Office* was published by the Hogarth Press. In 1950 Samuel Selvon (Trinidad) and George Lamming (Barbados) made their journey to an expectation: Selvon's first novel *A Brighter Sun* (published by Allan Wingate) appeared in 1952; Lamming's *In the Castle of My Skin* was published by Michael Joseph a year later; 1953 saw the publication of a first novel by yet another West Indian: Jonathan Cape

[1] April 1948 and November 1948 issues of *Life and Letters*.

published *The Hills Were Joyful Together*. Roger Mais had arrived from Jamaica in 1951. The deluge had begun.

The characters and settings of most novels by West Indians in England are drawn from the native islands they remember or imagine; the novels deal, moreover, with issues that are of immediate relevance to the West Indian people. The situation is ironic. Higher labour costs, greater individual spending power, and the existence of a vast network of institutions purchasing automatically have put the price of a novel manufactured in Britain beyond the means of most West Indians. The avid audiences for radio serials, and the energetic participation of West Indian audiences in the cinema suggest that there are imaginative capacities waiting to be exercised. But the present publishing situation does not encourage the growth of a cheap and even minor literature around which at least a habit of reading might be established.

West Indian writers deplore the poverty of cultural life in the islands, but the departure of so many gifted men from an area whose joint population hardly exceeds three million, has only aggravated the situation they sought to escape: 'This was the kind of atmosphere in which all of us grew up. On the one hand a mass of people who were either illiterate or if not, had no connection whatever to literature since they were too poor or too tired to read; and on the other hand a colonial middle class educated it seemed, for the specific purpose of sneering at anything which grew or was made on native soil.'[1] The West Indian artist in exile chafes at having to produce a literature disconnected from its sources, and complains of his 'irrelevance of function'; meanwhile, the island-dwellers, like their predecessors on the land for over three hundred years, are imprisoned in a life without fiction. The creation of a literate and responsive West Indian public would seem to be the only way to rout 'the Philistines (who) are encamped here'.[2]

[1] George Lamming, *The Pleasures of Exile* (1960), p. 40.
[2] Roger Mais, 'Why I Love and Leave Jamaica' (1950), reprinted in *Public Opinion*, Kingston, Jamaica (10th June 1962).

PART II

Approaches

VI

The Language of the Master?

(i) *Terranglia*

An approach which has made the literature of the West Indies part of a wider unit is conveniently illustrated by the publication *Terranglia: The Case for English as World Literature*.[1] Professor Jones's project attempts to cope with all the new literatures in English which have developed visibly in the first half of the twentieth century:

> When we talk about English (meaning British) literature, we are talking about a segment. When we add American literature, we have added only another segment. Until we are prepared to think of English as a world language expressing itself in a world literature we shall be getting farther and farther out of date. If we are to study 'English' literature—that is the literature of the English language—let us study all of it; every bit of it that has a legitimate claim to attention.[2]

This effort to make things bigger if not better is severely limited by arbitrary regional groupings, and by an undiscriminating disposition of authors in these groups. It is absurd to find Mabel M. A. Chan-Toon, Bankim Chandra Chatterjee and Sir Henry S. Cunningham in a region called 'India-Pakistan-Ceylon-Burma' for all the qualification that they are 'Older writers'. It serves no purpose to place Joseph Conrad, 'Han Suyin' and Alec Waugh in a section called 'Malaysia-Hong Kong'. But worse than *Terranglia's* bibliographic follies are its serious misconceptions about what is meant by 'the use of English'.

[1] Joseph Jones, *Terranglia: The Case for English as World Literature* (N.Y.: Twayne Publishers, 1965).
[2] *Terranglia*, p. 20.

(ii) *First Language or Second Language*

It is necessary to make the distinction that in some areas like the West Indies and Australia, English or a version of it is the first language, while in places like Pakistan and Nigeria it is a learned or second language. In the latter situation at least two kinds of possibilities have to be borne in mind. Firstly, there may be difficulties of expression arising from an inadequate grasp of basic features in the language—as when in Amos Tutuola's *The Palm— Wine Drinkard* (1954) the drinkard says 'I lied down there awake' (p. 14). Although, in Tutuola's fiction, it is not always possible to distinguish between a deliberately ungrammatical usage and what might be just a mistake which happens to be effective ('they were rolling on the ground as if a thousand petrol drums were *pushing* along a hard road', p. 22), it is nevertheless necessary to be aware that the distinction sometimes can be made.

The 'pushing' petrol drums above lead us into the second broad possibility that must be considered. An author who thinks in one language instinctively and can write in another is liable to modify the adopted language. A certain amount of this may be done unconsciously, but the Nigerian, Gabriel Okara, is all for a deliberate approach:

> As a writer who believes in the utilisation of African ideas, African philosophy and African folk-lore and imagery to the fullest extent possible, I am of the opinion the only way to use them effectively is to translate them almost literally from the African language native to the writer, into whatever European language he is using as his medium of expression. I have endeavoured in my words to keep as close as possible to the vernacular expressions . . . a writer can use the idioms of his own language in a way that is understandable in English.[1]

In his novel, *The Voice* (1964), Okara puts this principle into practice, drawing upon his native Ijaw. Three quotations may help us to see some of the advantages and some of the limitations of the kind of dubbing Okara proposes. The first, from the end of

---

[1] Gabriel Okara, 'African Speech . . . English Words' in *Transition* 10, Vol. 3, 1963. Published from Ibadan, Nigeria.

the novel, does not seem to carry any marks necessarily derived from the native language:

> When day broke the following day it broke on a canoe aimlessly floating down the river. And in the canoe tied together back to back with their feet tied to the seats of the canoe, were Okolo and Tuere. Down they floated from one bank of the river to the other like debris, carried by the current. Then the canoe was drawn into a whirlpool. It spun round and round and was slowly drawn into the cone and finally disappeared. And the water rolled over the top and the river flowed smoothly over it as if nothing had happened.
>
> (*The Voice*, p. 157)

From this, and other passages like it in the novel, it is evident that Okara does not follow his programme as fanatically as the article in *Transition* suggests.

The next passage contains examples of the novel's most obtrusive 'translation' feature. Most of the sentences have a verb form as their final word:

> It was the day's ending and Okolo by a window stood. Okolo stood looking at the sun behind the tree tops falling. The river was flowing, reflecting the finishing sun, like a dying away memory. It was like an idol's face, no one knowing what is behind. Okolo at the palm trees looked. They were like women with hair hanging down, dancing, possessed. Egrets, like white flower petals strung slackly across the river, swaying up and down, were returning home. And, on the river, canoes were crawling home with bent backs and tired hands, paddling.
>
> (*The Voice*, p. 13)

It takes a while to get used to the grammar of Okara's novel to the point where a sentence like 'Okolo at the palm trees looked' becomes normal, and it is arguable that a non-Ijaw reader cannot help being irritated by continuous exposure to such 'abnormal' structures where no special effects are being aimed at, but on the credit side no reader can resist the aptness of 'falling' in sentence two or fail to register the peculiar inevitability with which 'paddling' completes the brilliant evocation of 'canoes were crawling home with bent backs and tired hands'.

In the next passage, Okolo is given protection in the hut of the girl, Tuere, who had been driven out of the town previously, on the allegation that she was a witch. With the mob outside, Okolo revolves past events in his mind:

> *Inside* the hut Okolo stood, hearing all the spoken words *outside* and speaking with his *inside*. He spoke with his *inside* to find out why this woman there behaved thus. He knew her story only too well. She had been a girl of unusual habits, keeping to herself and speaking to herself. She did not flirt with boys though she had a hunger-killing beauty. So it was the *insides* of everyone that perhaps she had not the parts of a woman. They did not, because of these her strange behaviours call her a witch. They openly called her a witch when her mother and father died one after the other within a few weeks and after every young man who proposed to her died one after the other. All these Okolo remembered. He also remembered how in a circle of strong eyes and strong faces she stood being accused of taking witchcraft to kill her father and mother. They then from the town drove her. His *inside* then smelled bad for the town's people and for himself for not being fit to do anything on her behalf.
>
> (*The Voice*, p. 20)

Okara's 'translation' principle seems to produce an extraordinarily vivid effect in the sentence 'He also remembered how *in a circle of strong eyes and strong faces she stood being accused* . . .'. But the physical rightness of 'inside' in the final sentence does not, I think, cancel out our impression that the word appears (my italics) only as a result of Okara's modish insistence. In sentence one it is impossible to avoid feeling that the author is being clever.

In Achebe's novels there is a tighter artistic control over the incursions from the native language into English, but I do not want to illustrate this at any length. I shall take a convenient and authoritative example from *Transition* No. 18 (1965) where in an article 'English and the African Writer', Chinua Achebe himself writes:

> Allow me to quote a small example from *Arrow of God* which may give some idea of how I approach the use of English. The Chief Priest is telling one of his sons why it is necessary to send him to church:
>> I want one of my sons to join these people and be my eyes there. If there is nothing in it you will come back. But if there is something then you will bring back my share. The world is

The Language of the Master?

like a Mask, dancing. If you want to see it well you do not
stand in one place. My spirit tells me that those who do not
befriend the white man today will be saying 'had we known'
tomorrow.
Now supposing I had put it another way. Like this for instance:
I am sending you as my representative among those people—
just to be on the safe side in case the new religion develops.
One has to move with the times or else one is left behind. I
have a hunch that those who fail to come to terms with the
White man may well regret their lack of foresight.
The material is the same. But the form of the one is in character
and the other is not. It is largely a matter of instinct but judgement
comes into it too.

Tutuola, Okara and Achebe differ from one another as artists, but
these three writers are able to draw upon resources in their social
situation which do not exist for writers whose only language is
English.

In areas where English is a second language, the fiction produced in that tongue is not always the natural expression of a
whole society. And it may be limited by local factors like the
alternative literatures being produced in native languages; the
number of people able to read English and what proportion of the
total they represent; and the attitude of national governments to
the foreign tongue. In Pakistan, to take one example, the existence
of classics and highly developed written literatures in native languages has largely determined and fixed a process of compart-
mentalization:

> Though the English newspapers and journals print stories and
> poems at least once a week, generally writers like to write in Urdu
> and Bengali rather than in English. Our best writers do not like to
> write creative literature in English. English is reserved for jour-
> nalism, official use, use in law-courts and, occasionally, for literary
> criticism. In other words, it is treated as a medium mainly for
> non-literary communication and very rarely for creative self-
> expression.[1]

Pakistani writing in English is unlikely to become important at a
national level. In Nigeria, on the other hand, in spite of some

[1] S. A. Ashraf, 'The Study of English Literature in Pakistan' in *Commonwealth
Literature*, ed. John Press (1965), p. 139.

nationalistic demands in literary magazines that a local language should be used, the possibilities for the writer using English are enormous. 'Nigeria', writes a professional linguist, 'with a population of perhaps 48 million has according to conservative estimates, as many as 150 languages, none of which is spoken by more than six million people.'[1] In this huge artificial ex-colony, a Nigerian professional writer seeking a large audience, or a nationalist author committed to the task of helping to create a national consciousness has the strongest of incentives to write in English. Because there is no indigenous literary tradition in written form to which the writer may be drawn to contribute, a tradition in English stands at least an equal chance with any other language, both for expressing modern Nigerian experience (Achebe and Ekwensi) or for the re-casting of folk material (Tutuola).

Questions like these hardly arise in the West Indies. For the modern West Indian writer there is no possibility of a choice between English and another language. English is his native tongue and he uses it as a matter of course. I should like to look briefly at how this has come about.

(iii) *English in the West Indies: 'Bad English'*

A description by Edward Long in *The History of Jamaica* (1774) is a convenient point from which to look backwards at the way in which English became established among Negroes in the West Indies during the seventeenth and eighteenth centuries. The same description has a shape which helps us to anticipate the fluidity of the twentieth-century situation:

> The Africans speak their respective dialects with some mixture of broken English. The language of the Creoles is bad English, larded with the Guiney dialect, owing to their adopting African words in order to make themselves understood by the imported slaves; which they find easier than teaching these strangers to learn English. The better sort are very fond of improving their language by catching at any hard word that the Whites happen to let fall in their hearing; and they alter and misapply it in a strange manner; but a tolerable collection of them gives an air of knowledge and importance in the eyes of their brethren, which tickles their vanity

[1] John Spencer in *Commonwealth Literature*, p. 116.

and makes them more assiduous in stocking themselves with this unintelligible jargon. . . . This sort of gibberish likewise infects many of the White Creoles, who learn it from their nurses in infancy and meet with much difficulty, as they advance in years, to shake it entirely off and express themselves with correctness.[1]

To the three stages of 'Englishness' outlined by Long we have to add a fourth—the Standard English which he uses as a criterion of correctness. Individual Negroes had attained competence in this fourth type in the eighteenth and nineteenth centuries but it is only in the twentieth century, as a result of the establishment of popular education in the islands, that we can speak of a class of educated speakers of English from among the Negroes and other Black elements in the population. I would like to argue later that when this happens we have to propose a category called 'West Indian Standard', but it is necessary first to look at the earlier periods.

The three stages contained in Long's description help us to reconstruct the process by which English displaced the African dialects and became the basis of the language of West Indian Negroes. As the quotation shows, the stages may coexist at any given time, especially in the pre-Emancipation period when there was a continuous supply of newly arrived Africans. But we might dispose them chronologically by focusing on the language of the groups among which, at each point in time, the process of substitution was most advanced. The farther back in time we go, the greater the number of Africanisms we find in the language of these groups; as we move forward, the degree of Englishness increases.

In the first stage, African dialects predominate with only a mixture of broken English. As there is little evidence, we have to speculate about how the stage actually began, and we have to set a hypothetical point at which a new stage would have begun. A fifty-year unit seems convenient since it covers at least two generations. With Jamaica as field, the first stage would stretch to the end of the seventeenth century. To make orders and instructions understood, the Whites would have had to invent a species of essential English, partly made up of a number of formulaic words and phrases, and in general, showing fewer inflexional variations than

[1] Edward Long, *The History of Jamaica* (1774), Book III, Chapter 3, pp. 426–7.

would occur in exchanges between Whites. There would, however, be a compensatory increase in the reliance upon the extra-linguistic context, upon word order, and upon intonation to make necessary discriminations and to fill out meaning. One cannot help invoking the existence of an abbreviated language along these lines as one of the sources of the meagre inflexional content, and the heavy reliance upon syntactic directives in West Indian dialects of the twentieth century. However this may be, I would suggest that traces of a minimal English invented for practical purposes became lodged in the language of the slaves at an early period, and that in the slave context there would have been considerable motivation to pick up and practise the prestige language of the masters. We know that slavery was a scale by which all things African were devalued.

Only such pressure can account for the rapid transformation which had taken place by the early eighteenth century. Among the slaves born in the island, as the following quotation shows, stage two was well under way: 'The Slaves are brought from several places in Guiney, which are different from one another in Language and consequently they can't converse freely.... 'Tis true the Creole Negroes are not of this Number: They all speak English.'[1]

Although the plantation system restricted intercourse with the upper orders of the plantation hierarchy, there were areas of increased social contact, and consequently exposure to a wider range of English, between slaves and those Whites at the lower end of the social scale. In addition to general routine contact with the group and particular meetings with the Negro 'driver' for passing on instructions, there were intimacies contracted with slave women. Domestic slaves and personal attendants were exposed to a wider range of situations than field slaves, although it is worth remembering that not all the Creole ladies were literate. We can imagine that the individual contacts so far mentioned would have had some influence on the language of the participants and that the 'improvement' made by the slave would have been transmitted in some form to his or her immediate circle. But the most significant contact, because it would appear to have been between groups, was that

[1] Charles Leslie, *A New and Exact Account of Jamaica* (1739). Quotation from Letter I, p. 327, of the Third Edition of 1740.

between the Negroes and the White indentured servants[1] (mainly Irish and Scottish) in the seventeenth century and in the first half of the eighteenth. Leslie writes of these servants being ruined by combining with the Negroes: 'The great Thing which ruins most of these unfortunate Fellows, is the combining with the Negroes who tell them many plausible stories to engage them to betray their Trust.'[2] But Long (1774), describing them as 'the very dregs of the three kingdoms', states that they used to seduce the wives of the slaves and that the 'better sort of Creole Blacks disdain to associate with them'.[3]

Since there was no formal teaching of any kind, and since the models from which the slaves picked up what they could were themselves degenerate ones, it is not surprising that slave English was 'bad English'. Imperfect learning, imperfect forgetting, and the necessary fraternization with newly arrived Africans ensured that this 'bad English' would be 'larded with Guiney dialect':

> The Negroes seem very fond of reduplications, to express a greater or less quantity of anything; as *walky-walky*, *talky-talky*, *washy-washy*, *happy-happy*, *tie-tie*, *lilly-lilly*, *fum-fum*: to, *bug-a-bugs* (wood-ants) *dab-a-dab* (an olio made with maize, herring and pepper) *bra-bra* (another of their dishes) *grande-grande* (augmentative, size or grandeur) and so forth. In their conversations they confound all the moods, tenses, cases and conjunctions without mercy; for example, *I surprise* (for I am surprised) *me glad for see you* (I am glad to see you) *how you do* (for how d'ye do!) *me tank you; me ver well;* etc.[4]

The point to be emphasized, however, is that in stage two, in contrast to stage one, the base of the language is already English. Stage two seems to mark the period when we can begin to speak about Creole English, since the new combination is both English-

---

[1] Leslie gives an account of the deficiency laws of 1703 which demanded *inter alia* that 'Every Master of Slaves, for the first five working Slaves, shall be obliged to keep one White Man-servant, Over-seer or hired Man, for three months at least, and for ten Slaves, two Whites, and for every 10 more, one; to be resident in the Plantation where the Negroes are employed'. (See p. 214.)

[2] Leslie, p. 320.

[3] Long, Book III, Chapter 3, p. 411.

[4] Long, Book III, Chapter 3, p. 427.

based and literally island-born. From this point, however, the history of the Creole is a history of steady reduction in the number of obvious Africanisms. According to F. G. Cassidy, an editor of the authoritative *Dictionary of Jamaican English* (1966):

> ... There is no real evidence ... that any articulate African speech survives in any community in the island today, and it is doubtful whether any has been spoken at all within the twentieth century. A few snatches of African or African-like words are preserved in some songs and some of the revivalist cults keep up a terminology among themselves that has African elements, but these are all vestiges in a structure that is not genuinely African, but Jamaican. ...[1]

For while Creole English was appearing to draw closer to Standard English in vocabulary, its grammar, as Thomas Russell observed, was taking its own shape:

> Although it is evident that this, as every other corrupted form of language, is spoken by no previously well-planned system, yet as in course of time, every corruption resolves itself into certain very plain and distinct ones, which are, in not a few instances, in direct opposition to those of the pure parent language.[2]

Thomas Russell's *The Etymology of Jamaican Grammar* appeared in 1868. Russell is committed to a notion of correctness but his position was revolutionary in his time. More widely held than Russell's view in the eighteenth and nineteenth centuries, however, is the one, encouraged by the reduction of obvious Africanisms and by the closeness of vocabularies, that Creole English was simply 'bad English', spoken mainly by Negroes but sometimes by uneducated White Creoles.

By the time that Lady Nugent was keeping her Jamaica journal indeed, we are told that

> ... The Creole Language is not confined to the negroes. Many of the ladies, who have not been educated in England, speak a sort of broken English, with an indolent drawling out of their words, that is very tiresome if not disgusting. I stood next to a lady one night near a window, and, by way of saying something, remarked

[1] F. G. Cassidy, *Jamaica Talk* (1961), p. 20.
[2] Quoted by Cassidy in *Jamaica Talk*, p. 24.

that the air was much cooler than usual; to which she answered, 'Yes, ma-am, him rail-y too fra-ish.'[1]

With Lady Nugent's comment we are reminded that however fluid the situation may in fact have been, the crude ruling generalization of pre-Emancipation society was that there were two main varieties of English—the language of the illiterate Negro and the language of the literate master. But it follows from the limited social contact of the eighteenth and early nineteenth centuries that the grammar of slave English could neither be recognized nor generated by non-speakers of it. This gives great interest to the attempts of British writers in the eighteenth and early nineteenth centuries to represent 'Negro English' in their fictions. The way in which 'Negro English' became associated with certain stereotypes of the Negro is another concern of the next section. Both have bearings on modern West Indian writing.

(iv) *'Negro English' in British Fiction of the Eighteenth and Nineteenth Centuries*

The first example I would like to look at comes from a work by a writer who had actually been to the West Indies. In *Tom Cringle's Log* (1829), the prying narrator describes the behaviour of a Negro grave-digger left alone with a corpse and with the food and drink intended as an offering to the dead man's duppy (spirit):

> I noticed he kept looking towards the east, watching as I conjecture, the first appearance of the morning star, but it was as yet too early.
> He lifted the gourd with the pork, and took a large mouthful.
> 'How is dis? I can't put dis meat in Quacco's coffin, dere is salt in the pork; Duppy can't bear salt.'
> Another large mouthful.
> 'Duppy hate salt too much.'
> He ate it all up, and placed the empty gourd in the coffin. He then took up the one with boiled yam in it, and tasted it also.
> 'Salt here too—who de debil do such a ting? Must not let Duppy taste dat.'
> He discussed this also, placing the empty vessel in the coffin, as

---

[1] *Lady Nugent's Journal* (1839): entry for 24th April 1802. See p. 132 of 1907 edition.

he had done with the other. He then came to the calabash with the rum. There is no salt here, thought I.

'Rum! ah Duppy love rum—if it be well strong. Let me see—Massa Nigger, who put water in dis rum eh? No, no, never touch dat.'

Here he finished the whole and placed the empty vessel beside the others; then gradually sank back on his hams, with his mouth open and his eyes starting from the sockets, as he peered up into the tree, apparently at some terrible object.[1]

Scott's comic purpose is well served by his invented dialect. But there are two features of the passage that are of peculiar interest here. The first is the association of dialect with the stereotype of the comic Negro. The second has to do with the gap between the language of the narrator and the language of the fictional character. Bearing both of these in mind will help us to mark some significant points of growth in West Indian fiction. For as we shall see, the dialect is used in so many different human contexts by West Indian writers that it has been freed of the stereotype. And in different ways there has been a steady closing of the gap between the language of the narrator and the language of the fictional characters.

Another example of the use of dialect comes from the work of a writer who never visited the West Indies. The consequence is not, perhaps, a necessary one, but in this passage the dialect is totally invented and it is unconvincing.

White man tie me mother, and force her and me brother Tankey board ship, and bring them and sell them to me master: me mother take sick, and no able to work; so she sit down; white man see her, and whip me mother, whip her very much, and make her work; when he turn away she so sick she no able to stand, she sit down again; but white man, cruel white man, again see her, and whip her much, very much, till blood run. Tankey see it, me see it; me cry; Tankey no bear it: he come softly behind white man, and with big stone he knock him down; he make him dead; other white mans see Tankey and take him and hang him up by leg to tree, and whip him till he all bloody and blood run upon the ground. . . .[2]

[1] Michael Scott, *Tom Cringle's Log* (1829). Quotation from Vol. 1, pp. 219–20, of the 1894 edition in two volumes by Gibbings and Co. Ltd. The incident quoted follows a hilarious account of a Negro funeral in which it is possible to trace African cultural survivals.

[2] Cited by Wylie Sypher in *Guinea's Captive Kings* (University of North Carolina Press, 1942), see pp. 276–7.

Dorothy Kilner's *The Rotchfords* (1786) from which the passage comes has elements of both anti-slavery and cult-of-feeling traditions so its purpose should be evident. But there are again two features that I want to point out for the way in which they help us to measure the uses of dialect in West Indian writing. Miss Kilner's uncomplicated sentences with their monosyllabic words, their single tense, and their repetition to suggest paucity of vocabulary are intended to represent the simple speech of a simple man. It will be shown later how West Indian writers have complicated dialect to achieve less limited ends than this.

The two examples looked at reflect a limited knowledge of dialect and a limited conception of its possible artistic uses, the uses opted for coinciding with an external and stereotyped approach to the Negro. These were typical of British fictional representations in the eighteenth and nineteenth centuries. But that they were not inevitable may be argued from an interesting exception in William Godwin's *St. Leon* (1799), where the novelist-philosopher not only presents an unstereotyped Negro but protests against the habit of inventing a vulgar language to represent the socially inferior being. St. Leon, the hero, tries to bribe the gaoler, Hector:

> 'My good friend, are not you poor?'
> 'Yes, sir.'
> 'Would not you readily do me a kindness?'
> 'If my master give me leave, I will.'
> 'You mistake me. Would you be my friend?'
> 'I do not know what you mean, sir. I have been used to call the man I love my friend. If you mean that, you know I cannot choose whether I will be a man's friend; it comes of itself.'
> 'Can I not make you my friend?'
> 'That is, make me love you?'
> I was surprised at the propriety of his answers. I am unable at this distance of time to recall the defects of his language: and I disdain the mimic toil of inventing a jargon for him suitable to the lowness of his condition: the sense of what he said I faithfully report.[1]

Although this is lifeless fiction, it is fiction conscious of the possibilities of life. But in 1799, it is still a hundred and fifty years before

[1] William Godwin, *St. Leon* (1799). Quotation from pp. 234-5 of the edition of 1831.

the folk become full human beings in literature. When they do so, the 'jargon' invented for them will also have arrived. In the last part of this chapter there will be an examination of dialect in West Indian fiction. But first the ground must be prepared by a description of the contemporary linguistic situation.

(v) *The Contemporary Linguistic Situation*

There are varieties of West Indian dialect from island to island, but there are certain broad features in common, and it is to these that one refers in speaking about a West Indian linguistic situation. Once this is said it is convenient to concentrate on one territory, and since recent discussions have focused on Jamaica it makes for some continuity of exploration to choose the same field.

In the twentieth century we have to give up the notion of separate languages (Creole English and Standard English) and we have to envisage a scale. At one end of the scale is what we have been calling 'Standard English'. In the strictest sense, Standard English (SE) is the language of British expatriates, but quite apart from whether it is actually practised in the islands, it exercises a powerful influence. It exists as an ideal form to be aspired towards by mentally colonized West Indians, and it is the unknown norm by which even the illiterate measure social standing. An observant novelist, V. S. Naipaul, provides a comic illustration. In *The Mystic Masseur* (1957), Ganesh the mystic hero begins a small campaign:

> One day he said, 'Leela, is high time we realise that we living in a British country and I think we shouldn't be shame to talk the people language good.'
>
> Leela was squatting at the kitchen *chulha*, coaxing a fire from dry mango twigs. Her eyes were red and watery from the smoke. 'All right, man.'
>
> 'We starting now self, girl.'
>
> 'As you say, man.'
>
> 'Good. Let me see now. Ah, yes, Leela, have you lighted the fire? No, just gimme a chance. Is "lighted" or "lit" girl?'
>
> 'Look, ease me up, man. The smoke going in my eyes.'
>
> 'You ain't paying attention girl. You mean the smoke *is* going in you eye.'
>
> *(The Mystic Masseur,* p. 72)

The Language of the Master?

At this point in the novel, Leela is too concerned with life to bother about language, but with Ganesh's success and new importance, Leela becomes a lady:

> Every day Leela became more refined. She often went to San Fernando to visit Soomintra, and to shop. She came back with expensive saris and much heavy jewellery. But the most important change was in her English. She used a private accent which softened all harsh vowel sounds; her grammar owed nothing to anybody, and included a highly personal conjugation of the verb to be.
>
> She told Suruj Mooma, 'This house I are building I doesn't want it to come like any other Indian house. . . .'
>
> (*The Mystic Masseur*, p. 150)

Even beyond Leela and Ganesh, at the farthest end of the linguistic scale, and living in remote areas are the unschooled speakers of a number of closely related dialects that are the twentieth-century continuations of Creole English. The basic features are no different from those Thomas Russell had recognized in the language of the folk and had sought to describe in *The Etymology of Jamaican Grammar* (1868). But in the hundred-year interval, what was the language of the majority has become the language of a minority.

With the formal establishment of popular education in the latter half of the nineteenth century, we can trace the beginnings of a new connection on the grammatical level between the upper reaches of Creole English and Standard English. Once this connection was made, the long retreat of Creole as a separate language to its present minority position had begun. Another consequence of the connection was a multiplication of what I have called earlier 'stages or degrees of Englishness'. The emergent levels of dialect can be ranged in a continuous scale between Standard English and residual or hard-core Creole. At opposite ends we seem to have two different languages but they move towards each other by mutually intelligible degrees.

It is hard-core Creole which is analysed by Beryl Loftman Bailey in *Jamaican Creole Syntax: A Transformational Approach* (1966). Miss Bailey uses the term 'Jamaican Creole' to cover what we have been calling 'Creole English'. Miss Bailey seems to be inconsistent, however, since she adopts more rigid criteria for purposes of pure grammatical analysis than in the more nationalistic activity of estimating the number of speakers of Jamaican Creole. The coherent system she produces in her analysis would have been impossible if she had seriously held the position declared in the 'Introduction' to her grammar: 'There is a hard core—the un-schooled ranging from pre-school children to the elderly . . . but if we take into consideration the fact that every native-born Jamaican understands some form of Creole, an estimate of a million speakers would not be extravagant . . .'. This seems to be an excessive estimate which can only be accounted for by Miss Bailey's commitment to a view of Creole today as the people's language, and to her belief in an ur-Creole, 'some kind of Proto-Creole' whose 'prior existence in the Old World' and relexification in the New has spawned a knot of related Creole languages in the Caribbean area:

> By Jamaican Creole I mean the English-based Creole spoken throughout the island of Jamaica alongside the officially recognised English. It is a 'Mischsprache' in which the syntax represents the mixing of two related syntactic types—one English, the other some kind of Proto-Creole and the lexicon is predominantly English.[1]

In an earlier section I have proposed a theory of the origin of Creole English: I would suggest further, with Cassidy, that other Creoles developed under analogous conditions, hence their structural affinities:

> But structure is not everything and even the marked differences of grammar and sounds are not enough to over balance the large part of Jamaican folk speech that is English. If it is Creole, it is still English Creole as distinct from Spanish or French Creole. It co-exists with English and the two have more in common than apart.[2]

I want therefore to return to the concept of a linguistic scale and the fluid situation which even Miss Bailey recognizes (see pp. 1–2 of *Jamaican Creole Syntax*) to explain what is meant by 'West Indian Standard' and to suggest its significance for West Indian fiction.

West Indian Standard (WIS) lies nearest to Standard English (SE) on the linguistic scale in the islands. Its vocabulary is the same

---

[1] *Jamaican Creole Syntax* (1966), p. 1.
[2] F. G. Cassidy, *Jamaica Talk* (1961), p. 406.

as that of SE but with the addition of a small number of West Indianisms[1] which have passed from the dialect into educated usage. The grammar of WIS is practically the same as that of SE. In their written forms, therefore, SE and WIS are almost indistinguishable. The most obvious differences between SE and WIS exist on the level of actual pronunciation. In *Jamaica Talk*, Cassidy equates Jamaican Standard [a variant of WIS] with the way educated Jamaicans pronounce Standard English. I will want to make the definition a little more exclusive than that but Cassidy's impressionistic description of Jamaican pronunciation gives an idea of how one variant of WIS sounds:

> The educated Jamaican pronounces Standard English as well as the educated man anywhere—that is to say, according to his personal lights and attitudes, his interests and the impression of himself that he may seek to establish. Like everybody else he will have his local differences, yet no more of those necessarily than the educated Irishman, Welshman or Scot—or for that matter, than the educated Englishman who is not from the 'home counties'. These local differences are heard in Jamaica in individual words and turns of phrase, but perhaps most strikingly as a pattern of intonation and accentuation that is often very different from the levelness of many Americans on the one hand, or the hilliness of many Englishmen on the other. Jamaican speech is more accidented: it goes up and down more frequently, and by sharper rises and falls. In short, it has a decided and characteristic lilt, the origin of which we shall discuss in a moment.[2]

In the next paragraph, Cassidy seems to recognize a connection between the pronunciation in WIS and the pronunciation of the dialects. The one is only a less accidented relation of the other. At the point therefore where WIS resembles SE least, it is closest to the dialects.

---

[1] Formed by analogy from the term 'Jamaicanism' used and defined by F. G. Cassidy in *Jamaica Talk* (1961) thus: 'Most obviously this term would include any word, meaning or feature of grammar, idiom or pronunciation that has originated in Jamaica, or has been adopted here from a foreign source. It should also include any similar element that has survived in this island after dying elsewhere, or which has received a decidedly higher degree of use in Jamaica than elsewhere. Putting this into a more rational order, we may classify Jamaicanisms as belonging to five main types: preservations, borrowings, new formations, transferred meanings, and special preferences' (p. 3). The definition of 'West Indianism' would run along the same lines.

[2] *Jamaica Talk*, p. 26.

Approaches

Using the resemblance in pronunciation as a starting-point it is tempting to argue that there is an organic connection between the dialects and WIS. But this is only an intuition which would need more evidence, more delicacy of analysis, and more expertise than can be mustered here. If such an organic connection did exist, however, we might have been able to attribute to it some of the features of repetition and other rhythmic effects which seem to occur spontaneously in the narrative sections of West Indian novels, for we could argue that these are natural incursions from the oral tradition of the dialects. But my interest is less to advocate a distinctive linguistic variety than to describe a new class of speakers in whose usage the notion of an organic connection between WIS and the dialects may be validated.

I would propose the following criteria for recognizing speakers of West Indian Standard: they have been sufficiently educated to control the grammar and lexis of Standard English; they may learn to pronounce in other ways, but they retain ability to pronounce in their natural WIS way; above all, however, they are more or less instinctive speakers of or thinkers in a West Indian dialect or dialects. The third criterion suggests that the speaker of West Indian Standard is an educated West Indian whose social origin is in the dialect-speaking group or whose social contacts make him a dialect-speaker.

These criteria are not intended to increase nor diminish the number of speakers of WIS, but rather to help us to understand why the most distinctive speakers of West Indian Standard come from the Black or Coloured educated classes; the criteria also help us to see why such a class of speakers could not emerge as a class until the twentieth century. For until the effects of popular education could be felt, the numbers would be too small, and until there was a change in the social and psychological conditions, the Black or Coloured West Indian who was educated would be more than likely to seek to eliminate his dialect facility and imitate SE.

The range of the speaker of WIS, and a summary of the West Indian linguistic situation, are represented in the following diagram. The divisions are arbitrary but it is the general shape that I wish to impress.

A			
	B		
- - -		- - - - -	
		C	
		- - -	- - -
			D
SE	West Indian Standard	Dialects	Creole

Vertical lines mark off linguistic divisions but these are not mutually exclusive.
Horizontal lines indicate classes of speakers: broken portions indicate fluidity.

A = Speakers of Standard English   C = Speakers of Dialect
B = Speakers of West Indian Standard   D = Speakers of Creole

Speakers of WIS have a wide linguistic range. West Indian writers, as speakers of WIS, are also speakers of dialect.

A grammatical lapse which illustrates this in an accidental way is to be found in a short story *Afternoon in Trinidad*[1] by Alfred H. Mendes. At one point in the story, Dodo a cab-man suspects that his woman Queenie has been two-timing him:

> One night he *ask* Queenie about it and she *denied* it so convincingly that all *he could say* was that *he had found* it strange that she was not on speaking terms with Corinne and Georgie.
> 'Why you carn' *axe* straight out whey you wants to know ennh?' Queenie *said* indignantly. 'We did have some high words and den she pull dong me clothes line. I has a good min' to bring she up oui.'

Mendes's grammatical lapse 'he *ask*' (my italics) is made glaring by the correctness of his other verbs. The explanation would seem to be as follows: a tendency in West Indian dialects is to dispense with tense markers in the verb where context or where another grammatical feature is adequate. This tendency has passed into educated use to the extent that the speaker of West Indian Standard has to be on his guard (or thinks he has to be) when writing these forms. I would suggest that Mendes was tempted to say 'axe' with his character, resisted it but was so concerned about avoiding the most uneducated version that he slipped naturally into the intermediate form 'ask'.

But the West Indian writer's inwardness with the dialects is not

[1] In *Penguin New Writing 6*, ed. John Lehmann (1941), pp. 69–82.

revealed by accident in West Indian fiction. Although they do not have another language in the sense that Nigerians or Pakistanis do, West Indian writers have enriched their work by exploiting the possibilities of the folk dialect. How they do this is the subject of the next section of this chapter.

(vi) *Dialect in West Indian Fiction*

West Indian literature would seem to be the only substantial literature in which the dialect-speaking character is the central character. The conventional associations of dialect with comic characters or with characters on the periphery have not been eliminated, but they are disarmed of any stereotyping appearances or effects by occurring among other contextualizations of dialect. This characteristic feature of West Indian writing reflects the more obviously new event—the centrality of the Black or Coloured character and the articulation of this hitherto obscure and stereotyped person. It is important to add, however, that while the new contexts of dialect do not have a purely literary impulse in the way that Lawrence's use of dialect has in *Lady Chatterley's Lover*, neither are they to be accounted for in terms of the documentary demands of social realism. Most West Indian writers retain recognizable features of the dialects, but the literary inventions are shaped to meet wider expressive needs. In the works of a few writers dialect is put in for purposes of coarse realism, or to supply an anticipated exotic demand overseas, but the more interesting West Indian writers, like artists anywhere, are constantly opening up the possibilities of language, and in some of their works we can see the dialect being expanded in this exploratory way. It is at this growing process that I wish to look, but in order to clarify the discussion I would like to work under three main headings. In the first the focus will be on the relationship between the language of narration (the language of the implied author) and the language of the fictional character. In the second, the use of dialect to express the consciousness of the character will be looked at. In the third section, there will be a more rapid look at some other significant contexts where dialect is used by West Indian writers. The illustrations will be chosen in such a way as to reveal chronological developments, but I do not want to imply that each new possibility opened up eliminates an earlier usage. The emphasis must be on the variety of possibilities that have been created and that can still be drawn upon.

(a) *Dialect and Distance*

In the extract from *Tom Cringle's Log* quoted earlier, one of the sources of the comic effect was an incongruity between the language of the narrator (the implied author) and that of the fictional character. The incongruity was sharper for our awareness that the Standard English of the implied author belonged to a different social world from the world of the dialect-speaking character. We must begin therefore by making the observation that in West Indian fiction the two voices no longer reflect mutually exclusive social worlds. It increases the delicacy of our reading in fact if we can imagine the narrative sections in a West Indian Standard voice. This kind of delicacy is not always necessary, however, and is hardly called for, in the dialect novels of the White Creole, H. G. de Lisser, where the Negro is still a comic character and not much more, and where the author's attitude of withdrawal is reflected by an exaggerating of the distance between the narrator's language and that of the fictional character. An episode in *Jane's Career* (1914) is transitional in West Indian fiction in the way it combines an attitude of social superiority (recurrent in British presentations) with the West Indian's knowledge of the dialect. Jane is about to go to Kingston to pursue a career as a servant girl so she is taken to Daddy Buckram, the village sage. The description of the old man sets the scene in a revealing way:

> Like his audience, the Elder was black; he may have been about sixty years of age, and was intensely self-conscious. His close-cropped hair was turning grey; what chiefly distinguished him from all other men in the village was his glibness of tongue, his shoes, and his collar. Except on Sundays, every one else went bare-footed and collarless; but this Daddy Buckram would never consent to do at any time, holding that one who preached 'the Word' should be clothed in proper garments even though, as in his case, the shoes were usually down at heels and the collar dirty.
>
> (*Jane's Career*, p. 8)

Persuaded into an amused superiority, we witness next the recurrent device of writers handling the dialect-speaking character in a conventional way—a would-be impressive speech by the dialect-speaking character. Authorial markers of dissociation (my italics) are prominent, but de Lisser inscribes his dialect with obvious zest and with a dialect-speaker's understanding of dialect's capacity to absorb miscellaneous material (in this case the Bible):

> 'Jane', he continued *impressively* after a pause, 'Kingston is a very big an' wicked city, an' a young girl like you, who de Lord has blessed wid a good figure an' a face, must be careful not to keep bad company. Satan goeth about like a roaring lion in Kingston seeking who he may devour. He will devour you if you do not take him to the Lord in prayer. Do you' work well. Write to you' moder often, for a chile who don't remember her parent cannot prosper. Don't stay out in de street in de night, go to church whenever you' employer allow you. If sinners entice thee, consent thou not. Now, tell me what I say to you.'
> Jane hesitated a while, then answered.
> 'You say I mus' behave myself, sah, an' go to church, an' don't keep bad company, an' dat de devil is a roarin' lion. An' . . . An' dat I must write mumma.'
> The Elder *smiled his approval*. 'I see', he *observed benignantly*, 'that you have been giving my words attention. If you always remember dem like dat, you will conquer in de battle.'
>
> (*Jane's Career*, p. 9)

As a speaker of WIS, de Lisser was capable of more varied uses of the dialect than he settled for. But his repeatedly comic purposes merely followed the convention of European writers. In his novels, for all his inwardness with the dialect, the two voices come from two different worlds.

Daddy Buckram is a peripheral character, so it would be unjust to make too much of the comparison between de Lisser's presentation and Samuel Selvon's handling of a speech-making occasion by his peasant hero, Tiger, in *A Brighter Sun* (1952). But what I want to show is that social attitude has a great deal to do with the effects being pursued. Selvon is too involved with his character as an individual person to be distracted into superficial comedy. As a result, we find that the dialect is modified in the direction of the

Standard, and the authorial voice slips in and out of the speech without drawing attention to its greater 'correctness'. The episode occurs when Tiger's parents come to visit him on the birth of Tiger and Urmilla's first child. There is a small party, and Joe, the neighbour, has proposed a toast:

> Tiger saw a chance to prove he was getting to be a man. He said: 'I is the man of the house, and I have to answer Joe toast.'
>
> Urmilla moved with a sixth sense and filled the glasses again. Tiger looked at her and smiled and she knew she had done the right thing.
>
> But when he began to talk he found it wasn't going to be as easy as he thought, even with the rum in his head. 'Well', he began waveringly, '—we—glad to have family and friends here today, especially as the baby born. Is true we not rich and we have only a small thing here but still is a good thing. So let we make a little merry for the baby. I should really begin different, I don't know what happen to me. I should say: "Ladies and gentlemens" and then make speech. But I cannot speechify very good. I would learn though——' That was as far as he could go. He felt he would talk foolishness if he continued, and he gulped his drink.
>
> He wanted everyone to make a speech, but all the elders shook their heads. And it became awkward just standing and looking at one another, as if something had gone wrong.
>
> (*A Brighter Sun*, p. 52)

Writers since de Lisser have taken a less restricted view of the dialect-speaking character, and consequently of the dialect itself. The closer involvement of the implied author with the low-life character is reflected by a closing of the gap between the language of narration and the language of the fictional character. Further examples of this may be found in the next section called 'Dialect and Consciousness'. This section continues with a discussion of some attempts to draw the two voices together by techniques of narration.

The use of a dialect-speaking narrator by V. S. Reid in the novel *New Day* (1949) and by John Hearne in a short story *At the Stelling* (1960) remind us that few West Indian authors reproduce dialect precisely in their works. In these two cases invention is more obvious than in most. Both writers invent successfully, however, because they are intimate with the dialects out of which they are constructing, and have a keen eye for recognizable qualities and literary possibilities: as a result we feel that the language in the works is not a realistic reproduction of dialect as it may be spoken anywhere in fact, but it is a convincing extension of the familiar.

Reid's novel which links the granting of a new constitution to Jamaica in 1944 with the Morant Bay Rebellion of 1865 is narrated by the old man John Campbell who is a witness of the new and was an actor in the old. The novel opens in the later period and the new day unleashes the memory of the aged man. The whole is then unfolded more or less continuously from the earlier time to the later, but with regular returns to the present as the old man makes an interjection here or emphasizes a point there. Because the story is told as an oral performance by the reminiscing man, Reid is able to make a credible show of narrating in dialect. But what he actually does is to push WIS and dialect even closer together in the narrating voice of John Campbell:

> Mas'r, is a heavy night, this. Memory is pricking at me mind, and restlessness is a-ride me soul. I scent many things in the night-wind, night-wind is a-talk of days what pass and gone.
> But the night-wind blows down from the mountains, touching only the high places as it comes; so then, 'member, I can remember only these places which stand high on the road we ha' traveled.
>
> (*New Day*, p. 85)

Our sense of the speaking voice, rhythmic repetition, and personification imagery make this an impressive passage, but it is not dialect in the same way that the following from de Lisser is dialect:

> Who you gwine to send for policeman for? demanded Sarah, also at the top of her voice and with arms akimbo. 'Me! Y'u must be drunk! Look at the mallata (mulatto) ooman how she stand! Y'u t'ink I am a schoolgal, no? Y'u t'ink you can teck exvantage of me! If it wasn't for one t'ing, I would hold you in here an' gie y'u such a beaten dat you wouldn't walk for a week.'
>
> (*Jane's Career*, p. 118)

The stylized dialect in Reid's novel never sinks to such exotic vulgarity, although it does show signs of over-writing as in the pretentious homeliness of the following passage:

An old man now, me. Many years bank the flame that was John
Campbell. And down the passage o' those years many doors have
opened. Some o' them ha' let in rich barbecues o' joyousness, with
good things covering the bottom of the pot o' life and no thorns
there to give me pain. And others have opened into butteries of
hell, and me soul has been scarred with the fires.

(New Day, p. 42)

On the whole, however, Reid's experiment is a successful one.
Because the language of narration is pushed so close to the language
of the characters, the reader is seldom jerked into awareness of two
separate voices.

At less risk, since it is a much shorter piece, Hearne achieves
vivid effects with his dialect-speaking narrator in *At the Stelling:*[1]

I sink far down in that river and already, before it happen, I can
feel *perai* chew at my fly button and tear off my cod, or alligator
grab my leg to drag me to drowning. But God is good. When I
come up the sun is still there and I strike out for the little island
in the river opposite the stelling. The river is full of death that pass
you by, but the *stelling* holds a walking death like the destruction
of the Apocalypse.

I make ground at the island and draw myself into the mud, and
the bush and blood draw after me from between my legs. And
when I look back at the *stelling,* I see Mister Cockburn lie down in
him deck chair, as if fast asleep, and Mister Bailey lying on him
face upon the boards. . . .

And John standing on the path, with the repeater still as the
finger of God in him hands. . . .

(West Indian Stories, p. 62)

The first point to be made is that it would be impossible to feel the
full effect of this passage unless we imagine a speaking West Indian
voice. Repetition, monosyllabic rhythm and personification imagery make it resemble some in Reid's novel, but it is much less
obviously a dialect passage than any in Reid. Little more than the
pervasive present tense prevents it from being West Indian Standard.

Although both Reid and Hearne thus come close to making a
modified form of dialect do the work both of narration and dialogue, their use of narrating characters is a conservative device. It

[1] In Andrew Salkey (ed.), *West Indian Stories* (1960).

is in Samuel Selvon's works that the language of the implied author boldly declares itself as dialect differing little from the language of the characters. In the story 'Brackley and the Bed',[1] the author takes up the stance of the calypsonian or ballad-maker and both SE and WIS are abolished:

> Brackley hail from Tobago, which part they have it to say Robinson Crusoe used to hang out with Man Friday. Things was brown in that island and he make for England and manage to get a work and was just settling down when bam! he get a letter from his aunt saying Teena want to come to England too.
>
> Well, right away he write aunty and say no, no, because he have a feeling this girl would make botheration if she come England. The aunt write back to say she didn't mean to say that Teena want to come England, but that Teena left Tobago for England already.
>
> Brackley hold his head and bawl. And the evening the boat train come in at Waterloo, he went there and start 'busing she right away, not waiting to ask how the folks was at home or anything.
>
> 'What you doing in London?' Brackley ask as soon as Teena step off the train. 'What you come here for, eh? Even though I write home to say things real hard?'
>
> 'What happen, you buy the country already?' Teena sheself giving tit for tat right away. 'You ruling England now? The Queen abdicate?'
>
> (*Ways of Sunlight*, p. 151)

This is as far as any West Indian author has gone towards closing the gap between the language of narration and the language of the fictional character. It has been argued that social attitude has something to do with the closing of the gap. But this would be a misleading emphasis to end with. Writers like V. S. Naipaul achieve effects of incongruity by stressing differences between the two voices, and much of the fun of Alvin Bennett's *God the Stonebreaker* comes about in this way. A purely literary point on which to end, therefore, is that West Indian writers who possess WIS and dialect have a wide range within which to vary the distance between the voice of narration and the voice of the character. As we have seen, this can be of use in the hands of the artist who wishes to take advantage of it.

[1] In the collection *Ways of Sunlight* (1957).

The Language of the Master?

(b) *Dialect and Consciousness*

In *Corentyne Thunder* (1941), Edgar Mittelholzer's first novel, one of the centres of interest is Ramgolall the cowminder:

> A tale we are about to tell of Ramgolall, the cowminder, who lived on the Corentyne coast of British Guiana the only British colony on the mainland of South America. Ramgolall was small in body and rather short and very thin. He was an East Indian who had arrived in British Guiana in 1898 as an immigrant indentured to a sugar estate. He had worked very hard. He had faithfully served out the period of his indenture, and now at sixty-three years of age he minded cows on the savannah of the Corentyne coast, his own lord and guide.
>
> (*Corentyne Thunder*, p. 7)

It is an unpromising start, with the West Indian author doing his best to accommodate his prospective British reader by providing the geographical and historical background. The tone of the tourist guide combines with the stance of the superior omniscient novelist. But the work recovers from this disastrous beginning as Mittelholzer moves into his tale of fragile human endeavour in a vast inscrutable landscape.

Mittelholzer handles his dialect-speaking peasants with great compassion, but his use of dialect is in accordance with a strict realistic criterion of appropriateness to the character. This means that if he wishes to express anything complicated about the character, he has to work not directly through the character's consciousness, or in the character's language, but by a mediating omniscience.

I would like therefore to look at an episode in *Corentyne Thunder*, where an attempt is made to express Ramgolall's overwhelming sense of desolation. This will be followed by two examples from later West Indian novels where dialect is used, and the character's consciousness articulated in similarly complicated situations. There is no wish to imply that one method is necessarily better than the other. The purpose is to show by comparison how dialect offers alternative artistic possibilities to the West Indian writer.

Ramgolall and his daughter are returning home from work when the girl Beena is seized by pain:

Beena moaned softly and her breathing came in heavy gusts *as though her soul were fatigued with the things of this life and wished to leave her body in gasp after gasp of wind.* And Ramgolall, weak in body and in mind, could only look about him at a loss. His dark eyes seemed to appeal to the savannah and then to the sky. But the savannah remained still and grey-green, quiet and immobile *in its philosophy.* And the sky, too, would do nothing to aid him. Pale purple in the failing light and streaked with feathery brown and yellow clouds, *the sky watched like a statue of Buddha.*

'Ou! Bettay, you no go dead. Eh? Talk na? Is wh' wrong Bettay?'

But Beena moaned in reply, doubled up.

'Talk, no Bettay? Try. You' belly a-hurt?'

The moan came again, *like a portent, like the echo of a horn sounded in the depth of the earth.* 'The Dark gathers', *it seemed to tell the soul of Ramgolall* 'and Death cometh with the Dark. Be resigned my son.'

Ramgolall stood up in a panic, looking all around him. He saw the cows, a group of moving spots, headed for their pen and getting smaller as they went. He could smell their dung mingled with the iodine in the air. He could see the tiny mud-house, with its dry palm-leaf roof, where he and Beena and Kattree lived. It stood far off a mere speck.

(Corentyne Thunder, p. 10)

I have italicized some phrases which seem to be too crudely intrusive and which get in the way of the reader's imagination. But Mittelholzer works in other more acceptable ways. The evocation of empty savannah and vast sky against Ramgolall's appealing eyes are brought home in the final paragraph. Here distant objects express his desolation and panic at being cut off; and the faint smell in the air seems to suggest his wobbly hold upon existence.

But however effective Mittelholzer's indirect method may be, it remains an indirect method at its best. Ramgolall is little more than a figure of pathos: while *we* become aware of the meaning of his panic Ramgolall himself remains without consciousness. For, all the effects of the passage are achieved through devices in Standard English or in the West Indian Standard voice of the author. In this light, Ramgolall's words and dialect are flat counters out of touch with the experience he has undergone.

Because of Mittelholzer's limited view of Ramgolall's possibilities, *Corentyne Thunder* never really becomes the tale of a cowminder that it sets out to be. The peasant becomes increasingly peripheral as the novel advances. The peasant character is emphatically a central character in Samuel Selvon's *A Brighter Sun* (1952). And it is in this novel that dialect first becomes the language of consciousness in West Indian fiction. For Tiger is an introspective character and a dialect-speaking one. As we follow his development from premature Hindu wedding to turbulent fatherhood and responsible domestic anxiety, from Indian legacy to Trinidadian citizenship, and from obscure youth to naïve inquiring manhood, dialect becomes saturated with inner experience. Selvon does not present Tiger's consciousness exclusively through dialect; but authorial comment, reportage of the character's thought processes, and reproduction of these processes directly in dialect modulate into one another so smoothly that the impression given is of direct access to the dialect-speaker's raw consciousness:

> Life was beginning to get complicated, now that he was beginning to learn things. Sookdeo had promised to teach him to read. Boysie was going to show him many things in Port of Spain. Where was his life going to fit in? Perhaps, if he liked the city, he could get a job there, and give up the garden. Or Urmilla could keep it while he was at work. Anyway he wasn't sure. He wasn't sure about anything. . . . When Urmilla and the baby were asleep, he looked up at the roof and felt revulsion for his wife and child. They were to blame for all his worry. If he were alone, he could be like Boysie, not caring a damn. He would go to the city and get a job. . . . He would even go to school in the night and learn to read and write. . . . Look at Sookdeo, he argued, you think I want to be like he when I get old? Is only old age that I respect in him. All he could do is read and drink rum. When I learn to read, you think is only Guardian I going to read? I going to read plenty books, about America and England and all them places. Man I will go and live in Port of Spain, this village too small, you can't learn anything except how to plant crop.
>
> (*A Brighter Sun*, pp. 90–1)

If Tiger's thought processes are naïve, they are at least spread over a wide area of experience. In following the character's inner workings in a credible modification of dialect, Selvon helps to make dialect a more flexible instrument.

In Wilson Harris's *The Far Journey of Oudin* (1961) which also takes East Indians in the West Indies for its raw material, dialect becomes the dramatic language for articulating a complex process in consciousness. Mohammed and his brothers Hassan and Kaiser had deprived their crazy half-brother of his legacy and murdered him. After an initial period of prosperity the three brothers begin to feel their possessions crumbling and they become the prey of the ruthless money-lender Ram. The strange materialization of a wandering labourer called Oudin presents Ram with a longed-for accomplice and a willing slave. Ram sends Oudin to Mohammed, ostensibly as a useful helper but in fact Oudin's mission is to steal Mohammed's cattle, thus driving Mohammed even further into economic dependence upon the demonic money-lender. Oudin's resemblance to the murdered half-brother causes consternation in the Mohammed household and from this point Mohammed begins to feel himself visited by a curse:

'Is like if some kind of thing circulating me.' He paused.
'What you mean?' Ram was involved and interested.
'I don't know exactly how to explain. But time itself change since he come. Is like if I starting to grow conscious after a long time, that time itself is a forerunner to something. But Ah learning me lesson so late, is like it is a curse, and things that could have gone smooth now cracking up in haste around me. I so bewilder I can't place nothing no more. What I used to value and what I used not to value overlapping. Two, three, four face looking at me. Every face so different. I don't know which is private, which is public, which is past, which is future. And yet all is one, understand me?'
'I do,' Ram said softly, and almost inaudibly.
'I suppose I is an ignorant man. Ah lose me grip long ago. I wish to God ah could accept the fact that I changing. Ah feel that I, *me*, then is just a piece of moving furniture and something else, bigger by far, pushing me about until I don't know whether I standing 'pon me head, me backside, or me foot.'

(*The Far Journey of Oudin*, pp. 91–2)

The process of break-up of the known substances in the character's life under the weight of an intuition of something beyond complacent existence is a crucial stage in the experience of a Harris character. By boldly allowing the crumbling character to describe his condition in dialect, Harris enlists the urgency of the rhythmic speaking voice in suggesting the urgency of the experience. Here too, as throughout Harris's first five novels, the recognizable elements in the character's language offer the reader a foothold for coming to closer grips with a disturbing and unfamiliar state of consciousness. The successful use of dialect in a context like this in West Indian writing carries the conventionally simple language of the simple character to new levels of profoundity.

(c) *Some More Contexts of Dialect*

In the last two sections, there has been an attempt to show that dialect is a natural part of the equipment of the West Indian novelist, used as a means of narration, and for expressing the consciousness of the peasant character in a wide range of situations. It has been suggested that such a subtle and flexible use of dialect on such a large scale is probably unique in literature. In this section, it is proposed to consolidate the argument by providing some more examples of the varying contexts of dialect. It has possibly begun to appear already that the degree of Englishness of the dialect varies from situation to situation in the novels, and this impression will be confirmed by the passages to follow. But certain common features which have also emerged from previous examples will again be in evidence. These are: improvisation in syntax and lexis; direct and pithy expression; a strong tendency towards the use of image, especially of the personification type; and various kinds of repetition of syntactic structure and lexis combining with the spoken voice to produce highly rhythmic effects. It would be repetitive to accompany each extract below with a full description, and since my main purpose is simply to provide telling examples of the use of dialect in various contexts, analytic remarks will be restricted to a minimum.

Two examples of dialect used in a broadly political situation may be taken from works by George Lamming. Lamming's second novel *The Emigrants* (1954) brings together, on a ship bound for England, a collection of West Indians from different islands and of different social and educational levels. This gives Lamming scope to exercise a wide range of linguistic skills in differentiating the various dialects of his characters. For they all find themselves drawn into frequent council in which they discover the sameness of the islands and the sameness of their human quest for something better —national identity or personal freedom. The many discussions in the work are carried on in dialect. The example I want to quote is from a long speech by a Jamaican who begins with the generalization that 'West Indies people whatever islan' you bring them from, them want to prove something'. An account of the settling of the islands from different sources, and the state of disorientation this has produced, leads to this universal understanding:

> ... Them is West Indians. Not Jamaicans or Trinidadians. 'Cause the bigger the better. An' is the reason the West Indies may out o' dat vomit produce a great people 'cause them provin' that them want to be something. Some people say them have no hope for people who doan' know exactly w'at them want or who them is, but that is a lot of rass-clot talk. The interpretation me give hist'ry is people the world over always searchin' an' feelin', from time immemorial, them ain't know w'at is right, but them keep searchin' an' feelin', an' when them dead an' gone, hist'ry write things 'bout them that them themself would not have know or understand. Them wouldn't know themself if them see themself in hist'ry. 'Cause what them was tryin' to prove them leave to hist'ry to give a name.
>
> (*The Emigrants*, p. 68)

Lamming's 'Jamaican dialect' is not only credible as that, it is made to carry an extremely sophisticated notion—the kernel of the novel —without signs of strain or unnaturalness, and without announcing itself as dialect.

In the same author's *Season of Adventure* (1960), a novel concerned with different levels of freedom and the ways in which the political is also deeply personal, the following conversation takes place between Crim, who is grateful that the colonial powers have given freedom at last to San Cristobal, and Powell, who sees the matter in a different light:

> 'I say it was a real freedom happen when the tourist army went away', Crim said. 'It look a real freedom they give San Cristobal'.
> 'It don't have that kind o' givin' ' said Powell, trying to restrain his anger. 'Is wrong to say that, 'cause free is free an' it don't have

no givin'. Free is how you is from the start, an' when it look different you got to move, just move, an' when you movin' say that is a natural freedom make you move. You can't move to freedom, Crim, 'cause freedom is what you is an' where you start an' where you always got to stand.

(Season of Adventure, p. 18)

It is worth pointing out not only that the dialect is convincing and that it is being made to work in the context of a political philosophy but also that the emphatic and categorical quality of the language being used by Powell is appropriate to his character. Powell is in fact a passionate fanatic, a man who will not be handed his freedom by anyone and who has a violent distrustful attitude to the liberal gesture. Towards the end of the novel, when the white-skinned West Indian girl, Fola, wishes to free herself from the traditional denial by her class of its West Indianness, it is Powell the uncompromising fanatical victim of the history of his time who makes a murderous assault upon her:

'No noise', he said, rubbing his hand inside his shirt, 'no more than a sandfly can make, I warn you, no noise.'

'But . . . but . . . but what have I done?' Fola stammered.

'Enough,' said Powell. 'You an' your lot done enough.'

'Why? Why?' Fola's voice dribbled.

'It too late,' said Powell, rubbing the hand inside his shirt, 'it too late to explain, just as it too late for you an' your lot to make your peace with me.'

'You don't understand', she cried, 'You don't understand.'

'Exact, exact,' said Powell, 'I don't understand. An' what's more I don't want to. Where you an' your lot concern, I hope I never live to understand.'

Now Powell's hand emerged slowly from inside his shirt; but his fist was still hidden as it rubbed against his chest.

'What I do I do alone,' said Powell, 'no help from you an' your lot, 'cause I learn, I learn how any playing 'bout with your lot bound to end. You know the rules too good, an' it too late, it too late for me to learn what rules you have for muderin' me. So is me go murder first. Otherwise is you what will murder me, or make me murder myself.'

(Season of Adventure, p. 328)

The extraordinary power of the emotion in this incident might prevent us from realizing that Powell is a dialect-speaker whose way of speaking is precisely appropriate to his highly personal condition.

The advance which Lamming's artistic use of dialect represents may be illustrated by a quotation from an early West Indian writer who invested in the common language. In Alfred Mendes's *Black Fauns* (1935) set in a barrackyard in Trinidad, the women of the yard meet daily and have long conversations in dialect on miscellaneous subjects. An admiring remark about White people, and a denigration of Africans by one of the fauns prompts the following rejoinder from Ethelrida:

> 'I don't know why you say that, old lady' Ethelrida retorted, 'I see all the white people in civilised lands behaving worse than savage an' heathen. Look at de war in nineteen-fourteen. You ever see people made in God's image cut up and shoot up an' mash up each other like dat? I see Mister Pompom does like to go to the teeayter. What for? To see white girl upon white sheet behave like dressed-up worthless women. I hear white priest an' white parson does go to Africa in the forest to teach our own colour about Christ an' God. Day does call demself missionary. It look to me they got more than enough people in their own land to teach about Christ an' God. It look to me like niggers in Africa happy when white people leave them alone. As soon as white people, with Bible an' chaplet in hand go to our own people in Africa like they does bring trouble and unhappiness an' misery.'
>
> (*Black Fauns*, p. 194)

Although Mendes's usage is not as dynamic as Lamming's, the passage, a product of the 1930's, was a sign of things to come.

In Austin Clarke's *Amongst Thistles and Thorns* (1965) a sonorous dialect is used simultaneously for comic effect and to register social protest. In one episode, Nathan feels that he is qualified to describe the limiting society to his woman Ruby: 'I have come to a damn serious understanding during my travels in and around this blasted past tense village.' The conversation occurs when Nathan and Ruby are considering sending their son to the High School. Nathan argues that there is no hope of any but the least-considered white-collar jobs for the educated Black man:

. . . He could even come out a saniterry inspector and walk all through this blasted village in a khaki suit and white cork hat with a white enamel ladle in his hand' to dip down inside the poor people shitty closets with. But be-Christ! after all them school fees I pay out, and all them dollars spend on books, I hopes, I hopes to-hell that Milton do not come out as no damn inspector, looking for a million and one larvees in no blasted person' outdoor closet, or to see if they have young mosquitoes in their drinking-water buckets. That Ruby . . . that, Rube, is the lengths and advantages Milton could go in this kiss-me-arse island after he find himself in the possession of a high-school eddication.

(Amongst Thistles and Thorns, p. 105)

The zest with which Nathan puts this case and the rhythmic insistence of his language might be thought to distract from the force of the protest. But this would be true if direct protest were Clarke's sole intention. In fact, Nathan is an irresponsible character and his intention is to regain the favour of Ruby by attacking the things that threaten to thwart the boy. There is a protest element in his speech which is part of an authorial intention, but it is emphatically in the background.

The full measure of Nathan's deceptive oratory comes out when having argued against the futility of becoming educated, he insists that Milton must be sent to school. Aware of Ruby's vulnerability on this question, and of her yearnings for a better life for the boy, Nathan sweeps her along with the rhetoric of dialect:

'And if Milton is a boy what have a singing voice in his head, I want him to sing in the cathedral' choirs 'pon a Sundee. Oh Christ, I could see that bastard now, Rube, darling love! I could see Milton right this very now before my eye' wearing them red robes and that thing 'round his neck. . . .

Yeah . . . and walking up and down that cathedral' aisle with the choirs, and the Bishop o' the islan', and singing them psalms and carols and songs ancient and modernt so damn sweet, more sweeter than if he was a blasted humming bird!'

'That is our son, Nathan.'

'Be-Christ, Ruby, you have just say a mouthful! Milton is our son. Our own-own flesh-and-blood possession!'

(Amongst Thistles and Thorns, p. 105)

What I am trying to suggest with the quotations from Clarke, is that dialect has travelled so far in West Indian fiction that it is used to produce different effects simultaneously and that it can even go beyond lyricism to fake lyricism.

A fine example of the lyricism of dialect occurs in Jan Carew's *Black Midas* (1958). The novel as a whole is remarkable for the way it uses the vivid immediate qualities of dialect to suggest the speech of outdoor men, and to invoke a staggering landscape, but I shall confine myself to a lush moment when Rhodius and Shark (the Black Midas) are travelling up-river and Rhodius sees Shark sitting quietly:

> 'You hear the voices?' he asked.
> 'Which voices?'
> 'The river, man, the river. This water got more talk than the tongue in Babel. When night-time come all the dead man under the river does talk.' He spoke quietly, with his eyes on John Pye's shadow in the bow all the time. 'They got good people and bad one under the river, and me travel up and down so often me know them all. Me travel when star was bright, when moon hang low, when dark so heavy me couldn't spit through it. The good people does say 'Rhodius, Rhodius, don't take no chance with the power-god; Kusewayo sitting stony-still in he big chair. Steer clear of the living rock; they get tentacle-hand to pull you down ... don't take no risk by Topeco, the green spirit of the quiet water got whirlpool to suck you in ... don't make mistake at the looking Glass, is time of the year for sacrifice, that water deep with hungrying for you.' But the bad ones does say 'Come down, Rhodius. Come down, Rhodius. We will make you bones flute like weeping wood! Come down Rhodius; the river bottom smooth and we will roll you eye from here to Macharee." You hear them?' he said. 'You hear them?' And I pressed my ear against the gunwale, but all I heard was tongueless lisping and all I saw when I sat up was starlight dancing on the rim of whirlpools.

> *(Black Midas, pp. 177–8)*

In passages like this, Carew is able to suggest the haunting qualitise of his massive landscape, thus making credible the central faith of the novel, upon which much of its tension is built, that the pork-knocking characters are literally possessed, that the jungle is in their veins. In the final sentence we have an instance, I think, of WIS more than usually suffused with dialect rhythm and expressiveness.

The final example comes from Wilson Harris's *Palace of the Peacock* (1960). In his five Guyana novels, Harris follows a vision which demands to be worked out in unconventional ways: his characters do not exist in a recognizable social context; he is not concerned with the portrayal in realistic terms of the individual character; and there is a collapsing of our usual constitutive categories of time, person and place. We find in his novels, therefore, that the living and the dead, and people from different times and places coexist. Further, persons are constantly collapsing into one another and they frequently collapse into place and thing. Harris's vision is a vision of universality and transcendence running against our everyday notions about the nature of reality.

This means, taking the word in its common sense, that there is an air of unreality in these Guyana novels. There are two main ways in which Harris gives initial credibility to his strange fictions. The first is by the sensuous rendering of an intimate, felt Guyanese landscape. The second is by the use of dialect. This is true in general in the novels, but it is more sharply apparent at critical moments. At a time when characters are undergoing the most bizarre or extraordinary experiences, they express themselves in dialect.

In *Palace of the Peacock*, the crew of dead men pursuing their journey up-river beyond Mariella become aware of a flock of birds wheeling overhead. Each of the men has been dead once before, and they are all approaching their second death. Since Da Silva is the first to go, he 'sees' the most, and between him and Cameron who is still 'alive' (only once dead) there is a tense exchange:

'What in heaven name really preying on you sight and mind, Boy?' Cameron suddenly became curious. 'I only seeing vulture bird. Where the parrot what eating you?'

'Ah telling you Ah dream the boat sink with all of we', da Silva said speaking to himself as if he had forgotten Cameron's presence. 'Ah drowned dead and Ah float. All of we expose and float. . . .'

'Is vulture bird you really feeling and seeing' shouted Cameron. His voice was a croak in the air. Da Silva continued—a man grown deaf and blind with sleep—'Ah dream Ah get another chance to live me life over from the very start, you hear? He paused and the thought sank back into the stream. 'The impossible start to happen. Ah lose me own image and time like if I forget is where me sex really start. . . .'

'Fool, stop it,' Cameron hissed.

'Don't pick at me,' da Silva said. 'The impossible start happen

I tell you. Water start dream, rock and stone start dream, tree trunk and tree root dreaming, bird and beast dreaming. . . .'

'You is a menagerie and a jungle of a fool', Cameron's black tongue laughed and twisted.

(*Palace of the Peacock*, pp. 110–11)

Harris modulates the language in this passage so subtly that we might miss the way that we are made to move between Cameron's invective, da Silva's exultation and the discreet organizing touches of the implied author. Strange as the experience may be, and no matter bow undifferentiated the two men in a conventional way, the tension between them is laid bare, and da Silva's sense of a new beginning makes a vivid impression. Harris's use of the dialect in his novels is quite crucial from the point of view of their readability. Because the folk language is involved in such a complex imaginative world, the range and flexibility of the dialect are made greater.

To understand properly the certainty with which West Indian writers have turned the dialects to such literary account as I have tried to illustrate, we must remember that coexisting with the new literary growth in the West Indies, and pre-dating it, is a long oral tradition of story-telling and folk poetry in the dialect. A modern representative of this tradition is Louise Bennett of Jamaica whose dialect poems produced over the last twenty-five years have recently been published as *Jamaica Labrish: Jamaica Dialect Poems* (1967). In Trinidad, the oral tradition flourishes in the calypso whose most skilful exponent is Francisco Slinger, called 'The Mighty Sparrow'. What we are seeing in the West Indian novel, and in very recent West Indian poetry, is the assimilation of linguistic properties that have long been established in the oral usages of the folk. It is to be lamented that while local audiences have made Sparrow a millionaire and a popular hero because of his use of dialect, those who read either fail to recognize its subtle pervasive influence, or as Naipaul relates, 'object to its use in books which are read abroad. "They must be does talk so by you", one woman said to me. "Thy don't talk so by me".'[1]

[1] V. S. Naipaul, *The Middle Passage* (1962), p. 69.

VII

The Negro

(i) *Neo-African Literature—Neo-African Culture*

In the introduction to his massive catalogue *A Bibliography of Neo-African Literature* (1965), the German theorist Jahnheinz Jahn seems to define his subject in terms of style, but style closely related to cultural tradition:

> In contrast to Western literature . . . Neo-African literature has certain stylistic elements which stem from Negro-African oral tradition. It is this style which characterises Neo-African literature and not the author's language (for the most part European) birthplace or colour of skin. . . . Works written by Africans which lack these specific stylistic elements do not belong to neo-African but to traditional African literature. . . . The main centres of neo-African literature are Africa, South of the Sahara and the Caribbean, but we find it also in other areas of the world where African and Western traditions have mixed: Latin America, North America and even Europe.

In the same introduction, however, Jahn confesses that the criteria for recognizing neo-African literature are 'still under discussion' and that 'all the material which could be contained by such criteria has not yet been completely analysed'. But there is much less reticence in *Muntu: An Outline of Neo-African Culture*,[1] an earlier publication by the same author where, as it happens, the uniqueness and objectivity of these stylistic criteria, and their value as part of a critical method are put in serious doubt.

Discussing poetry written by Negroes in America, Jahn makes a distinction between 'the spiritual style' of an older generation like Paul Lawrence Dunbar and James Weldon Johnson, and the

---

[1] English translation published in 1961. German original 1958.

'agitation style' of poets of the 1930's like Sterling Brown and Robert Hayden. Between these two styles he locates the 'blues or Harlem style' of the 1920's exemplified by Langston Hughes and the *émigré* Jamaican Claude McKay: 'In the "spiritual style" the African component predominates, and in the "agitation style" the Western. In the "blues style" of Langston Hughes' poetry the two elements are evenly balanced.'[1] In the commentary on James Weldon Johnson's 'Negro National Anthem' with which Jahn follows this mechanical ordering of his material, the neo-African qualities are discovered in 'the imperative style', 'the intensification through repetition', the 'Nommo which transmutes the old Biblical images into new living actual images', and the 'responsibility of the word'. First of all, there is nothing specifically African about the stylistic features and the imaginative processes here enumerated. More damaging reflections arise when we look at the lines being 'analysed'.

> *Lift every voice and sing*
> *Till earth and heaven ring*
> *Ring with the harmonies of Liberty;*
> *Let our rejoicing rise*
> *High as the listening skies,*
> *Let us resound low as the rolling sea.*

The terms in which Jahn describes the stanza, and his enthusiastic tone, do not seem justifiable from the words on the page. What the example suggests is not only that Herr Jahn is a poor critic, but that 'stylistic criteria' are being advanced to give an impression of objectivity while the author pursues a more subjective hypothesis.[2]

In *Muntu* it is clear that Jahn's primary interest is in advancing a theory of neo-African culture of which neo-African literature is only a manifestation. In deliberate contrast to those ethnologists who stressed that there was a plurality of primitive cultures in Africa, Jahn envisages and gives prominence to a unified traditional

---

[1] Quotations from *Muntu*, pp. 200–4.

[2] The Neo-African theory does not appear to have passed without influence; it appears again in 'Jazz and the West Indian Novel' (*Bim*, 44, pp. 275–84; 45, pp. 39–51; and 46, pp. 115–26) where Edward Brathwaite advances the same 'stylistic elements', climaxing his case with a discussion of *Brother Man*, the worst novel by the near-White Jamaican, Roger Mais.

culture applicable to the whole of Africa, South of the Sahara: 'It will be objected that there has never been a traditional African culture as a whole, but only a plurality of different "primitive" cultures, and this objection will be supported by pointing to more or less accurate investigations by ethnologists. But the question of whether or not a plurality is understood as a unity is to a great extent one of interpretation.'[1] According to this interpretation, Neo-African culture arises out of the assimilation by the 'traditional African culture' of European influences—not, of course, Europe's spiritual decadence, but its modern technology.

It is worth noting that the author goes on to recognize that there is an element of myth in construing a single traditional African culture: 'Moreover, if it is not objective, the conception of the tradition as it appears in the light of neo-African culture is never-theless the only true one, since it is the one which will from now on determine the future of Africa. For several centuries Africa has had to suffer under the conception of the African past formed by Europe. As long as this was so, that European conception was "true," that is to say, effective. But the present and future on the other hand will be determined by the conception that *African* intelligence forms of the African past.'[2] By associating his myth of a single traditional African culture with something quite different, a *qualitative* revaluation of the African past, Jahn unwittingly de-values the solid achievement of historians and anthropologists of the late nineteenth and the twentieth centuries who have estab-lished, without recourse to myth, that far from being a land of savages from time immemorial, and long before the European incursions, Africa had been the scene of a number of advanced civilizations.

But my purpose is not to examine the correctness or the possible relevance of Jahn's views for the future of Africa itself. My concern is with how the West Indies and West Indian literature become involved in the neo-African theory. If in *Muntu* Jahn infers that the Caribbean[3] is a centre of neo-African literature, it is implied in *A*

[1] *Muntu*, p. 17.   [2] *Muntu*, pp. 17–18.
[3] There is not as yet any political unit called the 'Caribbean' and the existence of cultural community is inferred only from the majority presence of the Negro. I use the terms 'Dutch West Indies', 'French West Indies' and 'Spanish West Indies' to

Bibliography of Neo-African Literature that the area is one of neo-African culture. Behind the peculiar circularity with which Jahn protects himself is the *assumption* of African cultural survival in the Caribbean (and therefore in the West Indies). How the African cultures in the West Indies were modified physically and psychologically by the slave experience and the new geographical environment has already been demonstrated by historian-sociologists.[1] The treatment of African cultural survivals (secular and religious) by West Indian novelists consolidates such objective findings, and helps us to understand the range of attitudes to Africa and Africans in fiction from the West Indies.

(ii) *African Cultural Survivals in West Indian Fiction: Secular*

The earliest interesting case is to be found in a novel by the Jamaican W. G. Ogilvie. In *Cactus Village* (1950),[2] there appears to be evidence for those who argue that the system of exchange labour is an African survival, and for those who take the view that the system evolves in different parts of the world in response to analagous conditions. Ogilvie's villagers rally to the aid of the hero Hezekiah:

> Hezekiah was slim but wiry and strong. He was determined that none of these men who had given him a free day's labour should do more than he. His axe rang out with the best of them. His blows were measured and slower than those of some of his companions, but he was very accurate. He very seldom made a foul cut. As time went on the others noticed that his voice called most frequently when a tree was about to fall.
>
> During this time the women were not idle. As the cutlass-men cleared the bush, the women followed with long hooked sticks behind them. The fallen shrubs were hauled into large heaps; usually on some rocky spot, where they would be left to quail until they were dry enough to burn. All worked hard, but all were cheerful.
>
> (*Cactus Village*, p. 8)

A few paragraphs later there is an author's gloss which runs:

indicate the colonies and ex-colonies adjacent to the English-speaking West Indies. The word Caribbean, however, is used in its natural geographical sense to embrace all these territories bearing marks of association with the Imperial powers.

[1] See especially Orlando H. Patterson, *The Sociology of Slavery* (1967).

[2] Published by *The Pioneer Press*, Kingston, Jamaica.

Among the Jamaican peasantry it was an established custom that when a man was going to start a new cultivation he would call on his friends for a day's work. He was supposed to provide food and water. No other payment was necessary. Of course, whenever any of them called upon him for assistance he was expected to give it. Still, if a man were not very popular he would get only a few people to attend his 'match,' and those who came would not labour very hard.

(Cactus Village, p. 9)

The example from *Cactus Village* is of interest because in an earnest preface the author poured scorn on 'the "Negraryans" who wish the world to believe that all their ancestors come from Western Europe' and who 'dread any backward glance at our national beginnings'. Ogilvie, nevertheless, abstains from claiming that there is an African element in the system of exchange labour described in the novel. The rest of *Cactus Village* provides plenty of evidence that the abstinence is not an example of artistic self-control. If, as has been suggested,[1] exchange labour is an African cultural survival in the West Indies, Ogilvie was not sophisticated enough to be aware of it. Indeed, his seeming to celebrate this feature of peasant life as peculiarly Jamaican tends to imply at least an unconscious leaning to the 'analagous conditions' theory.

The ambiguous case in *Cactus Village* is not of literary significance in itself, but it does help to demonstrate how elusive African cultural survivals in the West Indies may be, or at any rate, how little scope there is for the West Indian novelist who wishes to evoke Africa in these terms. There is a different reason for glancing through fiction at another possible African influence in West Indian secular life. In many West Indian novels, Negro characters belonging to the socially depressed class (slum dwellers or labouring peasants) generally live together without benefit of Church marriage. Many main characters do this: Surjue and Rema in *The Hills Were Joyful Together* (1953), and Shine and Jesmina in *Brother Man* (1954), by Roger Mais; Joe and Rita in Samuel Selvon's *A Brighter Sun* (1952); Nathan and Ruby in Austin C. Clarke's *Amongst Thistles and Thorns* (1965); and Shark and Belle in *Black Midas* (1958), by

[1] By M. G. Smith in 'West Indian Culture', *Caribbean Quarterly*, Vol. 7, No. 3, December 1961.

Jan Carew. It is implicit in these novels from Jamaica, Trinidad, Barbados and Guyana that the background characters live in the same way.

Using historical and sociological evidence, Philip Curtin[1] advances Negro concubinage and the preference of the woman for this kind of marriage as 'one example of the adaptation of the African cultures to Jamaican life':

> The planters had little interest in the sexual mores of the slaves. The slaves made whatever sexual union they chose and these were usually more permanent than simple promiscuity. The Jamaican Negro normally had a 'wife', perhaps more than one. This family made a social unit that had nothing to do with the blessing of the established church. . . . By the time the missionaries arrived on the scene, Afro-Jamaican 'marriage' was too well established to be easily changed.

It is possible to argue even from Curtin's account that the conditions of slavery were by themselves enough to establish concubinage among West Indian Negroes, especially in view of the examples set by the masters and lamented by Lady Nugent:[2]

> Mrs. Bell told me to-day that a negro man and woman of theirs who are married, have fourteen grown-up children, all healthy field negroes. This is only one instance, out of many, which proves that the climate of this country being more congenial to their constitutions, they would increase and render the necessity of the Slave Trade out of the question, provided the masters were attentive to their morals, and established matrimony among them. But white men of all descriptions, married or single, live in a state of licentiousness with their female slaves. Until a great reformation takes place on their part, neither religion, decency nor morality can be established among the negroes. An answer that was made to Mr. Shirley, a Member of the Assembly (and a profligate character, as far as I can understand) who advised one of his slaves to marry, is a strong proof of this: 'Hi Massa, you telly me marry one wife which is no good! You no tinky I see you buckra no content wid one, two, tree or four wifes?'

[1] Philip D. Curtin, *Two Jamaicas* (Harvard University Press, Cambridge, 1955), p. 25. The title of a Jamaica Legislative Council report cited in a note by Curtin is highly indicative: 'Report of the Committee Appointed to Enquire into the Prevalence of Concubinage and the High Rate of Illegitimacy (Kingston, 1941).'

[2] *Lady Nugent's Journal* (1839), Entry for 8th April 1802.

But it is less important to determine the specific origin of West Indian concubinage than to be aware that it exists among a substantial section of the population. Among the same groups, however, there is an awareness of the marriage institution, and aspirations towards it either as a result of improved economic circumstances or in order to earn respectability. Some West Indian novelists turn this to comic purposes. But the most important effect of concubinage in the social situation is that marriage-adultery-divorce themes such as occur in the English novel are seldom treated in West Indian writing.

If African economic and social organizations were changed beyond easy recognition in the slave context, traditional arts and crafts were virtually wiped out. In this connection, it is useful to look at the only instance in West Indian fiction where an author allows a connection to be made between an element of West Indian secular life, and the African heritage.

Obadiah, the central character in Sylvia Wynter's *The Hills of Hebron* (1962), is possessed of an instinctive skill at woodcarving:

> One evening, he sat with Hugh on the pavement outside the shop. As they chatted together he whittled idly with his knife at a piece of wood. *He was unaware of what he was doing* until he realised that Hugh was nudging him and grinning slyly. He looked down at what he had made and saw a roughly-hewn miniature of his mother as she danced at a Pocomania meeting, her eyes wide and lost in a cold ecstasy, her breasts taut like thorns, her legs strong and powerful, the muscles raised and trembling as if with a fever—Obadiah had recaptured and imprisoned all this in wood forever.
>
> (*The Hills of Hebron*, p. 144)

Later in the novel Obadiah's self-discovery coincides with the end of a painful estrangement from his wife Rose. At this point, Miss Wynter introduces a second wood-carving episode:

> But as he sat waiting, he took up a fragment of wood and carved idly, thinking of making a toy for the child. Then as he shaped the rough outlines of a doll, he began to concentrate. For the first time in his life he created consciously, trying to embody in his carving his new awareness of himself and of Hebron. When he had finished

he put the doll in his pocket and left Hebron as twilight settled into the hollow spaces between the hills.

(*The Hills of Hebron*, p. 259)

Obadiah's adjustment to Hebron, and his self-discovery, are intended to symbolize the West Indian Negro's adjustment to the West Indies. That it is not Miss Wynter's intention to suggest that African wood-carving skills have survived in the West Indies is clear both from the presentation of Obadiah as unique in this respect, and from a later episode in the novel when a visiting German scholar (shades of Jahn and Ulli Beier) buys the carving from Obadiah:

'Tell me, what legend did you carve this doll from?'
Obadiah looked confused.
'You see this carving looks like ones that I saw in Africa . . . when I was there . . . I write books about sculpture . . . carvings like these . . . I make too, myself but in marble, not in wood . . . like you do . . . like they do in Africa, where your ancestors came from. And there they carve from father to son, and they carve out of the stories of their tribe, and their beliefs, their gods and devils. I bought a carving once that was made by the Dahomey . . . they made this out of a belief that each man has four souls, one given to him by an ancestor . . . one, his own, the third, the small bit of the Creator that lives in each man, the last one, that which joins him to the others in his group. The carving was one that I lost and yours is like it. That is why I ask, what belief did you carve this doll from? I would like to buy it from you . . . if you will sell it to me?'

(*The Hills of Hebron*, p. 274)

Having thus contrived that the African connection be made, Miss Wynter closes the incident with Obadiah's Hebron-orientated reply:

Obadiah nodded. This would mean food and water for Rose and the child. Besides, this man was no longer a stranger, for he had understood at once that there was more to the doll than the wood and the shape he had fashioned. So he told the man the story of Hebron, of their search for God, for it was out of this, the dream and the reality that he had carved the doll.

(*The Hills of Hebron*, p. 274)

Obadiah's wood-carving skill, the reader may conclude, is the instinctive expression of an obscure heritage preserved in the African personality. But Miss Wynter is careful not to show her hand.

(iii) Obeah and Cult Practices in West Indian Fiction

There are few indications in West Indian prose of the survival of African Cultures in West Indian secular life. But the frequent occurrence in novels of obeah and cult practices has sometimes been held as evidence of survivals in the religious field. Few West Indian novelists see these practices as anything more, in fact, than the incoherent remains of African religions and magic; and in all cases, obeah and cult manifestations are associated with socially depressed characters. It is possible, indeed, to be critical of the writers for having reproduced the social reality only too exactly, and without enough invention or imagination.

Obeah and cult practices occur in novels by West Indians of every racial origin; the degree of prominence given to them varies from novel to novel; and the authors' attitudes to their raw material differ widely. J. B. Emtage introduces Negro terror of the fetish in a mocking and comic spirit (*Brown Sugar*, 1966), but another White West Indian uses obeah differently in the novel of childhood *Christopher* (1959): the boy's increasing involvement with the Negro world around him, and his growing-up process, are subtly correlated with his development, away from an exotic view, to an understanding in psychological terms of how obeah operates. Sociological truth and a comic intention are both served in V. S. Naipaul's version of obeah in *The Suffrage of Elvira* (1958).

Some of the comic effects in this work derive from the doctrinal confusions of Hindu, Muslim and Christian in Naipaul's newly democratic Elvira: 'Things were crazily mixed up in Elvira. Everybody, Hindus, Muslims and Christians owned a Bible, the Hindus and Muslims looking on it if anything with greater awe. Hindus and Muslims celebrated Christmas and Easter. The Spaniards and some of the negroes celebrated the Hindu festival of lights.' In the political campaign around which the novel is built, the Hindu speculator Surujpat Harbans is up against a Negro candidate called Preacher. Harbans has the support of Baksh, a Muslim tailor;

Preacher's staunchest supporter is Cuffy, who runs a shoe-repair shop called 'The United African Pioneer Self-Help Society'.

When the 'big big dog' the drunken Baksh meets at night turns into a tiny puppy in the morning, the Elviran king-maker and his wife are convinced that the obeah-dog is an agent of Preacher's evil will, and that it forebodes death for the whole family. A visit by Mahadeo, one of Baksh's underlings, leads the forewarned proprietor of the shoe-repair shop to suspect that the Bakshes are counter-attacking:

> Mahadeo brought out his red pocket-notebook and a small pencil; 'I have to ask you a few questions, Mr. Cawfee.' He tried some elementary flattery: 'After all, you is a very important man in Elvira.'
>
> Mr. Cuffy liked elementary flattery. 'True,' he admitted. 'It's God's will.'
>
> 'Is what I think too. Mr. Cawfee, how your negro people getting on in Elvira?'
>
> 'All right, I believe, praise be to God.'
>
> 'You sure, Mr. Cawfee?'
>
> Mr. Cuffy squinted. 'How you mean?'
>
> '*Every*body all right? Nobody sick or anything like that?'
>
> 'What the hell you up to, Mahadeo?'
>
> Mahadeo laughed like a clerk in a government office.
>
> 'Just doing a job, Mr. Cawfee. Just a job. If any negro fall sick in Elvira, you is the fust man they come to, not true?'
>
> Mr. Cuffy softened. 'True.'
>
> 'And *no*body sick?'
>
> '*No*body.' Mr. Cuffy didn't care for the hopeful note in Mahadeo's voice. Mahadeo's pencil hesitated, disappointed.
>
> 'Nobody deading or dead?' Mr. Cuffy jumped up and dropped the black book. 'Obeah!' he cried, and took up an awl.
>
> 'Obeah. Loorkhoor was right. You people trying to work some obeah. Haul you tail outa my yard! Go on, quick sharp.'
>
> (*The Suffrage of Elvira*, p. 80)

Naipaul's Muslims are not only susceptible to the obeah-dog. They are capable, putatively, of terrifying the Negroes by an equally effective use of the black art. Both sides now begin to fear the fateful quadruped. The climax to Naipaul's obeah-dog episode, a brilliant parody of the Hollywood gunslinger's walk down the hushed main street at high noon, comes when the starving puppy

returns limping and wobbling along the road, causing consternation and awe among men, women and children, Hindus, Muslims
and Christians (pp. 115–19).

In Naipaul's fictional world, there is no attempt to restrict obeah
to Negroes. It would be a mistake to read from the novel back into
the society if one did not have knowledge of the society beforehand,
but Naipaul's fiction corresponds with fact at this point: in the West
Indies, belief in obeah may be found among the depressed and
illiterate, whatever their race or religion. This kind of truth to the
fact does not prevent Naipaul from making inventive use of sociological data.

The obeah man occurs as frequently as obeah, and in similar
contexts. Few writers have given him centrality or attempted to
explore his consciousness. Bra' Ambo, in Roger Mais's *Brother Man*
(1954), illustrates the general trend. He is a mercenary fraud who
sells ganja, and mints counterfeit coins. Early in the novel, it
seemed as if Mais was building towards a straight clash between the
Christian love of Bra' Man and the African superstition of Bra'
Ambo:

> Everybody knew that Bra' Ambo was a powerful obeah man.
> Bra' Ambo himself had given it out that he was a higher scientist
> than Bra' Man, for'—and he washed his hands before him, and
> smiled smugly—'Bra' Man study de science of de stars, astrology,
> an' I study de science of de stars too, but I study higher than dat,
> for I study de science of de Dead.'
> It was given to few 'scientors', he explained, to be able to read
> and understand the Book of the Dead. And he was one of them,
> and a man named De Lawrence, over the water, was another. And
> the way he said it, it might have been it was just the two of them,
> and no more—smirking like a cat before a saucer of milk, and
> washing his hands in the air.
> When people came and told this to Bra' Man he only smiled and
> said, 'Let Bra' Ambo go on studying his "Book of the Dead".'
> And he looked over their heads and said, 'There is the Book of
> Life open before him from cover to cover, let him seek to study
> that, if he will.'
>
> (*Brother Man,* pp. 84–5)

In the event, conflict never takes place. Ambo is flatly presented as
the type of the exploiting obeah man, and seen completely from the

outside. Mais settles to using him simply, as a foil to the Christ-like Bra' Man.

Mais's Ambo is constructed out of educated attitudes to the obeah man, and his presence in the novel is determined by the needs of an intention focused on the holy central character. Only one West Indian novelist has made an obeah man the central character in his fiction; although conventional attitudes to the obeah man appear in the novel, and although Ismith Khan allows Zampi some strokes of supernatural power, *The Obeah Man* (1964) grows away from the documentary and the spectacular to become a serious fictional study of self-definition. In the process, a highly personal view of obeah as a spiritual vocation is disclosed.

Zampi the fictional obeah man is not a Negro. We are told in fact that he 'has no race, no caste, no colour; he was the end of masses of assimilations and mixtures, having the eyes of the East Indian, the build of the Negro, the skin of the Chinese, and some of the colour of all' (p. 11). But Khan's creative intention is most clearly indicated by the use of the obeah man as the novel's centre of consciousness. Zampi comes over as a man ill at ease in a blighted world which he sees swallowing up all his people; 'It ain't have no place for we. The islands drowning and we going down with them—down, down, down. One day the clocks in the big church and them go stop and nobody here to fix them or wind them up. . . . We is nobody, and we ain't have nowhere to go. Everything leave me with a cold, cold feeling in my insides, and I ain't have no uses for you or nobody nor nothing—nothing . . .' (pp. 66–7). The obeah man's extraordinary sensitivity puts him at odds with himself and with his woman Zolda. It also alienates him from the unthinking people whom he wishes to serve. It is only when Zampi learns to accept alienation as the painful condition of art that a kind of peace comes into his life:

> . . . An obeah man had to practise at distancing himself from all things. He had to know joy and pleasure as he knew sorrow and pain, but he must also know how to withdraw himself from its torrent, he must be in total possession of himself, and at the height of infinite joy he must know with all of his senses all that lives and breathes about him. He must never sleep the sleep of other men,

he must have a clockwork in his head. He must at a moment's notice to be able to shake the rhythm from his ear, to hold his feet from tapping. He must know the pleasure in his groin and he must know how to prevent it from swallowing him up.

If *The Obeah Man* fails, it fails because too much is made to depend upon a naïve philosophy of self-control. This is not too obtrusive in the presentation of Zampi, since Khan expresses the conflict within his central character in dramatic terms and makes the acceptance of partial withdrawal a logical act of choice that was always latent in the hero's attitudes and behaviour. But when the relationship between Zampi and Zolda is done in terms of aspiring spirit and voluptuous flesh, such a crude externalization does little justice to Khan's own intuitions embodied in the actual presentation of Zampi. As a result, the end of the novel is confused. Zolda's decision to return to the hills with Zampi in pursuit of higher life strikes the reader as too arbitrarily contrived. And Khan slips uncertainly back to the pre-conversion state of the character by allowing her to wish (in another of the lurid patches of writing that mars the work) 'to have him possess her with thrusts like lightning bolts that would scorch her loins' (p. 186).

Khan's imagining of an obeah man who sees himself as an artist is a reminder, if such is needed, that the creative writer can and often does distort the facts to suit his own ends. With one complex exception,[1] however, the writers who use the cults in their novels stay close to the social reality. Sylvia Wynter's *The Hills of Hebron* (1962) documents the wide range of cults in the islands, including a pocomania cult (corresponding to the Haitian voodoo worshippers): 'the Believers' (corresponding to the break-away Afro-Baptist cults which Philip Curtin and Orlando Patterson[2] describe as having first formed themselves in the 1860's); and the 'New Believers' (a cult invented from two related creeds—Marcus Garvey's Black God religion and the Jamaican Ras Tafarians'[3]

[1] George Lamming's *Season of Adventure* (1960) discussed below, pp. 135-149.
[2] Philip Curtin, *Two Jamaicas* (Harvard University Press, 1955); Orlando H. Patterson, *The Sociology of Slavery* (1967).
[3] For a sound account of the Ras Tafari movement in Jamaica, see *Report on The Rastafari Movement in Kingston, Jamaica*, published by the Institute of Social and Economic Research (1960).

belief in the divinity of the Emperor of Ethiopia). When the Believers' movement collapses with the ignominious failure of their leader to take flight to heaven, some of the brethren join the orthodox Christian Church: 'There was something atavistic about their singing as though they were shouting to recall lost gods from the primeval forests of Africa. And at times their singing stirred up secret urges in the Reverend's own heart which had been slumbering through centuries of civilisation' (p. 120). Reverend Brooke's disturbance at his flock's hearts of darkness corresponds with the uneasiness of nineteenth-century missionaries at the incursions of rhythmic singing and other 'African' manifestations into the orthodox Church.

Miss Wynter comically deflates the cults depicted in her novel. A good illustration of the method used is Moses's confession to his first convert of how the Lord inspired him in a vision: 'It was just a day like any other, Sister Edwards. No sign to mark it as different. I was watering the flowers. I came to a rhododendron bush that stood alone by itself. As I poured out water at the root, I see the whole bush light up with fire before my eyes. I step back, I stand still, I watch. The bush flamed orange and green fire. The presence of God was all round about me. I fall on my knees, I bow my head to the earth. I make to take off my shoes but as it wasn't Sunday I wasn't wearing any. And the ground on which I was standing, Sister Edwards, was holy, holy ground' (p. 107).

But the author does not simply make fun of her cultists. The novel shows a passionate concern about the void in the lives of the socially depressed cultists, and sees part of the solution as lying in socio-economic adjustments. This socio-economic leaning is given emphasis by Miss Wynter's allowing Moses to become unnerved when a labour leader rouses the people to take stock of 'the extent of their misery, the hopelessness of their poverty, the lack of any future for their children' (p. 204). He advises them to have nothing to do with churches ('All that is finished and done'), rather, they should believe in organized labour, and Man.[1] The weight of the

[1] A similar impulse is to be found in Ralph de Boissiere's *Crown Jewel* (1952), where Cassie is freed from her belief in the Orisha by the love of the labour leader LeMaitre whose movement she joins. De Boissiere's account of a Shango meeting in Chapter 36 is of great exotic as well as documentary interest.

presentation leads the reader to think that this is Miss Wynter's advice too.

The socio-economic depression of the masses and the 'great emptiness, somewhere in their life, that gnawing at them and begging for plenty plenty satisfaction' (p. 59), underlie Andrew Salkey's handling of pocomania cultists in *A Quality of Violence* (1959). The spectacular elements of drums, rhythm, sacrifice, flagellation and spirit possession occur. But Salkey sets the novel in a period of drought and aridity in the land: this is the clearest of indications that the author has larger artistic uses for the frenzied manifestations of the cultists.

The pocomanians find the substance of their lives breaking up beyond control in the endless drought. Dada Johnson their leader sees their faith in him collapsing, and the deputy is looking around for the right moment to make a bid for primacy. These motives operate in the spectacular dance ('the Giant X') in which the dancers equate their bodies with the land, each whipping himself in an attempt to banish the barrenness of the land and that of the earthly body: 'We must lash the devil out of the land. We must lash good water into the land.' The rivalry between Dada and his deputy spurs each man to more and more incisive self-laceration until both collapse exhausted and expiring. The Giant X claims both as sacrificial victims. But the rains do not come.

This fierce vision of human aberration under burning stress, and the deafness of the gods is placed within a more conventional ordering of experience in the novel. But although the solid virtues and values of the Marshalls and the Parkins help to disperse the pessimism in the work, it is Salkey's exploration, through the sacrificed and suicidal cultists, of the irrational element in human existence that makes the work such a powerful one.

Another kind of approach to the cultists is represented by Orlando Patterson's interpretation of Ras Tafarians in *The Children of Sisyphus* (p. 196). The objects of derision in J. B. Emtage's lampoon, *Brown Sugar* (1966), are handled realistically and with compassion by Patterson. The progress of Sammy the garbageman, for instance, as he drives his cart through the dungle allows the author to describe the shacks and huts of the slum-dwellers and to express the socio-economic causes of Ras Tafarianism in harrowing terms.

But the novel intends to be more than just a socially realistic fiction. Through the consciousness of the Ras Tafarian leader, Brother Solomon, Patterson seeks to portray Rasta destitution and unavailing struggle to escape as the fate of man in an absurd world. When Brother John and Brother Ezekiel bring the news that the delegation to Ethiopia has failed and that the Rastas would not be received in the Emperor's kingdom, Brother Solomon reveals that he had known it all along but had deliberately left all the other Brethren undeceived; the deception must be maintained for as long as possible. The deceived are not just poor and wretched people:

> 'Then what else them is?' Brother John's voice broke in impatiently. 'They are gods. You can't see? Every wretched one of them is archetype of the clown-man, playing their part upon the comic stage so well they are no longer conscious of playing. You can't see, Brothers? Everyone of them is a living symbol full of meaning and revelation. Look! They have before them one hour, two hours, five no twelve, before the ship come. Twelve hours of unreality. Twelve hours of happiness. Who else but the gods could enjoy such happiness? For the moment they are conquerors. For a moment they have cheated the dreary circle. And it's only the moment that counts.'

When his audience object that, with a crowd outside waiting to receive the news, meditations on life are inappropriate, Brother Solomon continues to expound:

> 'Life,' Brother Solomon repeated, and he had half retreated from them again. 'Life, you say, Brother. You speak of the long comic repetition, don't it, Brother? But you don't feel yourself that it's only them that's tried; that have their hopes raised an' then shattered only to start again. No, Brother, no. They you see outside are just the gods that make plain by magnitude what ordinary mortals fear to face and run from. Everywhere in everything, there is the comedy you see before you now, Brother.'
>
> (*The Children of Sisyphus*, p. 202)

The studied nature of these passages from the penultimate chapter (the doctrinal heart of the novel), and Brother Solomon's thinly concealed bearing of the authorial message illustrate the difficulties of a West Indian novelist who is intelligent enough to know that social documentation is not sufficient but whose creative inspiration is a received philosophy rather than an evolving personal vision. For while Patterson's avowedly inherited doctrine is not inapplicable to the life depicted in his fiction, the obtrusive manner in which the interpretation is given makes it seem unnatural. This is not the case in Roger Mais's *The Hills Were Joyful Together*, for instance, where the technique is just as clumsy but where one's sense of the experienced author's deeply felt intuitions seeking to express themselves prevents the declared philosophy both from being everything, and from seeming to be intellectually imposed. Patterson's handling of his cultist raw material none the less represents an ambitious and interesting attempt to translate social reality into some of its possibilities by fictional means. The attempt would have appeared more successful if George Lamming had not shown larger possibilities in *Season of Adventure* (1960).

(iv) *Devaluation and the Response*

The African cultures in the West Indies did not alter simply in the sense that all transported cultures change; nor were the physical limitations imposed by slavery the only unnatural determinants of change.

In the New World, a degrading system of slavery defined the initial relationship between the Negro and the European, 'the white rulers having the highest status, and their culture the greatest prestige. Things African were correspondingly devalued, including African racial traits'.[1] Philip Curtin's lucid *The Image of Africa* (1965) bears out Frantz Fanon's rousing description of the alienating work of slavery and colonialism: 'Colonialism is not satisfied merely with holding a people in its grip and emptying the native's brain of all form and content. By a kind of perverted logic, it turns to the past of the oppressed people and distorts, disfigures and destroys it. . . . For colonialism this vast continent was the haunt of savages, a country riddled with superstitions and fanaticism,

---

[1] M. G. Smith, 'West Indian Culture' in *Caribbean Quarterly* (Vol. 7, No. 3, December 1961).

destined for contempt, weighed down by the curse of God, a country of cannibals—in short, the Negro's country.'[1]

After Emancipation, the West Indian Negro's attempts to define a national and cultural identity have been complicated by what has been felt as a necessarily antecedent need to undo the colonial devaluation of Africa, Africans and the African past. Fanon continues: 'The past is given back its value. Culture, extracted from the past to be displayed in all its splendour, is not necessarily that of his own country.... The Negro, never so much a Negro as since he has been dominated by the Whites comes to realise that history points out a well-defined path to him: he must demonstrate that a Negro culture exists.'[2]

In the first half of the twentieth century, a number of broadly social and political movements took place in the Caribbean and in North America. Mutual influences cannot be ruled out, but what is impressive about these movements is the way they spontaneously coalesce around a common interest in Africa and how in each case the interest in Africa arose because New World Negroes were not at ease in societies to which they belonged, but in which they were at the squalid bottom of the socio-economic ladder. The earliest of these was Haitian nationalism[3] beginning in the 1850's, but becoming more militant with the American occupation of 1915. From a base in Harlem, the Jamaican Marcus Garvey became the First Negro leader to have an international following, and the first man to organize a mass movement among American Negroes. His 'Universal Negro Improvement Association' rallied Negroes everywhere in the 1920's.[4] The third recognizable movement was less overtly racial in its appeal. 'Pan-Africanism',[5] the political

---

[1] *The Wretched of the Earth* (1965), pp. 170 and 171.

[2] *The Wretched of the Earth*, p. 171.

[3] For details about Haitian nationalism and the celebration of Africa as a cultural matrix, see 'The French West Indian Background of Négritude' in G. R. Coulthard's *Race and Colour in Caribbean Literature* (1962).

[4] A good account of Garvey's half-visionary half-crackpot programmes and his impact on the Negro world is E. D. Cronon's *Black Moses* (University of Wisconsin Press: Madison, 1955). Two essays by West Indians are also valuable: Claude McKay, 'Marcus Aurelius Garvey' in *Harlem: Negro Metropolis* (N.Y., 1940), and George Padmore, 'Black Zionism or Garveyism' in *Pan-Africanism or Communism?* (1956).

[5] George Padmore, *Pan-Africanism or Communism?* (1956), pp. 105–85, is the most reliable guide to the understanding of Pan-Africanism by one of its leading exponents.

ideal of a united and free Africa, was the intellectuals' expression
of Negro brotherhood: it began as early as 1900 in London, and
closed with the historic Fifth Congress in Manchester in 1945 which
was virtually a conference of future heads of African states. These
movements coincided with the beginnings of more disciplined
approaches by Europeans to African history and cultures, and with
the cult of the primitive in the arts.

The movements were accompanied by literary manifestations
which they seem to have inspired. Coulthard speaks of the drums
beginning to beat in the literature of Haiti; and three years after
dismissing Garvey as 'a West Indian charlatan', Claude McKay
connected his fellow countryman's activities with the 'Harlem
Renaissance', the Negro literary upsurge of the 1920's: 'The flower-
ing of Harlem's creative life came in the Garvey era. . . . If Marcus
Garvey did not originate the phrase, "New Negro," he at least
made it popular.' From the Caribbean came Aimé Césaire's great
poem 'Cahier d'un Retour au Pays Natal' (1939) in which the
catching word 'Négritude' appears for the first time. All these
literary manifestations share certain features: a celebration of Africa
as a cultural matrix; a favourable interpretation of the African past;
a pride in Blackness; a contrast between a harmonious way of life
and a decadent White civilization lost in materialism; and a joyful
proclamation of the sensuous and integrated African or Negro
personality. The word 'négritude' has come to imply this complex
of facts, attitudes and myths especially as they appear in works of
literature by Negroes throughout the Caribbean.

To consider négritude and the broad social and political movements of the century together in this way is not only to recognize
their overlapping ideas and emotions, but to remind ourselves that
they all relate to the same historical necessity. But if Caribbean
négritude was a phase in the development of Caribbean nationalisms, the word has come to have other implications.

Mainly responsible for this was the Senegalese, Leopold Sedhar
Senghor, who became the leading theorist of négritude after the
Second World War. For Senghor, a man from Africa, who did not

Colin Legum's *Pan-Africanism* (1962) contains useful information but misinterprets
this political movement.

need to prove that he was of African origin, the négritude of a poem is to be found more in its style, essentially image and rhythm, than in its content. This style, however, is bound up with the Negro's sensuous apprehension of the world and his immediate participation in the Cosmos. (Senghor construes this as an exclusive racial quality of the Negro, the opposite of the White analytic mode.) These sensuous qualities which, according to Senghor, represent the essence of Negro civilization, are the properties of Negro writers everywhere, whether they are conscious of it or not: 'The Spirit of African Negro civilisation consciously or not, animates the best Negro artists and writers of to-day, whether they come from Africa or America. So far as they are conscious of African Negro culture and are inspired by it they are elevated in the international scale; so far as they turn their backs on Africa the mother they degenerate and become feeble.'[1] For Senghor, it is not necessary to hunt out survivals of African cultures in the usual senses. The survival of the descendants of Africans is the same as the survival of Negro civilization.

There are differences in emphasis and purpose between the négritude associated with the Pan-Negro and Pan-African movements originating in the Caribbean and North America, and that négritude based on the theory of the culture-bearing person as outlined by Senghor. But it is better to recognize the different contexts and meanings of the word 'négritude' than to choose one version as the 'real thing'. In so far as it stands upon a theory of culture, however, it is worth bearing Frantz Fanon's warning in mind:

> . . . The unconditional affirmation of African culture has succeeded the unconditional affirmation of European culture. On the whole, the poets of Negro-ism oppose the idea of an old Europe to a young Africa, tiresome reasoning to lyricism, oppressive logic to high-stepping nature, and on one side stiffness, ceremony, etiquette, and scepticism while on the other, frankness, liveliness, liberty and—why not?—luxuriance: but also irresponsibility.
>
> The poets of Negro-ism will not stop at the limits of the continent. From America, black voices will take up the hymn with

[1] 'The Physio-psychology of the Negro' in *The 1st International Conference of Negro Writers and Artists* (Paris, 1956, pp. 51–64).

fuller unison. . . . The historical necessity in which the men of African culture find themselves to racialise their claims and to speak more of African culture than of national culture will tend to lead them up a blind alley.[1]

By the time that most West Indian works come to be written (after 1950), social and political developments have robbed négritude of much of its urgency on a practical level. The movement has also become international and changed in character. In the West Indies, the consciousness of race and of Africa has been awakened by the movements of the preceding decades, and the nationalist spirit is stirring. There is an implicit racial appeal in the socio-economic persuasions, but the interest is clearly in the Negro in the Caribbean.

Although it is a mistake to speak about négritude in West Indian fiction, it is nevertheless worth recognizing that attitudes to Africa and Africans, some of which are inspired by the movements of the preceding decades, play a considerable part. In the next sections, therefore, it is proposed to examine a number of novels in which West Indian authors show an interest in Africa and things African. George Lamming's *Season of Adventure* (1960) is set on the imaginary island of San Cristobal, newly independent and lacking in orientation. The most interesting character is the girl, Fola, a member of the light-skinned middle class. Lamming's use of a religious ceremony makes this novel a convenient starting-point for a discussion which wants to look at the artistic qualities of those works in which attitudes to Africa and Africans are expressed, while making the point that lying behind these attitudes is a more important interest in the West Indies.

(v) *The West Indian Interest in Africa* (*Literary*)

(a) *Season of Adventure*

On his terrified visit to Trinidad in 1960, V. S. Naipaul observed of Port of Spain: 'The city throbbed with steel bands. A good opening line for a novelist or a travel writer, but the steel band used to be regarded as a high manifestation of West Indian culture, and

---

[1] 'On National Culture' in *The Wretched of the Earth* (1965), pp. 172-3.

it was a sound I detested' (*The Middle Passage*, 1962). George Lamming's nationalistic novel, *Season of Adventure* (1960), begins: 'Beyond the horizons of the trees, it was too black to see the sky. But the music was there, loud as a gospel to a believer's ears. It was the music of Steel Drums, hard strident and clear. . . .' In a sense, *Season of Adventure* is a celebration (the first literary one) of the steel band. Not only does the sound of the steel drums hang in the air throughout the novel: at the climax is a glorious parade of all the bands marching on to Freedom Square celebrating the coming of a new government:

> Gort led in solo with the calypsoes and digging songs that had first christened his master's name: Never never me again; Glory, Glory, King Coca-Cola; Doctor Say you Pay to Earn But Lantern say you Pay to Learn; The Queen's Canary Fly Away; River Ben Come Down; Goin' to see Aunt Jane; and not the native folk-songs alone. The paradox of their double culture was no less honoured with rhythm. For they changed as the mood assailed them; and a mood had soon taken them back to childhood and the hymns of their chapel days: Hold the Fort For I am Coming, I Got a Sword in My Hand, Help me to Use it Lord; and back again the music would swing as though their moods were magnet which the rhythms had waited for. Now it was a noise of: Never, Never Me Again, and Daylight Come and I Wanna Go Home. And each time the change came, the bass drums would wait to hear from Gort who led in solo and on no other than his dead master's drum.
>
> (*Season of Adventure*, p. 358)

But Lamming's nationalism is not the local-culture-waving Naipaul goes out of his way to snipe at.

Season of Adventure is an analysis of the failure of nationalism in the newly independent San Cristobal. 'In the colonial countries, the spirit of indulgence is dominant at the core of the bourgeoisie; and this is because the national bourgeoisie identifies itself with the Western bourgeoisie from whom it has learnt its lessons. It follows the Western bourgeoisie along its path of negation and decadence without ever having emulated it in its first stages of exploration and invention. . . . It is already senile before it has come to know the petulance, the fearlessness or the will to succeed of youth.'[1] Fanon's

---

[1] Frantz Fanon, '*The Wretched of the Earth* (1965), p. 124.

description of the new ruling class in the ex-colonies is a convenient statement of one of Lamming's starting-points in *Season of Adventure*. So too is the Martiniquan's picture of the disillusion of the poor and underprivileged with the new order: 'The peasant who goes on scratching out a living from the soil, and the unemployed man who never finds employment do not manage, in spite of public holidays and flags, new and brightly-coloured though they may be, to convince themselves that anything has really changed in their lives.... The masses begin to sulk; they turn away from this nation in which they have been given no place and begin to lose interest in it.'[1]

The dilemmas on both sides are the ambitious substance of *Season of Adventure*. Throughout the work, however, Lamming contrasts the outcast Drum Boys' instinctive and immediate possession of the language of the drums with the insecure hold of the middle class upon the European culture they wish to imitate. 'Is like how education wipe out everythin' San Cristobal got except the ceremony an' the bands. To teacher an' all who well-to-do it happen. Everythin' wipe out, leavin' only what they learn.' Crim's remark (p. 17) draws from Powell, another Drum Boy, a declaration which may be said to be the pulse of Lamming's novel: 'A man must got somethin' that he can't let go ... like how Gort hold that drum.' Lamming's vision of the inter-relationship of politics with other aspects of life allows the novel to run from political inertia to the theme of cultural loss. The reader's expectation that this theme will involve Africa in some way is not disappointed. The rhythms of the drums, although clearly belonging to the West Indian Steel band, are made to suggest an African heritage. At the end of the novel after the triumph of the drums and the establishment of the Second Republic, the new president makes a speech in which the symbolic implications of the steel band are more or less declared: 'It was language which caused the First Republic to fall. And the Second would suffer the same fate; the Second and the Third unless they tried to find a language which was no less immediate than the language of the drums.' The Second Republic and the West Indian nation, Lamming is urging, must not only take

[1] *The Wretched of the Earth*, pp. 136-7.

a backward glance at its origins, it must use the personal relation of the Drum Boys to their drums as a model for the creation of a language, and for the meaningful and relevant appropriation of their double cultural heritage.

It should already be clear enough that Lamming's purpose goes beyond a mere satirizing of the middle-class West Indian condition. That he is neither sentimentalizing the peasants nor invoking Africa as a convenient fetish are explicit both in the details of his presentation of a voodoo ceremony, and in the use to which he puts this ceremony (it is one for the resurrection of the dead) in *Season of Adventure*.[1] But before focusing on this key element it is necessary to map out the broad pattern of *Season of Adventure* and notice some of the obstacles to a just appraisal or satisfactory reading of it.

The novelist dealing with political issues differs from the political analyst in that he aims to create a sense of life—the impression of a society in which there are individuals involved in relationships with one another. Unlike the novelist mainly concerned with the subtleties of manners and morals playing upon the individual con-science, he usually tries to portray whole societies (as distinct from particular classes), and he tries to show the whole weight of history behind the society being described. The honesty and force with which the society is described are of great consequence, for society in the political novel is not simply a background in which the characters move. Because the novelist's intention is to deal in the

---

[1] A ceremony described in *The Pleasures of Exile* (1960), pp. 9–10, would appear to be the basis of the ceremony in the novel: 'In the republic of Haiti . . . a native religion sometimes forces the official Law to negotiate with peasants who have retained a racial and historic desire to worship their original gods. We do not have to share their faith in order to see the universal significance of certain themes implicit in the particular ceremony of the Souls I witnessed four years ago in the suburbs of Port-au-Prince. . . . The celebrants are mainly relatives of the deceased who, ever since their death, have been locked in Water. It is the duty of the Dead to return and offer on this momentous night, a full and honest report on their past relations with the living. . . . It is the duty of the Dead to speak, since their release from that purgatory of Water cannot be realised until they have fulfilled the contract which this ceremony symbolises. The Dead need to speak if they are going to enter that eternity which will be their last and permanent Future. The living demand to hear whether there is any need for forgiveness, for redemption. . . . Different as they may be in their present state of existence, those alive and those now Dead—their ambitions point to a similar end. They are interested in their Future.'

not so obvious processes by which public issues become translated into personal ones, society is as important as character in this kind of novel. Indeed, while the characters in political novels may be presented as unique individuals, they carry an unusual degree of typicality or representativeness in relation to that society.

The central character in *Season of Adventure* is Fola, an educated West Indian girl who visits a voodoo ceremony in the slum section of her island and finds herself participating in the rites. 'Part product of that world, living still under the shadow of its past disfigurement, all her emotions had sprung from a nervous caution to accept it as her root, her natural gift of legacies. Fear was the honest and ignorant instinct she had felt in the *tonelle*. Her shame, like that of all San Cristobal was unavoidable' (p. 94). The visit to the *tonelle* arouses Fola to a consciousness of the incompleteness in her life, and sets the girl off on a single-minded and at times cruel search into her origins, both personal (she has known only her step-father, Piggott) and racial (her mother Agnes is uncertain whether Fola's father is European or Negro). Lamming explores Fola's crisis through several sets of relationships in the novel: with her mother, Agnes, whose secrecy Fola interprets as guilt, and whose sexual attractiveness Fola harshly condemns as vulgarity and cheapness; with Piggott, whose physical sterility tightens the affection he feels for his step-daughter and who becomes a destructive beast when the girl begins to slip away from him and the privileged world in which he has sought to capture her; and with Charlot, the European teacher, who instructs her in history and who in a strange mood of self-contempt and unconscious superiority takes his pupil/mistress to witness the voodoo ceremony.

On the other side of the fence, Lamming studies the development of Fola's relationship with the peasant world of the deprived masses. He does this through her particular involvements with Chiki, an artist full of compassion but troubled in his own right by an apparent drying up of inspiration; and with Powell, the political fanatic who finally makes an uncompromising and murderous assault upon the light-skinned girl because he thinks it impossible, and too late, for people of her type to break with their traditional attitudes to the black masses.

Each of these relationships is presented with such realistic particularity, and each is so urgent, as to become absorbing in itself
rather than as a segment of Fola's complex problem of adjustment.
Further, each relationship carries a symbolic burden which Lamming wants us to respond to as intensely as we do to the literal
situation. Agnes is not only a secretive mother unable to com-
municate with an impatient rebelling daughter, she is, like the
islands, both the willing prostitute of the ages and the passive
victim of a rapacious history, waiting now, like the islands, to be
made respectable to those she has nourished. And Powell is as much
an embittered individual as the extreme, somehow subtle spirit of
Black Power repudiating a class whose capacity to betray it has
experienced only too often: 'What I do I do alone,' said Powell,
'no help from you an' your lot, 'cause I learn, I learn how any
playing 'bout with your lot bound to end. You know the rules too
good, an' it too late, it too late for me to learn what rules you have
for murderin' me. So is me go murder first. Otherwise is you what
will murder me, or make me murder myself' (p. 328).

The reader has to accustom himself to responding at the same
time to the fullness of each relationship and to its being part of a
larger web; its realistic particularity and its symbolic representativeness. A further source of difficulty is that although Fola is given
most exposure in the novel, each of the other characters (whether
Belinda the prostitute, or Piggott one of the new exploiters of the
people) becomes a centre of interest in turn. The author's compassion for his characters in the toils of a pressing set of social and
political circumstances never permits the reader to rest on a selec-
tive principle in the way it is possible to rest with one character in
Naipaul's *A House for Mr. Biswas*, for example. This kind of
compassion is impressively witnessed at the end of Chapter XIV,
where an Author's Note on the character, Powell, seems in theory
to break the fictional illusion but in fact serves to strengthen it. The
last paragraphs of this note run:

> I believe deep in my bones that the mad impulse which drove
> Powell to his criminal defeat was largely my doing. I will not have
> this explained away by talk about environment; nor can I allow my
> own moral infirmity to be transferred to a foreign conscience,

labelled imperialist. I shall go beyond my grave in the knowledge
that I am responsible for what happened to my brother.

Powell still resides somewhere in my heart, with a dubious love,
some strange, nameless shadow of regret; and yet with the deepest,
deepest nostalgia. For I have never felt myself to be an honest part
of anything since the world of his childhood deserted me.

(Season of Adventure, p. 332)

This autobiographical strain, although not operating as explicitly
as in the case of Powell, gives intensity to the presentation of yet
another character—Chiki the painter with four works behind him
but now suffering a block to his creativity as the confusing implications of his double cultural heritage begin to work themselves out
in his consciousness. The reader approaching *Season of Adventure*
with set principles about what the art of the novel is or ought to
be will find many of the work's best effects achieved at times when
those principles are most blatantly flouted.

Fola's process of self-discovery, which begins with her experience at the voodoo ceremony, takes place in a difficult and ambi-
tiously crowded novel. Her process is at once an example of 'every
man's backward glance', and a representation of the middle-class
West Indian's relationship to the peasantry. The social cleavage
with which Lamming begins is best expressed in the conversation
between Crim and Powell, two Drum Boys who notice her in the
crowd at the *tonelle* where the meeting is taking place:

'Is what my eyes seein'?' Powell said. 'Over there, first row.'
They both looked at the girl whose elegance was no less con-
spicuous than the solitary white face beside her.

'Is the stranger man who bring her,' Crim said, 'or else she won't
be here.'

'Look at her good,' said Powell, 'education an' class just twist
that girl mouth right out o' shape. Like all the rest she learn fast
how to talk two ways.'

Crim couldn't resist admiring the novelty which her presence
had created in the *tonelle*.

'Is great she look,' he said, 'almost as great as Gort.'

'She got open-air talk an' inside talk,' said Powell. 'Like tonight
she go talk great, with the stranger man. Grammar an' clause,
where do turn into does, plural and singular in correct formation,

an' all that. But inside, like between you an' me, she tongue make the same rat-trap noise. Then she talk real, an' sentences come tumblin' down like one-foot man. Is how them all is.'

(*Season of Adventure*, p. 21)

But Fola's alienation from the Reserve has a broader parallel. The *tonelle*, where the West African serpent cult has persisted, though undergoing change over three hundred years, is a stark reminder of Africa and the slave migrations. In exploring Fola's attitude to the *tonelle*, Lamming is also writing about the West Indian Negro's attitude to Africa. This becomes obvious in the novel when Fola, after her 'awakening' experiences at the ceremony suddenly realizes why her visit to the *tonelle* is more problematic than the visit of American tourists to European monuments:

> It was because, for Liza and herself it was because their relation to the *tonelle* was far more personal than any monument could ever be to an American in his mad pursuit of origins. *Personal and near.* . . . Her relation to the *tonelle* was *near* and more personal since the conditions of her life to-day, the conditions of Liza's life in this very moment, could recall a departure that was near and tangible: the departure of those slaves who had started the serpent cult which the drums in their dumb eloquence had sought to resurrect. . . .
>
> Part-product of that world, living still under the shadow of its past disfigurement, all her emotions had sprung from a nervous caution to accept it as her root, her natural gift of legacies. Fear was the honest and ignorant instinct she had felt in the *tonelle*. Her shame, like that of all San Cristobal was unavoidable.
>
> (*Season of Adventure*, pp. 93–4)

Pages 93–4 of *Season of Adventure* are very similar in content to pages 161–2 of *The Pleasures of Exile*. In the latter work, a paragraph on Americans in quest of Europe is followed by an analysis of the West Indian Negro's attitude to Africa:

> The West Indian Negro who sets out on a similar journey to Africa is less secure. His relation to that continent is more personal and more problematic. It is more personal because the conditions of his life to-day, his status as a man, are a clear indication of the reasons which led to the departure of his ancestors from that continent. . . . His relation to Africa is more problematic because he has not . . . been introduced to it through history. He knows it

through rumour and myth which is made sinister by a foreign tutelage, and he becomes, through the gradual conditioning of his education, identified with fear: fear of that continent as a world beyond human intervention. Part product of that world, and living still under the shadow of its past disfigurement, he appears reluctant to acknowledge his share of the legacy which is part of his heritage.

(Season of Adventure, pp. 160–1)

In the novel *Season of Adventure*, Lamming explores the problematic relation to Africa in terms proper to works of fiction. The middle-class West Indian's denial of the masses, and his shame of Africa are seen as obstacles to the fulfilment of the person, and the inauthentic existence of the unfulfilled person is a kind of death. Fola is imagined as such a dead person, and the creative task of the novel is to probe this condition and to feel for the problems and possibilities of re-birth.

The ceremony for the resurrection of the dead is projected as a symbolic occasion, and as an actual experience shocking Fola into her journey of self-discovery. Lamming, the novelist, insinuates the idea of Fola's 'hidden parallel of feeling' with the 'coarse exuberant faces' at the *tonelle* through the European's words. Charlot makes the observation that Fola responds to rhythm like the worshippers:

'You want to suggest that I believe in all "that",' she said. Her voice was low, distinct, closing on a note of quiet disdain.
'But I've seen you dance, Fola.'
'What's that got to do . . .'
'It's the same rhythm,' he said. 'And the music of the Steel Drums. You yourself have said no music makes you feel the same way.'
'But what's that got to do with holding ceremonies?' she challenged, 'and talking to the dead?'
'There couldn't be any music without the ceremonies,' said Charlot. 'You couldn't do your dancing without those women. It's from being so near to them that you have learnt how to move your body.'
Fola felt a sudden resentment towards him. Her triumph would have to be as large as the families whom she was about to defend; for the civilised honour of the whole republic was now in danger.
'Near?' she said subtly.

'In feeling you are,' said Charlot, 'you can deny them anything
except the way you feel when the same rhythm holds you.'

(*Season of Adventure*, pp. 27–8)

This comes close indeed to saying 'all your lot have rhythm'. But
Lamming makes brilliant use of the European cliché. The novelist's
problem, at this point, is to create in the reader an expectation that
something is about to happen to Fola, and that the something has
to do with a special relationship that exists between Fola and the
cultists, but not between the cultists and Charlot. At the same time,
the specialness of Fola's relationship with the cultists must not
preclude the possibility of a more remote but equally valid kinship
between the cultists and Charlot, who is human after all. By associating the voodoo drums with the more familiar and pervasive
steel band music, Lamming gives an air of truth to Charlot's initial
observation. If Charlot's insistence upon his lack of affinity with
the cultists strikes the reader as being too glib, however, Fola's
strenuous denials only serve to confirm that she is aware of more
than she cares to admit as yet.

Lamming builds upon this rhetorical ploy by filtering realistic
descriptions of feverish dance, monotonous chanting and spirit
possession through Fola's disturbed consciousness, so that we are
left to feel that a combination of Charlot's superior nagging and
the mass-belief of the devotees have made her vulnerable:

> The voices were all raised in prayer, answering to the grave sup-
> plications of the priest. Fola looked to see if there was movement
> in the tent; but her glance was intercepted by an old woman who
> still watched her. Was the old woman's glance an accident? The
> voices had wrought a gradual contamination of Fola's senses. Was
> she becoming a part of their belief? Would they really hear the
> sound of dead voices in the tent? Her questions were other than
> an interest to examine. She became aware of their contagion in her
> mind. The prayers were a conspiracy against her doubt. The voices
> grew loud and louder in their prayers, each prayer like a furious
> bargain for her faith.

(*Season of Adventure*, pp. 33–4)

At this point it is possible to locate some major differences in
intention and tactics between H. G. de Lisser and Lamming, for
in *The White Witch of Rosehall* (1929), too, a main character, Ruther-

ford, witnesses a ceremony. He is accompanied by a friend, Rider. The first thing to notice is that Rutherford is at a distance, not in the crowd. Nevertheless he is given the beginning of an experience:

> A shudder passed through Robert; to his surprise he found that he too was slightly moving his body to the rhythm of the sound. Rider had himself better in hand, but the hypnotic influence of the scene did not leave him entirely unaffected. It had an appeal to the more primitive emotions. It stirred up something in the depths of one's being. He could understand how devotees in pagan lands were moved at times almost to madness by the call and compulsion of their strange and horrible religions.
>
> (*The White Witch of Rosehall*, p. 202)

After the appearance of Kurtz in Conrad's *Heart of Darkness* (1902), episodes dealing with the European character affected by the primitive become a must in the second-rate literature of tropica. Once de Lisser makes the gesture towards this convention, a gap rapidly opens up again between the civilized Englishman and the pagan cultists. Rutherford resumes a function as the enlarging eye upon an exotic rite which it is de Lisser's object to 'write-up'.

The detailed and spectacular ceremony described in *Season of Adventure*, on the other hand, is subservient to a process of dissolution in the observing character. The episode is divided into omniscient authorial description of the ceremony, subjective impressions from Charlot and Fola, snatches of conversation between Crim and Powell, and a continuing argument between Fola and Charlot. Expectations are early set up with regard to Fola, and because each return to her consciousness finds her further on towards a crisis of 'conversion', each retreat to another perspective becomes charged either with suspense or with an indirect bearing on the girl's subjective state.

The details of the ceremony are every bit as exotic as those in de Lisser's novel, but by making Fola such an intense focus of interest in a psychological sense, Lamming forces the exciting events into a corrosive background. We become aware of the feverishness of the dance as an aspect of the girl's growing hysteria:

... The atmosphere of the *tonelle* had increased in its effect upon her. There was something intimidating about the women. The dance had become more feverish. Fola recognised what they were doing, but there was too much tension in their bodies. She expected something to collapse inside them. Fola had lived in the shadow of two terrors: hypnosis and the sight of rats. She thought of both and the dancing made her shudder.

(*Season of Adventure*, p. 25)

In a similar fashion, the case of spirit possession is not used as a spectacle in itself. Indeed, Lamming seems to throw away spectacular possibilities by allowing the possessed woman to go into her swoon behind Fola's back, while Fola's eyes are fixed upon the approaching procession led by the high priest or *houngan*:

It seemed there was no order to his giving. Fola could feel the pimples swelling over her arms. She studied the faces of those who had drunk from the bottle of gin so that she might detect some order in the *Houngan's* benediction. But a sweat broke under her eyes as she heard the swoon of a woman's voice behind her. She wanted to ask Charlot what he would do if the *Houngan* ordered them to drink. But the woman's voice was reaching cold and sticky as a hand into her skull. Her breath blew a staleness of gin odour round Fola's ears. Fola's attention was divided between the crippled swoon of the woman's voice and the progress which the procession was making towards the bamboo pole.

Would Charlot drink of the gin? And what would happen if she refused? Was the woman behind her going to be sick? It was the sound of a voice in some near stage of asphyxia, crying: 'Spirit, ride! ride! An' come, come, come sister, come, hold sister, hold and let it come, inside O! Spirit, let it, inside O spirit come! An' kind let it O O O come, come.'

(*Season of Adventure*, p. 31)

Lamming's controlling purpose frees him to write in a manner that could be described as sensational if seen out of context. The description of the *houngan* is a good example, especially when compared with this description of Takoo at the climax of de Lisser's attempted spectacular:

Takoo was clothed from head to foot in flaming red, robed as a high priest of Sassabonsum or some other potent God of the African forests. In this robe of office he loomed taller than Robert or Rider had ever seen him before, and there was dignity in his

gait and a gloomy earnestness in his gaze that seemed to inspire
that crouching silent audience with awe.

(The White Witch of Rosehall, p. 203)

Lamming's high priest is much more fantastic:

> He was a short, black man, narrow around the waist, almost
> fragile in the spareness of his arms. He wore a pair of snake-skin
> sandals. The straps parted and crawled in a bright black radiance
> lapping around his toes. The smell of cemeteries rotted his hands.
> His eyes were the colour of burnt hay. Delirious in their gaze, they
> sparkled and cracked into splinters of light like glass. He carried
> an axe in his right hand, a bracelet of black bones was swinging
> freely round his wrist when he waved the axe in worship above his
> head. The gods resided in every tooth of point and blade.

(Season of Adventure, pp. 31–2)

This is not a piece of lurid writing, however, because we are seeing
from Fola's point of view, her senses have almost been overwhelmed by the strange sights and sounds and the mass hysteria
around her, and the frightening *houngan* is face to face with her. The
compelling presence of the *houngan* completes the temporary confusion of Fola's senses, and she is led into the tent where the gods
seem to possess her.

The sensational use of an African ceremony in *The White Witch
of Rosehall* is accompanied by a revulsion against what is presented
as African paganism, and the fictional character's revulsion is
shared by the author. In *Season of Adventure*, the 'dark continent'
view is located in a character who is to be disburdened; the sensational aspects of the ceremony are used as a corrosive force, mes-
merizing Fola into participating in the rites at the *tonelle*. Lamming
does not try to present Fola's actions as arising from anything more
than fear, shock, and a confusion of the senses. Fola does not come
to share the faith of the cultists. But when the girl begins to reflect
on her experience later, she recognizes that her fear and ignorance
in the *tonelle* are closely related to her revulsion from the peasant
masses. From this point, she starts to free herself from shame,
seeking desperately to add to the known 'Fola', the 'other than'
which her education and privileged upbringing have conspired to
bury.

147

As the ceremony is one for the resurrection of the dead, it lends itself symbolically: the 'dead' Fola finds the opportunity to break out of her purgatory and gain a new future. Expanding in her season of adventure, Fola sees the privileged families of the republic as forever locked in water, 'decrepit skeletons near Federal Drive polluting the live air with their corpse breathing'. When she catches herself hesitating between the safety of denial and the shame of acknowledging her new friends at the Reserve, Fola guiltily accuses herself too, of being a corpse trapped in purgatory: 'Like the dead souls that could not trespass beyond their recorded lives, she had cut herself off from her own future.' On the other hand, when Fola intervenes to save Chiki from arrest, she is seen as a dead coming to bear witness, as well as like a believer possessed by the gods:

> The women watched Fola as though they had seen Guru's soul recover in flesh and stand in the *tonelle*, shouting what he knew about the diamonds which had disappeared again. Fola stood there, her eyes now closed, fist knotted like Aunt Jame's in her possession. They thought the girl was a corpse until the corporal disturbed her sleep.
>
> (*Season of Adventure*, p. 274)

But while Lamming uses the cult and the cultists to image lost meanings, and to shock Fola into her season of adventure, the author deliberately refuses to take a sentimental view of the *tonelle*. At the end of the novel, the meeting place is destroyed by fire, and the *houngan* has lost command and self-command. The politician Baako, in looking forward, expresses a proper sociological view:

> He said he would ask the citizens of the Reserve and all like them to think again about their relation to the *tonelle*. He would not order them to change, but he would try to find a language which might explain that the magic of medical science was no less real than the previous magic of prayer. The difference was one of speed. Injections worked faster than a bribe for knowledge they could not guarantee.
>
> (*Season of Adventure*, p. 365)

The 'no less real than' hardly conceals a recognition by this authorially approved character that the practice of the cultists can also be seen as a symptom of social and economic frustration.

Season of Adventure is the most significant of the West Indian novels invoking Africa, and a major achievement, for several reasons: because it does not replace a denigrating excess by a romanticizing one; because it embodies a corrective view without making this the novel's *raison d'être*; because it is so emphatically a West Indian novel—invoking the African heritage not to make statements about Africa but to explore the troubled components of West Indian culture and nationhood; and because it can do all this without preventing us from seeing that Fola's special circumstances, and by implication those of the West Indian, are only a manifestation, although a pressing one in the islands today, of every man's need to take the past into account with humility, fearlessness and receptivity if the future is to be free and alive.

(b) *Black Albino*

It is a sharp drop from Lamming's intensely wrought novel to the wish-fulfilment in Namba Roy's tribal presentation of poetic justice. In *Black Albino* (1961), Roy combines the theme of the recall of the exiled leader with that of the vindication of the unjustly despised. By merit, Tomaso the former Chief returns to favour with the tribe; his albino son, Tamba, proves to his young companions that, in spite of his strange colour, he is a worthy son of a worthy chief. The moral satisfaction in which Roy indulges is to be seen at the end of the novel when Tomaso is allowed, gracelessly, to remind his people of their injustice:

> 'Hear me now!' continued Tomaso, relentlessly. 'My son has not changed the colour of his face since you drove us from the village. Go back to thy huts and tell thy picnies that what you taught them was a lie, that he has the same blood, the same laughter comes from his mouth, the same water in his eyes as they, and only when I have seen with my own eyes that they the little ones, have taken to my child, only then shall I, with my Kisanka, and the two little ones, come back to thy village, and I be thy chief once more. I have spoken!'

Roy's moralizing strain is not always as obtrusive as this, but it often leads to an over-sentimental presentation of the oppressed, and a vindictive categorization of the villains in his novel.

But if the novel does not bear probing of this kind, it is a rich bed of African cultural survivals. In the Foreword to *Black Albino*, Tom Driberg, therefore, writes:

> I first heard of the Maroons shortly before going to Jamaica some years ago. It was Katharine Dunham, that wonderful impresario of Caribbean dance and song, who told me about them and said that I must visit one of the villages—Accompong—in which a remnant of them still proudly maintained their autonomy and their ancestral traditions. I did so, and shall never forget the strange fascination of that remote hill-village, or the courteous hospitality which seemed to take one back through the centuries.
>
> Katherine Dunham—a qualified anthropologist as well as a woman of the theatre—eagerly traced back to their African origins many of the cultural patterns of the Maroons. By a coincidence, I am writing this foreword in West Africa; and around me in real life are so many of the sights and sounds and customs that occur, too, in Namba Roy's story—the cottonwood trees, the delicious paw-paws, women pounding herbs for healing, the greedy ants, the talking drums, the stool of chieftainship . . . and so many of the human characteristics, found in his Maroons, that go to make up what is beginning to be called the African personality.

These cultural survivals are well sign-posted in the novel or explicated with varying degrees of self-consciousness. Instead of attempting to catalogue them, I shall look at three features— nostalgia for the lost land, the physical descriptions of the African character, and Roy's attempt to fashion an 'African' language in the novel. These elements will reappear in some novels to be looked at afterwards.

The novel opens with Tomaso and five of his men sitting on a mountain top, comparing their new land with the old:

> 'You speak truly, Tahta. This Jamaica is indeed a strange land, with no lions and no animals with hides to break the point of a spear. Some crocodiles it is true, and some snakes and wild hogs; but neither the lightfooted antelope nor asunu, the heavy-footed one, whom the bakra named elephant, have ever set foot on this place.' He sighed as he passed his eyes over the wooded hill above him.
>
> 'True, there are woods here, and the mighty rocks and steep mountains give good hands to our fighting and hiding from the bakra of the plains; but sometimes I long for the forest so thick and

high that the face of the sun cannot be seen beneath and where even the mighty asunu, with teeth as tall as a warrior must bellow for fear of getting lost.'

There is some obvious sub-Biblical writing here, but what is interesting is how, although Roy is writing in the post-1950 period, he is able to control the references to the native continent by allowing the character to express nostalgia by a recall of commonplace things. In fact, the passage does not contain more than a contrast through negatives between the two natural environments. The sigh which does not quite avoid being a stereotyped gesture, nevertheless, manages to be less melodramatic than it might have been. And in the final sentence, ('but sometimes I long . . .'), the emotion is much more poignant for being expressed in an image of vast enclosure which could by no means be mistaken for an unequivocal declaration of the superiority of the old land to all other lands. What I am arguing, in other words, is that Roy succeeds in part, for the very simple reason that the emotion being expressed is appropriate to the condition of the fictional character, and not a function of the author's sentimentality. The use of negative terms in the contrast intensifies the feeling for the other land but it indicates, further, an acceptance of the present one, an acceptance which is also implied in the 'sometimes' of the 'I long' sentences. Roy's Maroons, as the novel shows, are interested in coming to terms with the new land, not in returning to Africa.

In the description of the physique of his Africans, Roy shows a race pride but not race exclusiveness. The references to 'the bull-necked one' at the beginning and at the end of the following description prevent us from thinking that any race has the monopoly of beauty:

He was tall and well proportioned, and though he looked almost slight in build opposite the bullnecked one, yet the width of the chief's great shoulders and the power beneath the shiny black skin of his arms and leg muscles showed even in his most relaxed state. He was dressed like his companions in brown loincloth, only, and his only distinction was a band of cloth around his forehead which proclaimed him their chief and leader. Everything about him—his nose, lips, hair and colour, proclaimed him a full-blooded son of Africa. As he leaned his head to one side, meeting the eyes of the warrior who had just spoken, his calm and dignity did not seem to please this bullnecked one, judging by the sudden change on the face of the latter.

(*Black Albino*, pp. 10–11)

This description of the African person, as is obvious from the passage itself, is not a gratuitous one but works naturally in the developing tension between Tomaso and Lago. It is a simple virtue, but sometimes, in the high fever of négritude, lost sight of. The description of Tomaso's wife Kisanka offers a significant variation and an accommodation, however concealed, to other standards of beauty. Roy seems to enjoy the paradox of a theoretically ugly heroine, but one who is attractive nevertheless to the other characters:

> From her countrymen's view, there would be three things to prevent her being the most beautiful girl in their midst; she was not plump, and her nose and lips, though flat and full as befitting a daughter of Africa, were not flat and full enough to make her the undisputed beauty of the village. Apart from this she would have been voted beautiful by any people of any race, with her largish eyes, graceful neck and figure, and a face tapered beautifully to match. Her hair, bunched together by its fine curls, excluded any doubt of her pure African strain, and her skin with the colour and texture of fine black satin, helped also to confirm this.

(*Black Albino*, pp. 18–19)

It is useful to point out that Kisanka's three 'blemishes' draw her closer to a European standard. But I do not think we could accuse the author of *Black Albino* of being a psychological victim of the devaluative process.

I want to look now at Roy's efforts to suggest an 'African' language in English. The first characteristic that Roy gives to his Maroon language is personification. Describing a rough sea, Tahta the old bush-doctor says that 'the water was bitten with madness. It lifted itself and threw its body against the land as if the land had covered it with insults. It was many days and nights before its anger was spent' (p. 9). This is not necessarily African, but Roy makes his intention more explicit in a description of the trees of Twin Sisters, where the personification works by analogy with tribal custom: 'The aged leaves passed along with dignity and without *fuss*, and the young ones, full of respect for their elders, took the places of their predecessors without a blare of horns to announce their coming' (p. 52). Personification of landscape is a characteristic trick of West Indian writers dealing with Africa, and we shall see some more examples later.

For the rest, Roy depends upon Biblical patterns ('It shall be a man-child Tomaso! And none shall call thee childless afterwards', p. 23); the use of expletives ('Rejoice with me, O my people!', p. 23); vivid periphrasis ('Speak and tell me why I have been spared from the beaks of the vultures', p. 12) which are not always appropriate; hyphenated phrases ('brother-with-the-empty-loins', p. 12) and words yoked without hyphens ('mouthslayer') that work best in contexts of invective; the use of parables and proverbs ('a ram goat . . . tried to fool all the animals in the forest that he was a lion until one day the real lion came and only the horns of the ram were left', p. 11); and finally the use of vivid metaphor (Tomaso going 'into the bakra's mouth' to get information, p. 57). It needs saying at this point that in disconnected extracts and in descriptive analysis of technique, Roy's novel seems to be better than it is. Continuous exposure to its simple effects, however, and the underlying moral imperatives mar some good moments.

The next work to be looked at faces some of the very problems Roy solved in a workmanlike way. But *The Leopard* has been acclaimed by most commentators on West Indian literature. It is admired by C. L. R. James and Wilson Harris. More academic figures like Coulthard, Jahn, and J. A. Ramsaran have also seemed to give their approval. Ramsaran does not go beyond the statement that its 'language is marked by a freshness and individual quality which cannot be missed by any sensitive reader'[1]; Jahnheinz Jahn pronounces that Reid 'understands African philosophy in all its depth and makes it come to life'.[2] And Coulthard says that 'whatever the symbolic or allegorical significance of the novel, Reid has tried to pour himself into a completely African character. The background too, naturally, is African'.[3] These views will not be

[1] J. A. Ramsaran, *New Approaches to African Literature* (Ibadan University Press, 1965), p. 102.
[2] *Muntu*, p. 208.
[3] Coulthard, p. 77.

referred to explicitly, but it is useful to bear them in mind in what follows.

(c) *The Leopard*

The Leopard may be seen in two lights. In the first place it is the West Indian novel of imaginary Africa and the African personality *par excellence*. In the second, and more significantly, it is a precursor of *Season of Adventure*. I shall deal with its more popular aspect first.

By opting to narrate much of the novel through a series of flashbacks seen from Nebu's point of view, Reid commits himself to projecting his central character's personality from the inside. In doing so he utilizes stock ideas of romanticism and primitivism. Like Senghor, and like people who do not come from any of the countries of Africa, Reid refers to Nebu as an 'African', and he uses this term in free variation with the word 'Negro'. Although we learn in Chapter Twenty-three that Nebu is 'an effigy . . . fixed forever in gray stones', and in Chapter Thirteen that he is 'a blue black god squatting quiet beyond comprehension', he is saved for humanity (and as we shall see below, for the msabu Gibson) by the 'rich warm blood [that] was pumping along the African's veins'. Indeed, even when asleep he is in rhythmic communion with the earth-force: 'His eyes were closed and only the gentle heaving of the blanket showed that life was thereabout. His sleep was in rhythm with the land, and if the rain had ceased or the wind had died, he would have instantly waked' (p. 86). Little wonder that when, armed at last with a rifle, he runs to the bush, 'the bush was waiting and drew him in with a hundred green arms in heat for him' (p. 52). Our response to one whole side of Reid is a response to a highly sensuous prose in the service of decadence.

One of the key sections of the novel has to do with the dance at the coming of the rains, a solo performance by Nebu the houseboy in the Gibsons' bedroom. Nebu's dance is interrupted by the entry of a rain-soaked Mrs. Gibson. Intercourse takes place on this highly charged occasion (the only time) and later Mrs. Gibson gives birth to the fertile African's son. Since Nebu's relationship with his son is a genuinely imagined human relationship, the one that makes *The Leopard* more than a self-indulgent exercise in black romanticism, it might be argued that the episode is a functional one. But while admitting this, I want to show how Reid uses it for quite other purposes. The passages I would like to quote come from pages 17–19 and from page 21. As quotation is continuous through the first five extracts, page references will be omitted.

Over the whole stretch of text there are three features that recur: a mystic view of person and place; a vein of sexual imagery of a violent kind; and a mixture of over-writing with superb imaginative effects. The three features cannot exist separately, but what I want to follow is the way in which, by the last two passages, Reid declines into the crudest predictable confrontation, with a reduction in the imaginative quality of the writing.

In the first passage, the wind sweeps into the room, the rain draws nearer and then bursts upon the house:

> Vast, cold, furry hands instantly clamped themselves on every inch of his wet, naked body. He shivered violently at the first touch and then the bush flesh, that knew the elements with the primary acquaintance of a forest tree, accepted the wind with a gust of soft laughter. His head arrogantly cocked back on the column of ebony throat, Nebu laughed mirthfully. Miles away he heard the swiftly growing roar of the rain as it exploded on the sounding board of this wide and cushioned land. Then the flood struck down on the trees outside and the house fell on his ears.

In sentence two, the coming of the wind is felt by Nebu in a female position as a taking by force ('shivered violently') joyfully accepted after the initial revulsion. In the same sentence, the 'bush flesh that knew . . . tree' has to do with the African one-ness with the earth-force; and the slightly illogical 'column of ebony throat' in the following sentence is part of Reid's view of the African as sensuous sculpture. In the opening sentence, there is an adjectival overloading, 'vast, cold, furry' followed by 'wet, naked', but the passage closes with the brilliant 'house fell on his ears' to create the sense of the crashing in of the rain upon Nebu's consciousness.

In the next passage, Nebu dances the dance of creation to the thunder of the rains and the whistle of the wind: the final sentence with its repetitive co-ordinate opening clauses (from which the 'although' clause breaks to return to the repetitive unifying 'all the tribes in all the land') closes with the sonorous place names of 'Ethiopia and Uganda to beyond mighty Kilimanjaro'. However much we may be aware that Reid is working from a theory of the rhythmic African and of the collective unconscious of the race, it is impossible not to be swept along by the imaginative enactment:

> Nebu flung the squegee away from him, opened his arms wide and bellowed laughter into the darkly wet void which his land had become. And suddenly it was a ngoma, but a ngoma that not the wisest master dancer among the Somali or the Masai or the Kikuyu could conceive. For the thunder of the rains was the drums, the whistle of the wind was the pipes, and although he was the only dancer at this ngoma, he was all the tribes in all the land from the borders of Ethiopia and Uganda to beyond mighty Kilimanjaro.

The trouble with this brilliant evocation, however, is that Reid throws it away on the common-place. The beginning of stylistic collapse can be seen in the over-explicit violence of the sexual imagery of the rains raping the earth:

> He danced full of power and able to perform impossible feats of agility in time to the rhythm of the rain-drums. The wind blowing on his nudity was the sweet-skinned girl whom the elders of the tribe had chosen for him at that half-forgotten Dance of Puberty when he had proved his maleness. Outside the windows the earth was in a joyous uproar beneath the rape of the long rains. The rain found all its hollows and embraced the hillocks. It soaked the trees to the roots.

Although the closing image is what remains in our minds, it is worth noting the felicitous 'rain-*drums*' in sentence one, stretching into the 'sweet-*skinned*' used in relation to the girl in the next sentence.

In the fourth passage Nebu's exultation is reduced to a more worldly fingering of female garments:

> Nebu danced nude, narrow-hipped, the strong calves and plough-widened shoulders like dark old wine catching what light there was about. In an odd way as he glided, a tiger grace to his flanks, he seemed to claim the room: running his hand over the bedsheets, touching with his finger-tips the things of hers on the dresser, the lacy small clothes thrown on a chair—and then his dream world

lurched. Nebu hooked his head round and stared into the eyes of the woman.

The sexual suggestions of the opening sentence in this passage are caught up in the 'sculptured hard young manhood' of the next. The hollows and hillocks of the raped land reappear in the 'shoulder hollows and breasts proud as Babylon' of the White woman:

> She had ridden in through the rainstorm and her clothes were soaked and clung to her horsewoman's body so that she was all long flat legs and shoulder hollows, and breasts proud as Babylon. The water-stiffened felt hat was in her hand. Brown hair flecked with water tumbled to her shoulders. The black, posed catlike on his sprung knees, was sculptured in hard young manhood. With the tip of her tongue, the msabu touched the rainwater on her lips.

Locally, the 'water-stiffened felt hat' in the msabu's hand is a brilliant stroke, but it is used indiscriminately with the less original rain-soaked clothes and the inviting flick of the tongue over the lips to bring about this climax:

> And even now he remembered the rough thrusts of the msabu's hips when she fought for him to fill her, using the rich language of the body to talk away his fears.

It is clear that Reid wants us to see this event as a re-enactment of the dance by Nebu and the 'joyous uproar' of the earth under the rains, fertilization of the woman by mystic force of Nebu. But what we actually read through the clichés is an unoriginal description of sex on a stormy day. The passage, moreover, cannot sustain any other interpretation because we are never taken into the consciousness of the woman, and because Reid does not even attempt to develop her as a character after what we are being asked to see as almost a cosmic experience.

But if our response to this part of the novel is of imaginative power held back from opening up possibilities by its commitment in the long run to a stereotyped confrontation, Reid moves towards a more interesting parable in the relationship between Nebu and the child born of this meeting of Europe and Africa.

When Nebu finds that he has killed Bwana Gibson, the man he had wronged many years before, he determines to make restitution by taking back to the town, at great personal risk, the crippled boy who was Gibson's companion. In the ironic situation which Reid develops it is the boy who has the upper-hand. The boy knows that Nebu is his father but he is ashamed of the Kikuyu. Insecure and perverse, he insults and abuses Nebu. Nebu, on the other hand, believing that the boy does not know the truth, maintains a deeply grieved silence. As they journey through the bush, the boy's ambivalent attitudes to Nebu, and Nebu's desire both to please him and to find value in him, displace Reid's previous interest in romanticizing the race. Without a conscious authorial striving, the journey in the bush becomes a symbolic journey, reaching its climax in a cave on the outskirts of the town, where with the leopard of hate ready to pounce, Nebu's self-control and his love for the boy, concealed as duty, break down the half-bwana's revulsion at last:

> 'Nebu,' the boy said softly. The black looked curiously at him.
> 'You love me very much,' the boy said.
> The boy's eyes were opened wide, stretched boldly wide so that they were two huge, strangely lit rooms into which the black almost wandered. Nebu was glad that the great bow on his back snubbed on the threshhold and halted him. His legs were sleek and firm once more and he backed away proudly on them. The negro laughed in his belly; it was unseen on his face.
> '*I* love you, toto?'
>
> (*The Leopard*, p. 170)

What is impressive about this moment of acknowledgement is the factualness of the presentation, and the way in which, in the narrative section, Reid moves naturally from observed and realistic detail ('the boy's eyes were opened wide') to expressive metaphor 'strangely lit rooms . . . *almost* wandered') and back to realistic detail ('the great bow . . . halted him'). The legs 'sleek and firm' are the dramatic outcome of reconciliation, not the celebrating terms of racialism. Nebu's seeming question carries the unheard sound of human fulfilment. Because of the emotional dynamics in the situation, Reid's most extravagant effects in the following passage remain under strict control:

> 'Father,' the boy said softly, grinning at him.
> Through the soles of his feet, he could hear the ocean at Mom-

basa. The great waves stood straight up in the water, fifty yards out, and tossed their shaggy heads and reared in and shook the beach in their teeth.

(The Leopard, p. 171)

So inspired is Reid by the truth of the situation he has created that when, later, the father–son relationship is broken by the long history of mistrust between them (Nebu will not use the gun because it has failed him once on account of the half-bwana's trickery) we return to the ironic appropriateness of the 'almost' wandering into the strangely lit rooms, and the disruptive presence of 'the great bow on his back [which] snubbed on the threshold and halted him'. Lamming's *Season of Adventure* is a more substantial work than *The Leopard*. And Lamming operates from the point of view of the alienated character, but it is impossible to avoid the resemblance between Fola and Reid's half-bwana. *The Leopard* is in its finest aspect a parable on the relationship between alienated West Indian and embarrassing African ancestry.

(d) 'The Scholar-man' and 'Other Leopards'

There are some similarities at first sight between the two novels written by West Indians who have lived in Africa. By coincidence, both Dathorne and Williams come from Guyana, and in the fictions the central characters, Adam Questus (*The Scholar-man,* 1964) and Dennis Williams's Froad (*Other Leopards,* 1963), are Guyanese on the African continent. Both novels satirize aspects of life in Africa, and in both the central characters move towards resolutions that concern the individual rather than the race or the nation.

Of the two, Dathorne's is the more explicit and the less interesting. Questus comes to Africa in order to claim a distant kinship which will make him whole, but *The Scholar-man* suffers from Dathorne's disbelief in the dilemma of his mechanically named hero. This is reflected in the pretentiousness of Questus's dialogues with himself, and in Dathorne's easy distraction into cheerful deflations of expatriate University staff and self-important native dignitaries. But instead of satirizing his hero or making him too a comic figure, Dathorne pretentiously follows his fashionable theme of communion with Africa. This leads to some lurid over-writing locally as for instance when Quested is motoring to a dance: 'The dark-green trees kissed the tip of the road, brushed its lip of leaf against the side of the car'; and a few lines later: 'The night ran beside the car like a tiger on the edge of the forests, as dark as sleep, and naked like a black man spitting out his soul'; and two sentences on: 'The headlights undressed the folds of dark, and the car pricked at the womb of virgin night' (p. 146). Dathorne's actual knowledge of Africa does not seem to have cured such bad taste. But it is at the conclusion that the quest for origins leads to the worst kind of mystification. By some quite arbitrary strokes in characterization, Dathorne converts the tarty daughter of the Head of the English Department into a soul-mate for the hero. Adam and Helen plan to meet in England where they will have a more familiar feel for the surroundings. (The point, it seems here, is that the West Indian is more English than African.) But before this can take place, Questus drives into the night and has intercourse with an outcast mud-woman:

> Then the rain fell and he lay lost in this, his third baptism of mud and water; and he lay flat clutching her, feeling the shape of her huge breasts and the rain tickled his eyes and smoothed his face and the blessing of water poured down his mouth and his nostrils and the lightning itched and thunder eased and the wind blanketed them; and in the madness of that rainy moment, in the slush and the lighted dark, the wet and the testimony of thunder, he knew.
> (*The Scholar-man*, p. 180)

Relying on the repetition of 'and', the incantatory use of words like 'baptism', 'water', 'lightning' and 'thunder', and the conclusive placing of 'he knew', Dathorne wishes to suggest that his hero has returned to the rejected earth rhythms of the pre-expatriate Africa. But this attitude to the continent is not very different from the one displayed in Reid's extravaganza quoted earlier, and it is much less skilfully written. Since the symbolism of the woman is never suggested elsewhere in the novel (she is realistically described on page 140 where she provokes disgust), and since this incident seems to take place quite gratuitously, the reader is left mystified. Questus 'knew', and so presumably does Dathorne, but neither can tell, for this is the end of the novel.

Williams's central character, Froad, declares his problems in the first two pages of *Other Leopards*:

> I am a man, you see, plagued by these two names, and this is their history: Lionel the who I was, dealing with Lobo the who I continually felt I ought to become, this chap, this *alter ego* of ancestral times that I was sure quietly slumbered behind the culti-vated mask. Now on that afternoon I came consciously to sense the thing that has made this story: that not enviable state of being, the attitude of involuntary paralysis that made them know me in Africa—the more intelligent that is—as the Uncommitted African.
>
> (*Other Leopards*, pp. 19–20)

The first point to notice in this is that Williams gives up the easy possibility of leading his character from hope to dramatic dis-illusion. The novel opens with the sense of disorientation.

Williams's purpose in narrating the novel through Froad's con-sciousness is clearly to explore this disturbing state: 'The past was ashes; a mystical future sending wave-impulses back to a hopeless past' (p. 74). This comment on the political slogan 'Africa will be free' is also Froad's comment on himself. It becomes a direct judgement when egged on by Hughie his methodical English superior, he tries to appropriate the past in the gold figurine of Queen Amanishakatee, and fails:

> . . . I wished for words to assault those stone ears with some claim of my very own, mine, me! But time passed, wind blew, sand settled, gloom deepened, and I could think of nothing; nothing at all . . . I knew now, with the relief of a criminal accepting the process of law, that I had to condemn myself. That was that! What could Hughie's measurements and contrivings mean to me now; or ever! There was no man, no brother, no Mother of Time, no people, nobody. There were only vessels; whole or broken, full or empty. At the heart of the mirage there was no water.
>
> (*Other Leopards*, p. 155)

Froad's tension arises from his longing to escape this inner sense of hollowness and his honesty in resisting what he despises in some moods as sham consolations in politics, religion, love, or tradition. Thus he vacillates between supporting Muslim Negroes and help-ing Christian Negroes; between admiring the certainty of Chief, his compatriot from Guyana, and despising the older man's missionary attitude; he is impotent before Catherine, the Welsh girl who offers to mother him, and Eve the sensuous Guyanese whose appeal is the appeal of 'dark silent creek-water' and sullen impenetrability. Above all, it is in Froad's violent swinging from hate to love for Hughie, the master of events, that Williams seeks to reveal the shattered being of his fraudulent men. Although Froad is at some points the agent of Williams's satire, the total impression of the character that is conveyed is of cynicism and longing:

> Catherine and her granite hillsides and ruins and legends and history flitted through my mind. Now what the hell does it really feel like? Hughie and his traditions and his burden and his conscientious fanaticism. The Chief and his certainty and his duty and truth and all that. Every man a place! I'm like the bloody scavengers; no shadow.
>
> (*Other Leopards*, p. 96)

The power of Williams's novel is the power to suggest in concrete terms the menace and the comfort of discovering origins. Its honesty leads to a conclusion that is in stark contrast to the bogus exoticism of Dathorne's consummation for Questus. By the end of *Other Leopards* the need either for roots or for spiritual transcendence has been concretely established, but the central character has achieved neither:

> Now, having removed my body and the last traces of it, I am without context clear. Going up this new tree, picking the thorns bare, one by one, I am in a darkness nowhere at all. I am nothing, nowhere. This is something gained . . . Hughie has not found me; I have outwitted him. I have achieved a valuable state: a condition outside his method. . . . Only remains now to remove my consciousness. This I can do whenever I wish. I am free of the earth. I do not need to go down there for anything.
>
> (*Other Leopards*, pp. 221-2)

The agitated, repetitive sentences act out the obsessive nature of Froad's desire for escape and annihilation, but the negative satisfaction of outwitting Hughie makes it impossible for us to imagine that the climax represents a spiritual or philosophical triumph. Froad's madness, indeed, is evident in the impossibility of what he

The Negro

claims to have done to his body and to be able to do with his consciousness. It is a measure of Williams's triumph that although the novel is set in Africa and works through African material, it is the universal dimension of Froad's case—the abortive quest for origins—that emerges from this fiction.

VIII

Aborigines

'It's all so blasted silly and complicated. After all I've earned a right here as well. I'm as native as they, ain't I? A little better educated, maybe, whatever in hell that means.'

(Palace of the Peacock, p. 58)

At the beginning of *The History of the Caribby Islands* (1666), translated from the French by John Davies, the author writes: 'In the first place we shall speak of the inhabitants thereof who are strangers . . . which having dispatched we shall descend to a more large and particular consideration of the Indians [the Amerindians] the natural and originary inhabitants of the country.'[1] With the European discoveries 'the natural and originary inhabitants' of the West Indies were virtually eliminated; the small communities which survive in Dominica and Guyana today are regarded as marginal to the society. This would seem to account for the fact that the aboriginal Indian seldom appears, and is not a centre of social or political interest either in verse, in drama, or in fiction by writers from the West Indies. Indeed, the fiction in which the contemporary Indians do appear[2] either registers them as detribalized individuals in the towns ('Bucks') or portrays them as exotic groups in the interior; two 'historical' novels[3] in which they are prominent seek to picture a primitive already degenerate people living in a remote time, there being no evidence in these

[1] As there is no danger of confusion with Indians from India in this section, the word 'Indian' will be used here in free variation with 'Amerindian' to include the different tribes in Guyana, and the Caribs and Arawaks who dominated the islands.

[2] See especially Christopher Nicole, *Shadows in the Jungle* (1961).

[3] H. G. deLisser, *The Arawak Girl* (1958), and Edgar Mittelholzer, *Children of Kaywana* (1952).

works of felt continuities between the present generation of West Indians and their ancestors on the land.

In *Palace of the Peacock* (1960) and *Heartland* (1964), on the other hand, Wilson Harris discovers relevance in the Indians, involving them in three of the basic themes in his fiction: the unity of all men, the theme of re-birth, and the search for ancestral roots. At the same time, the author from Guyana makes the 'historical' Indian 'come alive' in a way that no other West Indian novelist or historian has been bold enough to imagine.

The historical action lying behind *Palace of the Peacock*—the European pursuit of gold and the Indians in the sixteenth century—is never far from our consciousness as we read the novel. Harris evokes the emotions roused by the coming of the invaders to the aboriginal village with great vividness, suggesting both Indian excitement and European misgiving:

> Our arrival at the Mission was a day of curious consternation and belief for the colony. The news flew like lightning across the river and into the bush. It seemed to fall from the sky through the cloudy trees that arched high in the air and barely touched, leaving the narrowest ribbon of space. The stream that reflected the news was inexpressibly smooth and true, and the leaves that sprinkled the news from the heavens of the forest stood on a shell of expectant water as if they floated half on the air, half on a stone.
>
> We drove at a walking pace through the brooding reflecting carpet unable to make up our minds where we actually stood. We had hardly turned into the bank when a fleet of canoes devoured us. Faces pressed upon us from land and water. The news was confirmed like wild-fire. We were the news.
>
> (*Palace of the Peacock*, p. 37)

Harris's presentation of the meeting between invader and invaded does not allow us to make a stock response either to the historical conflict or to the peoples involved. A passage from *The Arawak Girl* may help to show the significance of this. As the invaders' caravels approach, the Arawaks come to meet them with spears and shouts. Columbus wishes to be moderate:

> 'We must pacify, not antagonise, these savages; by pacific methods we shall bring them to do whatever we wish.'
>
> 'But if they attack us Admiral?' demanded one fellow, glancing

from the deck of the Nina down to where the Indians in the canoes were brandishing their spears.

'That is another matter; then indeed we shall have to teach them a lesson they will not speedily forget. But remember, we are Christians, and we are here, among other things, to spread the doctrine of Holy Church. We must forgive our enemies.' At the moment it did not occur to Don Christopher that he and his were really the enemy and that the people of the island could have no need of forgiveness from them. But then the Admiral already looked upon the Indians as his King's subjects and therefore necessarily obedient to the governance of himself as His Majesty's Viceroy in these parts.

(*The Arawak Girl*, p. 16)

The authorial intrusions and the heavy-handed irony in the dialogue are part of an attempt to turn the reader against the invading Spaniards. Historical novels which re-create conflict situations from the past run the risk of persuading us to take sides, thus perpetuating those conflicts. But although historical novels raise this problem in an acute form, it exists for most writers of fiction.

For while particular novelists may manage to make us identify with some of their personages without blocking our sympathy for the others, it is one of the limiting qualities of conventional novels dealing with characters in a social context (involving manners, morals, politics etc.) that they can force us to take sides so exclusively, it sometimes becomes tempting to describe this kind of fiction as 'divisive'. In *The Arawak Girl*, cited less as an easy target than as a convenient illustration, de Lisser portrays the girl Anacanoa both as a fierce nationalist heroine against the Spaniards—persuading us to share her hostile attitudes to 'these brutal pale-faced men . . . of another breed altogether'; and as a beautiful and exceptional Indian set apart from a decadent race—so that we approve of her and despise her people in the mass.

Wilson Harris's novels deliberately steer away from such divisive possibilities. The Amerindian woman captured by the invading crew in *Palace of the Peacock* is not cast as a heroine. She is un-named and aged; forced to accompany the crew in pursuit of the flying folk she shows no antagonism to the foreigners:

Aborigines

We had in our midst a new member sitting crumpled-looking like a curious ball, old and wrinkled. Her long black hair—with the faintest glimmer of silvery grey—hung in two plaits down to her waist. She sat still as a bowing statue, the stillness and surrender of the American Indian of Guyana in reflective pose. Her small eyes winked and blinked a little. It was an emotionless face. The stiff brooding materiality and expression of youth had vanished, and now—in old age—there remained no sign of former feeling. There was almost an air of crumpled pointlessness in her expression, the air of wisdom that a millenium was past, a long timeless journey was finished without appearing to have begun, and no show of malice, enmity and overt desire to overcome oppression and evil mattered any longer.

(Palace of the Peacock, p. 71)

But the reader's fear that Harris might be about to foist an equally hackneyed contrast—between European materialism and greed on the one hand, and native spirituality on the other[1]—is quickly dispelled.

As the vessel enters a particularly dangerous section of the river casually named in the novel 'the straits of memory', the use of the initially visual 'tiny embroideries' as a metaphor for the disturbed surface of the river is the means by which Harris leads the reader through further sense impressions to blur the distinction between the passive wrinkled woman and the possessive river, and to perceive a more dynamic relationship between them:

Tiny embroideries resembling the handiwork on the Arawak woman's kerchief and the wrinkles on her brow, turned to incredible and fast soundless breakers and foam. Her crumpled bosom and river grew agitated with desire bottling and shaking every fear and inhibition and outcry. The ruffles in the water were her dress rolling and rising to embrace the crew.

Harris depends upon the reader's capacity to feel the connection, visually and in terms of energy, between the woman's long flowing hair and the lively stream for a reinforcement of this identification:

This sudden insolence of soul rose and caught them from the

[1] Pancho, the half-Amerindian in Jan Carew's *Black Midas* (1958), tells the hero of the novel: 'Me mama was an Indian woman and gold-fire never light in she eye nor in she people eye. If it wasn't for you skipper, me would have lef' the gold just where it born in the earth belly.'

powder of her eyes, and the age of her smile and the dust in her hair all flowing back upon them with silent streaming majesty and abnormal youth and in a wave of freedom and strength.

(Palace of the Peacock, p. 73)

At this point the reader is aware that the Amerindian woman wishes to possess the crew just as much as the crew wish to possess the tribe they are risking death to pursue. But another process begins in the sentence. The boat is in 'the straits of memory' and it is about to crash, so it is not difficult for us to accept that at this psychological moment the woman should return to 'an earlier dream of distant centuries . . . the Siberian unconscious pilgrimage' (p. 72), from which it follows that she should become young and majestic again. This process seems to insinuate that in spite of the apparent differences in time and person and place, the present crew's quest is in the same spirit as that of the pre-Columban Amerindians.

Meanwhile, the literal fact that both the crew and the old woman are in the grip of the death-dealing river precipitates the crew's and the reader's recognition of an ultimate unity existing at the heart of the most bitter historical oppositions:

The crew were transformed by the awesome spectacle of a voiceless soundless motion, the purest appearance of vision in the chaos of emotional sense. Earthquake and volcanic water appeared to seize them and stop their ears dashing the scales only from their eyes. They saw the naked unequivocal flowing peril and beauty and soul of the pursuer and the pursued all together. . . .

(Palace of the Peacock, p. 73)

Harris's imaginative use of the nameless Amerindian woman in one of his major themes—the unity of man—is remarkable enough considering contemporary West Indian attitudes to the Amerindians. Yet it is worth noting as well that far from purchasing his effects by ignoring historical accounts of the aboriginal Indians, Harris faithfully uses these as stepping stones. Because of this, it is quite easy to extract an accurate historical picture of the relationship between Amerindians and Europeans from *Palace of the Peacock*, but the author makes us aware that to do so is to promote only one of the many possibilities latent in any historical situation. His handling of Petra the pregnant woman in *Heartland* is equally uninhibited, and equally faithful to the familiar facts.

Like Mittelholzer's Kaywana, Petra is only part Indian. The other side of her ancestry is given uncertainly as 'Portuguese or Spanish'. Her tribe, however, accept her fully, 'repressing the fact of her mixed racial stock'. But when it is discovered that she is with child 'no one knew for certain for whom', she is cast out and begins a long flight which brings her to steal daSilva's rations, and with an imaginary pursuer on her trail to seek rest at Kaiser's shack. Here her labour begins. Stevenson, the novel's central consciousness, discovers her at this stage and helps in the birth. But as soon as he leaves the house to search for food for her, Petra collects her movable belongings and her child and resumes flight.

To extract Petra's story in this way is to show how much Harris the novelist is willing to forego (there is no story of Petra as such in the novel), and the extent to which his fiction is grounded upon what is easily credible and literal. But when Stevenson comes upon Petra he is suffering from the shock of a mistress's betrayal and flight, a father's death, and a consciousness growing in the jungle of undeveloped capacities and possibilities in his own life—as if he is himself pregnant with an uncertain, unborn self. On the simplest level, therefore, the confrontation with Petra, and Stevenson's participation in the ritual of birth images forth the introspective process in which Stevenson has been involved: it is after the meeting with the Amerindian woman that Stevenson's new self is released. It is not difficult for the reader to grasp further that the image is not static, for we are made to feel that while Stevenson is literally assisting Petra in her labour, she is, in a less describable but none the less intimate way, being instrumental in his birth.

Yet, while the work seems to give ancestral status to the Amerindians we must be careful to notice that Harris is not advancing the sentimental proposition that the Amerindians are our true ancestors and once we make contact with them we will discover ourselves. For it follows from the author's conviction of the unity of all men that the ancestors may be discovered in any race, and that to restrict them to any one race, as is fashionable in some West Indian writing, is to reduce man's complex heritage. The most straightforward expression of this view takes place in *The Far Journey of Oudin* where Hassan's hankering for India is ridiculed by his brother Kaiser, the latter seeing himself as being able to pass more easily for a Negro:

> Hassan had just got the obstinate idea in his burning head that he wanted to return to India to circulate his ashes on mother-soil.
>
> Kaiser protested. If he returned he would be looked upon as an outcast and an untouchable ghost. What language had he save the darkest and frailest outline of an ancient style and tongue? Not a blasted thing more. Remember too how much he had forgotten, Kaiser scolded him. The ceremonies and sacraments he fitfully observed were not a patch on the real thing. It was a dim hope, dimmer than their father's childhood and innocence.
>
> 'No', Kaiser said, 'I shall become a richer man than you. I am giving up rice and sugar for gold and diamonds. I can pass as a negro pork-knocker and I shall take a passage to the goldfields of Cuyuni and Mazaruni. I shall steal into Venezuela, and swim across oil.'
>
> (*The Far Journey of Oudin*, pp. 72–3)

In *The Secret Ladder* (1963), on the other hand, so scrupulous is Harris's approach to truth, he allows the surveyor Russell Fenwick to distrust the way in which his mixed ancestry seems to be a mechanical and therefore parodic form of a desirable integration of races:

> He had never known his father who had been in his middle fifties (his mother being at the time in her late thirties) when he was born. Soon after, his father died suddenly. His mother possessed a very good snapshot: it had acquired a sub-aqueous background look over the years but still revealed a dark big man of vivid African descent. His mother—on the other hand—was a delicate almost aerial figure of a woman, half French, half English. Her skin was like a fair East Indian's shadowed by night-black wings of hair. It was rumoured that along with her European stock she possessed a fraction of Amerindian blood, as well, and that her grandmother was as Arawak as her husband's grandfather had been uncompromisingly African.
>
> Fenwick smiled. He had grown to discern a curious narcissistic humour and evasive reality in the family myth. He was not ashamed of the unique vagaries and fictions of the ancestral past. Far from it, he was proud. Nevertheless it made him profoundly uneasy at

times. There was something guilty and concrete he had to learn to face, after all. Possibly it was all coming to a head and he would have no way of escaping in the end. Still he longed for an easy way out.

(*The Secret Ladder*, pp. 36–7)

But it is in the relationship between Fenwick and the aged African Poseidon that Harris's critical approach to the question of ancestral roots emerges most tough-mindedly. The surveyor and his men find their preliminary work on an irrigation project obstructed by the runaway slave villagers who resent these agents of technology and government as the latest threat to the freedom they have fled into the bush to preserve. It is within this frame that Harris explores the dilemma of Fenwick, the middle-class West Indian with the refined upbringing. The first meeting with Poseidon, the leader of the free villagers, is described as a confrontation with something from a deliberately forgotten primeval world:

At first Fenwick saw nothing. But as he peered closely into the barely perceptible door of vegetation he discerned Poseidon's small upturned boat or corial buried in the grass. It could have been the black startling back of a boa-constrictor, many of which often lay like this in the swamps and then vanished. There was the faint hoarse sound of an approaching body swimming in the undergrowth. Fenwick adjusted his eyes. He could no longer evade a reality that had always escaped him. The strangest figure he had ever seen had appeared in the opening of the bush, dressed in a flannel vest, flapping ragged fins of trousers on his legs. Fenwick could not help fastening his eyes greedily upon him as if he saw down a bottomless gauge and river of reflection. He wanted to laugh at the weird sensation but was unable to do so. The old man's hair was white as wool and his cheeks—covered with wild curling rings—looked like an unkempt sheep's back. The black wooden snake of skin peeping through its animal blanket was wrinkled and stitched together incredibly.

(*The Secret Ladder*, p. 23)

Writing melodramatically to his mother, Fenwick tries to grapple with this ancestral skeleton:

'What will you say when I tell you I have come across the Grand Old Man of our history, my father's history in particular? . . . He has a Greek name—Poseidon. . . . I wish I could truly grasp the

importance of this meeting. If I do not—if my generation do not—
Leviathan will swallow us all. It isn't a question of fear it's a
question of going in unashamed to come out of the womb again.'

(*The Secret Ladder*, p. 38)

Fenwick must accept and come to terms with a debased African
heritage, but Harris shows the character as equally aware of the
necessity to avoid setting up this heritage as a fetish. In the critical
handling of Bryant who worships Poseidon unreservedly, Harris
issues a politic warning against being carried too far by emotion
('To *misconceive*[1] the African, I believe, if I may use such an expression as *misconceive*, at this stage, is to misunderstand and exploit
him mercilessly and oneself as well'). Simultaneously, the tension
that exists between Bryant and Fenwick is an externalization of the
very real conflict in Fenwick's mind. The surveyor's impulse to
worship the old man is balanced by his realization that although
Poseidon and his fellows have avoided enslavement in their maroon
settlement, nothing new has come of their escape; their static
freedom 'has turned cruel, abortive, evasive, woolly and wild
everywhere almost' (p. 39). The maroon villagers are in fact en-
slaved again, frozen in their posture of freedom.[2] Poseidon himself,
as the humane Fenwick frustratedly declares, remains incapable of
responsiveness to anything external to himself: ' "I can see in your
eyes you don't care about anything I have said. Why don't you?" '
(p. 52).

As *The Secret Ladder* develops, Fenwick and the reader come to
see that Poseidon is important ultimately as a symbol of man's
frail endurance and as testament to the need for a better humanity
partly dependent upon 'the digging up and exposure of the buried
community he represented':

> 'I confess I am appalled at his condition', Fenwick spoke inwardly
> to himself. The sound of his voice had been buried in the spirit of
> his avowal, so abstract and farfetched it seemed, it vanquished the
> pride of speech. 'Yes, I confess I owe allegiance to him because of
> his condition, allegiance of an important kind, that of conscience,
> of the rebirth of humanity. And this is the highest form of alle-

[1] Author's italics.
[2] It is instructive to compare Harris's treatment of the maroons with Namba Roy's
idealizing reconstruction in *Black Albino* (1961).

giance of all. It is the kind a man gives to a god. But surely this does not mean I must reduce myself to his trapped condition, become even less human than he, a mere symbol and nothing more, in order to worship him! I would be mad.' He smiled woodenly at last—like someone who had been humoring a hidden intractable child—and began to speak openly again:

'Plain wholesome understanding of history and facts and possibilities is important, Bryant. Take the unadorned facts of science, the plain economic structure of society shorn of worshipful emotion, shorn of this fiction of freedom you claim Poseidon alone possesses. I am glad we can see him as he is so that we can know what this life is, the hard business of this life, here and now (do you follow me?) and indeed we can see—beyond a shadow of doubt— the necessity for human freedom.' Fenwick stopped abruptly, trying to dam the flood of expression. He was filled with mounting uncertainty and an excess of misgiving.

(*The Secret Ladder*, p. 51)

Harris's refusal to see the discovery of the African heritage as the solution to West Indian problems arises in part from his conviction of the unity of all men, and in part out of his habitually critical attitude to over-simplifications of experience. Because he is that phenomenon in contemporary writing, the author with an individual vision not needing to be propped up by the more obvious social and political themes, he is able to use as symbols not only the topical African presence but the socially 'irrelevant' Indians. Returning to Petra in *Heartland*, it should now be possible to see how her ambiguous parentage stands for ignorance of real origins and for the difficulty of coming to terms with national or racial heritage. Similarly, her uncertainty about the fathering of her child means that she does not know what she will give birth to, or by what midwife's agency. In this sense, Petra's history is that of man over the centuries and of the modern West Indian in particular searching for the true self:

At the time when her expulsion from the body of the tribe occurred, it left her dazed and beaten, immersed in the heart of a painful brooding insensibility, like one beginning to learn to live on technical scraps of stunned memory in a way she had only glimmeringly perceived before in a series of losses, raids and deprivations.

(*Heartland*, p. 68)

IX

The Commonwealth Approach

wo recent publications stand for the last general approach
from which I would like to develop an argument. In 1961
there was published in America a volume of essays by
separate hands—*The Commonwealth Pen: An Introduction to the
Literature of the British Commonwealth*;[1] this was followed in Britain
four years later by *Commonwealth Literature: Unity and Diversity in
a Common Culture*[2]—papers from a Conference sponsored jointly by
the publishers William Heinemann Ltd. and the University of
Leeds. Neither of these books is as committed to the theory of a
Commonwealth culture as their subtitles may seem to imply. The
first is a useful country by country account; the Leeds-Heinemann
venture is made up of a number of individual essays grouped
around selected topics.

But there are some assumptions in the Commonwealth label
which need to be examined, as we can see in the following words
from an introductory speech at the Leeds Conference:

> Local critics know the local literature and the local situation; their
> comments on both would be richer if they could see them both in
> comparison with other similar situations in other countries and
> see, too, the treatment given to them by writers in those different
> countries.[3]

Professor Jeffares's 'other countries' is restricted to Commonwealth countries. But if comparisons are to be made, there is no
literary reason why they should be confined to books from within

[1] Cornell University Press, New York. Edited by A. L. McLeod.
[2] Published in 1965. Edited by John Press.
[3] A. N. Jeffares in *Commonwealth Literature*, p. xiv.

the colonies and ex-colonies. If we are interested in how imaginative literature works, a comparison between Defoe's *Moll Flanders* (1722) and Cyprian Ekwensi's *Jagua Nana* (1961) is just as likely to be illuminating as one between the Nigerian's novel and *God the Stonebreaker* (1962) by the West Indian, Alvin Bennett. And V. S. Naipaul's *A House for Mr. Biswas* (1961) might well be illuminated by a comparison with *King Lear*. Analagous human situations and analagous states of society occur at widely different times, and between people who do not necessarily fall under the same social or political order.

A comparative approach based on the notion of Commonwealth would imply a restriction on the universalizing power of literature, and would inhibit the comparing critic. If we were to give this up and take the Commonwealth viewpoint as an attempt, rather, to suggest the shaping influence on literature of common background realities in these areas, we would still be obliged to find it unsatisfactory. For the synthetic principle ignores too many social, cultural and political differences between the countries it seeks to hold together:

> The speakers from the older Dominions have told us much that we might not have known, and have allowed us to make some comparative deductions, but the observations they had to offer could hardly have the novelty of those made by the delegates from the younger Dominions. . . . The older Dominions—Canada, Australia, New Zealand are clearly tied to the British tradition and share the same problems together.[1]

The euphemisms 'older Dominions' and 'younger Dominions' point to the first major division to be made—into Black Commonwealth and White Commonwealth. To elaborate in a crude way, colonials in the White Commonwealth were never a subject people in the sense of being held in check by an alien oppressor on the land itself. However outcast some of the transportees may have been, and however alienated the voluntary exiles, these colonists were not psychologically or physically cut off from their original country, nor were they violently deprived of a cultural tradition. But in the Black Commonwealth, colonization has meant the im-

---

[1] Douglas Grant in *Commonwealth Literature*, p. 207.

position by one people of its institutions and values upon another, as well as the denigration of the subject people as race, nation and as individuals. The process of decolonization is therefore more dramatic in the Black Commonwealth:

> Decolonisation is quite simply the replacing of a certain species of men by another species of men . . . a whole social structure being changed from the bottom up. The extraordinary importance of this change is that it is willed, called for, demanded. The need for this change exists in its crude state, impetuous and compelling in the consciousness and in the lives of the men and women who are colonised. . . .
>
> Decolonisation never takes place un-noticed, for it influences individuals and modifies them fundamentally. It transforms spectators crushed with their inessentiality into privileged actors with the grandiose glare of history's floodlights upon them. . . . Decolonisation is the veritable creation of new men . . . the thing which has been colonised becomes man during the same process by which it frees itself.[1]

Fanon's vivid writing does not describe what actually happens in the areas where European master and colonized Black confront each other. But it seems to suggest a sense of dissolution and regeneration in these areas which cannot be said to be as striking or as widespread in the settled atmosphere of the 'older Dominions'.

Once a broad distinction is made, however, we have to give up the notion of a Black Commonwealth too. There is little sense of tradition or social convention in the West Indies, for example, no equivalent to the tribal world and traditional life which the Nigerian Chinua Achebe draws upon in *Things Fall Apart* (1958). As we shall see later, commentators on West Indian literature are only too aware of this particular distinction.

But it is at this point that it is necessary to bring forward the main objections to the idea of the Commonwealth as a way of approaching literature. In the first place, it forces us to concentrate on political and social issues to a degree that invests these with a disproportionate influence upon our attempts to offer critical opinions on what are, above all, works of imaginative literature. In the second, it consolidates a tendency to over-simplify the

---

[1] Frantz Fanon, *The Wretched of the Earth* (1965), pp. 29 and 30.

relationship between literature ('local literature') and the society ('the local situation') from which it takes its stimulus. These misdirections are particularly harmful in the West Indies where the death-marks of slavery are still to be seen in the economic condition of the masses, and in race and colour tensions only on a more subtle scale than in pre-Emancipation society. So many West Indian writers make these the inspiration and the substance of their fictions that in the first critical book on Caribbean writing in general we read:

> Even the most cursory glance at the literature (and the painting, sculpture, music and dancing) of the Caribbean, in Spanish, French or English, reveals a constant concern for what I have called race and colour. *The Negro in Caribbean Literature* might, at first sight, have seemed a more appropriate title for this study. . . . However . . . [such a title] suggests a simplification. . . . *Race and Colour* on the other hand embraces a diversity of social, cultural, and historical relations between the man of colour (Negro or mulatto), who thinks of himself and writes consciously as a coloured man, and the white world.[1]

In an earlier part of the book a racial aspect of this boring socio-literary phenomenon was examined in detail and in a head-on way. Here, avoiding the more obvious race, colour and social protest themes, it is proposed to work by indirection. The next four chapters are essays in illustration of the wide range of relationships that may exist between a society and the literature which draws upon it.

[1] G. R. Coulthard, *Race and Colour in Caribbean Literature* (1962), p. 5.

X

The Achievement of Roger Mais

S hortly after the publication of his first novel *The Hills Were Joyful Together* (1953), Roger Mais declared that his intention had been 'to give the world a true picture of the real Jamaica and the dreadful condition of the working classes'.[1] We find in the work, accordingly, a stark and realistic picture of impoverished people trapped in a squalid slum that is identifiably Jamaican. The work has been received in the spirit in which it was passionately submitted, and Mais's second novel, *Brother Man*, consolidated the author's reputation as a novelist of social protest. The reputation has persisted in spite of his third novel, *Black Lightning* (1955), in which there are no signs of organized society and not the slightest expression of a protesting attitude. The work has been virtually disregarded in the West Indies, but I would like to contend that it is in *Black Lightning* that Mais's art and understanding are in greatest harmony, and that it is upon this his last published novel that his reputation must rest.

I do not wish to imply that *Black Lightning* must be kept separate from the other novels, nor would it be proper to take the view that it is unrelated to the Jamaican social situation. But there is a progressive movement from novel to novel of a kind that can only be described as exploratory, and I would like to trace this movement as a way of showing how *Black Lightning* develops out of, and imaginatively transcends the local situation.

The first novel, *The Hills Were Joyful Together*, is set in a yard which is a microcosm of Jamaican slum life. The characters are differentiated from one another, but the author is more interested

[1] *John O'London's Weekly* (1st May 1953).

in projecting the life of the yard as a whole than in creating individual characters. Supplementing what we make of the expressed life of the yard are authorial intrusions of two kinds, advancing two main 'philosophies'. The first has to do with Mais's social protest intention, and may be described as materialistic determinism. It is usually put in the mouth of the prison chaplain: '. . . What happens to people when their lives are constricted and dwarfed and girdled with poverty . . . things like that and that and that come out of it . . . moral deformity, degradation, disease . . .' (p. 197). The second philosophy declared in the novel occurs in authorial choruses at the beginnings of chapters. It is a philosophy of Chance, or the indifference of the Universe: 'The trifling sprigs of chance confound our footsteps . . . the events that make tomorrow quit themselves today outside our ken . . .' (p. 242), and 'The dark shadows beyond our ken crowd in upon us and stand and wait unseen . . . they wait in silence and drink us up in darkness . . .' (p. 150). As Mais declares them, however, these philosophies clash, and his art is at its least convincing when he tries to show them working together. The episode dealing with the death of Surjue at the end of the novel is illustrative. Surjue is just about to make good his escape from prison. It is a dark and cloudy night, but just as the escaping character reaches the top of the prison wall, the wind parts the clouds and the moon shines through. Mais also contrives that at this precise moment, Surjue's enemy, warder Nickoll, writhing with toothache, should lift his head, see Surjue, and bring him down with the one gunshot that would have been possible in the circumstances. As Surjue falls to the ground on the free side of the wall, the perverse clouds return to cover the moon, and a seemingly disconsolate dog bays in the distance. Mais's over-deliberate manipulation at this emphatic point in the novel is neither in keeping with the life-qualities he expresses in his characters, nor does it do justice to his intuitions about life suspended in expressive scene and image.

In contrast to Mais's self-conscious demonstrations, there are images of distress and vulnerability which *express* more than the author can state. These appear notably in his presentation of the women, Rema and Euphemia. Then there are scenes in which the sheer perplexity of being human and not in control of the inner heartland is in evidence. Such a scene occurs after the adolescent Manny has been rejected by the older woman, Euphemia. His friend Wilfie is helping him to fix the frame of a chicken coop:

> Wilfie held the wire in place, and Manny drove home the straightened nail, using more force than was necessary. He clinched the nail head over the wire to make it hold. His hands seemed extra big and awkward, and they were trembling a little.
>
> He took his upper lip between his teeth and bit it until he could taste the salty taste of blood in his mouth. He beat on the ground with the hammer, and Wilfie just looked at him, still without saying a word. He opened his mouth as though he was going to speak, and shut it again.
>
> (*The Hills Were Joyful Together*, pp. 162–3)

Mais's recurrent expressive quality works to great effect in *Black Lightning*, not least in the section dealing with Estella's crucial elopement. On the story level, Estella leaves Jake because she prefers Steve. We have to wait till the end of the novel to realize that she still loves the hero, and had left him only because his unconscious resentment of his dependence upon her had begun to show. The scene in which Estella tries to choose between Steve and Jake, however, prepares us for complications by showing Estella as a creature pained and baffled not simply about what choice ought to be made, but bewildered by the strange contrarieties that exist within:

> She stretched out her arms above her head, and her fingers clutched at the tufts of scrubby grass that grew there, and tore at them.
>
> And then she lay still.
>
> The sound of the pea-doves calling to each other under the sweetwood trees, the song of the axe, the wind soughing through the branches were the only sounds in the wood.
>
> A shudder passed through her. She turned over on her side again, sat up, pressed her fist into it, bending over as though taken with pain.
>
> The first brown smudgings of dust shook out over the silent wood. She stood up, looked about her as though she had lost her way, turned and went to the edge of the wood where it met the common beyond, this side of the house.
>
> (*Black Lightning*, pp. 32–3)

These are the dilemmas Mais is really interested in as an artist, and as he develops, he finds they are attributable neither to society nor to an external and malignant Chance.

In *Brother Man*, the setting is again the Kingston slums, and the theme is still an obviously social one, but there are significant shifts of emphasis. The authorial intrusions are not only reduced in frequency, they are disciplined into the form of a Chorus placed at the beginning of each act in a five-act novel. While the details in each act are identifiably local, the Chorus neither insists upon the specialness of the Jamaican yard-dwellers' situation nor offers indignant 'philosophical' generalizations. Rueful and detached, it abstracts the essential repetitive humanity of what goes on among the urban proletariat: 'The tongues in the lane clack-clack almost continuously, going up and down the full scale of human emotions, human folly, ignorance, suffering, viciousness, magnanimity, weakness, greatness, littleness, insufficiency, frailty, strength' (p. 7). Mais is clearly standing back from his 'case', but his commitment is no less than in the previous novel.

To some extent, the pessimism and pathos of *The Hills Were Joyful Together* were modified by a number of un-emphasized positives in the novel: charity, embodied in Mass Mose the clarinet-player, the kindly Zephyr, and Ras, the serene and compassionate cultist; the healing power of *eros*, seen in the relationship between Surjue and Rema, and recalled with idyllic force by Surjue at the time of greatest despair (p. 245); and an elemental and rhythmic energy which binds the yard-dwellers in community, as on the night of the fish-fry (pp. 48–52) when they enact in song and dance the miracle of catastrophe overcome—the crossing of a swollen river. In *Brother Man*, Mais gives prominence to one of the positives latent in *The Hills Were Joyful Together*: the novel hopefully explores the protective possibility of Messianic leadership. It differs further from its predecessor in being built around a central character. But in the presentation of Bra' Man, Mais fails.

The extended parallel between the life and crucifixion of Christ and that of Bra' Man shows Mais's determination to universalize his work, but it leads to the introduction of arbitrary visions and apparitions, miracles, naïve moralizing as in the incident of the crab and the little boy, and an unfortunate pseudo-Biblical prose. Some of these elements are present in the description of Bra' Man among the multitude:

> And through him blessing came to the people in the lane, even to those who did not go out to receive it. People came up to him in the crowd, and touched their handkerchiefs against his clothes, and came away again, and laid the handkerchiefs on their sick, and they became well. *And Bra' Man didn't even know it was done.*
>
> He went among them blessing them and healing them, and a crowd followed him one day *from the market at the foot of King Street, the principal street in the city,* because one woman had recognised him, and she called the attention of the others, pointing him out.
>
> (*Brother Man*, p. 109)

I have italicized places where Mais tries to make Bra' Man viable as a separate character, not a copy of Jesus, but the parallels are too strong for the differences to make any impact on the reader. The passage, incidentally, illustrates the obverse side of Mais's intensity: no other West Indian writer would have created a scene like this without a comic intention.

A consideration of the relationship between Bra' Man and the girl Minette throws further light on Mais's failure with the central character. Bra' Man rescues Minette from the desperate beginnings of prostitution and brings her to live in his house. Certain episodes suggest that Minette has been introduced as a sleeping temptation to the prophet:

> Minette woke up in the middle of the night to find Brother Man, holding a lighted candle in his hand, staring down into her face.
>
> She started up, frightened, her blood suddenly racing.
>
> What's the matter Bra' Man?' she said.
>
> 'Nothing, daughter,' he murmured, unmoving. 'Hush, go back to sleep.'
>
> He still held the candle aloft, looking down into her face intently, as though searching for something there.
>
> She felt oddly shaken, disturbed, she knew not how or why.
>
> (*Brother Man*, p. 99)

When Minette's nightdress falls open to reveal her breasts, Bra' Man 'rested the candle on the table, drew up a stool beside her cot, and sat down. She saw that he had the Bible in his hand. He opened it and read aloud . . .' (p. 99). Although clearly worried about the sexlessness of his hero, Mais feels it necessary to keep him Christ-like and chaste. Later, when the artist's instinct for fidelity to the situation he has created leads to Bra' Man's succumbing to Minette, Mais's design for a Christ also manages to make itself felt. Minette kneels beside Bra' Man's seat and takes his hands to the once rejected temptations:

> He looked down at her, started to shake his head . . . their eyes met, held an instant. Something like an involuntary spasm shuddered through his flesh.
> His hands jerked away suddenly. He got to his feet so quickly that the stool went over behind him. He stumbled rather than walked away, leaving her kneeling on the floor.
> He turned, looked at her, saw that she was sobbing, her hands pressed to her face; her shoulders were shaking with her sobs.
> Something like an animal cry went from him. He blundered back across the distance that separated them, went down on his knees beside her on the floor.
>
> (*Brother Man*, pp. 136–7)

Mais will not allow intercourse by passion, but intercourse through compassion is allowable for the Christ-character. Mais's failure with Bra' Man as a fictional character lies in this: the conflict which ought to have been located in the character registers only as an uncertainty of intention in the author.

With the inevitable 'crucifixion' of Bra' Man ('When they had mauled him to the satisfaction of their lust, they voided on him and fouled him', p. 188), Mais's exploration of the redeeming power of a secular Messiah comes to a disappointed end. Yet Mais does not allow disillusionment to be registered in this novel. The shock of Bra' Man's failure is plastered over by an ambiguous 'vision of certitude':

> 'They'll all come crawlin' to you yet, an' beg you to forgive them.'
> He just bowed his head before her. His heart was too full to speak.
> He saw all things that lay before him in a vision of certitude, and he was alone no longer.

'Look at me', he said.

Her gaze met his, unfaltering.

'You see it, out there, too?'

She looked up above the rooftops where that great light glowed across the sky.

She said: 'Yes, John, I have seen it.'

'Good' he said, and again, 'Good'.

(Brother Man, p. 191)

The only certitude here, however, is that Bra' Man and Minette love each other. Unless we are meant to imagine that Bra' Man is indulging in a superior irony over Minette's understanding, the novel ends over-optimistically as far as Bra' Man's public prospects are concerned.

The rejection of Bra' Man by his followers, like the crucifixion of Christ, was a revelation of human contrareity. The wild impulse by which they become a mob to destroy the one upon whom they found themselves dependent was the result of inner, not outer pressures. It is the inner, private world that Mais explores in *Black Lightning*. There is no social density; the setting of the novel is remote, self-contained, rural.

In a small cast, the central character is Jake, an artist-blacksmith, and the central symbol is Samson. But whereas the parallel between Bra' Man and Christ had been imposed externally by the author, Mais now invests in the consciousness of his fictional character; it is Jake who fastens upon Samson as a model of man's independence:

> There were times when Jake, too, used to take long walks by himself into the woods, and he knew what it was that Amos got from that feeling of being withdrawn from the world. He got the same feeling from being alone with his carving. Healing went with it, and a sense of stillness and peace. And a feeling too that a man is alone in the world and sufficient, and not dependent upon anyone.

(Black Lightning, pp. 90–1)

It is ironic that Jake should identify with Samson, for Samson is a symbol of both strength and weakness, an archetype of the human person. Mais is able to unfold Jake's growing awareness of this irony as the dramatic, disconcerting process of the novel.

When the novel begins, Jake is at work on a carving of Samson in solid mahogany, but progress is slow because his artist's hands are struggling to express a truth not in accordance with his pre-conception of Samson. After Estella leaves him, Jake's complacency starts to crumble, the carving begins to take 'its own end into its hands', becoming 'what it wants to be . . .'. The finished work Jake contemptuously reveals to Amos is not Samson in his prime, but the blinded Samson, a figure of ruined strength leaning on a little boy:

> Amos looked, and he tried to say something, but words would not come to him.
> 'Do you see what I see?' said Jake. And without taking his eyes off the statue: 'Why don't you say something? Are you dumb?' His hand reached out, and clutched the other's shoulder. 'You are shaking like a leaf! Are you afraid? There's nothing here to be afraid of. There's nobody going to hurt you. . . .'
> And Amos said slowly: 'I see it, Jake. What—what you wanted me to see. Yes, I see it now. I see what you mean. It ain't Samson anymore, is what you mean; ain't it?'
> 'What is it then?' tensely. 'Tell me. Perhaps you can tell me.'
> (*Black Lightning*, p. 112)

The lesson of Samson is driven home when Jake is blinded by lightning and he is brought to depend upon Amos and Bess. Although Mais does not see the sense of purpose which now comes into these characters' lives as negligible, he makes us share Jake's contempt for the shabby process of salvage to which men must resort in the world. It satisfies our sense of the protagonist's stature that with the tragic discovery of his own and Samson's dependent humanity Jake should move inevitably to an aristocratic suicide.

Through his central character, Mais expresses a tragic view of life, and a dignified response to it. In the developing relationship between Glen and Miriam which he runs alongside the story of Jake, a more practical positive merges.

The prevalence of concubinage in the social milieu from which his characters derived, and Mais's uninhibited and realistic transfers into *The Hills Were Joyful Together* and *Brother Man* must have made it easier for the writer from Jamaica to observe the natural conflicts and instinctive compacts that are constituents in sexual love. And the drawing together of Bra' Man and Minette after Bra' Man's public failure in *Brother Man* must have led the author to wonder about the possibilities of men and women coming to terms with their world through sexual relationships. However all this may be, the relationship between Glen and Miriam is presented as a wayward succession of approaches and retreats until Jake's suicide drives them to the final step of accepting the need to be dependent upon each other.

By combining the suicide of Jake with the growth of love between Glen and Miriam, Mais discovers a pattern of renewal after destruction. The natural setting of the novel reinforces this impression. For Jake's alienation occurs in a world which includes George's spontaneous affinity with nature (climaxed by the youth's exulting ride on the mare Beauty), and the human crises in the novel are made to coincide with phenomena in nature. All these motifs are caught up in the final movement of the novel.

Jake had asked about Samson: 'Where will he take that burden to its last resting-place and set it down? And be restored to himself again, whole?' (p. 110). It is by a strict logic to the situation and the character that for Jake as for Samson the resting-place should be self-destruction. Jake must pull down his own self and hostile temple to be whole again. A more generalized sense of renewal is suggested by Jake's suicide taking place in a burgeoning wood after the flood: 'Birds sang from the wood again, and little by little it lost the dank peaty smell of sodden rotting vegetation. It smelled again sweet and fresh like the face of a young girl' (p. 201). At the same time as Jake embraces his death, moreover, Amos and Estella make their compact in the wood; George and Beauty are exulting in that gallop across the common; and Glen and Miriam draw together:[1]

> 'The wood is so full of peace. . . . If I had to die, I think I would like to die out here.'
> His arm tightened about her waist.
> 'Don't talk about dying. We want to live. Ain't it?'

[1] In this quotation and in the one following, Mais's dialogue, never quite convincing, sounds like a Hollywood script. But the context seems to distract us from niggling.

'Yes, Glen. We want to live . . . for a long, long time. . . .'
'That's the way to talk, girl, that's the stuff.'

(Black Lightning, p. 221)

As Jake's suicide shot sounds from one part of the wood, life asserts itself in another. This is a long way from the death of Surjue in *The Hills Were Joyful Together*:

> He fell spread-eagled on his back and lay still.
> A scudding, shapeless mass of filmy clouds drew over the face of the moon. The stars put out again.
> A dog howled in the darkness outside the wall.
> He lay on his back, his arms flung wide, staring up at the silent unequivocal stars.

(The Hills Were Joyful Together, p. 288)

And there is more conviction in Glen's and Miriam's tentative embrace than in the 'vision of certitude' of *Brother Man*.

Mais's sense of the tragic in life, and his compassionate understanding were stimulated by the society in which he lived. In his most assured fiction he attained to a genuine tragic vision by separating the stimulus from its special social context.

XI

The World of *A House for Mr. Biswas*

V. S. Naipaul's *A House for Mr. Biswas* (1964) takes the form of fictive biography, beginning with the inauspicious birth of Mr. Biswas in an obscure village, and ending with his death in the city forty-six years later. But Naipaul elects to explore and interpret the life and achievement of Mr. Biswas against a dense and changing background: the fiction also represents, in less depth, the life of the Tulsis, an Indian family into which Mr. Biswas came to be married. Inevitably the novel has been seen as providing a picture of Indian life in the West Indies, with Hanuman House, the Tulsi family residence at Arwacas, becoming representative: 'Before *Mr. Biswas*, the West Indian East Indian was without form features or voice. Now we know more about Hanuman House than we do about Brandt's Pen [in John Hearne's novels] or the Village of Love [in a novel by Merrill Ferguson].'[1] In fact, the kind of family life represented at Hanuman House no longer exists in Trinidad. A brief account of the outer sociohistorical situation upon which the novel draws may be useful.

After Negro Emancipation, India became the main overseas source of cheap labour for the British sugar islands: between 1839 and 1917 no fewer than 416,000 indentured Indians were imported as substitutes for the freed Negroes. These new slaves were procured in the poverty-stricken districts of India; most of them were transported to Guyana (239,000) and to Trinidad (134,000) where labour problems had been particularly acute.[2] Today, descendants

[1] L. E. Brathwaite, 'Roots' in *Bim*, July–December 1963.
[2] A simplified account of the labour situation in the islands after Emancipation is to be found in F. R. Augier and Others, *The Making of the West Indies* (1960), pp. 182–210. Indian immigration figures are taken from this textbook.

of Indians comprise 49 per cent of the population of Guyana and 35 per cent of that of Trinidad. Writing about the social structure of Guyana, a sociologist who has spent many years in the area generalizes about the Indians: 'In 1917, the system of organised immigration ceased, and after that time very few people entered the country from India. Even during the nineteenth century there had been a marked tendency for Indian languages to be replaced by the Guianese lower-class dialect of English, and now this process was accelerated until today Indian languages are practically never used except on ritual occasions when they are about as widely under-stood as Latin is among Roman Catholics in England. The same thing happened in other fields of culture, such as dress, home furnishing, and recreational activities. This process of "creolisa-tion" affected nearly all aspects of life so that customs and forms of social structure which superficially appear to be entirely "Indian" are in fact sharply modified by the local environment.'[1] The same general process of 'creolisation' has taken place in Trinidad, pos-sibly at a faster rate than in Guyana.

But at first, the Indians kept to themselves, and the better-off ones retained a family life in many respects similar to that fictional-ized in *A House for Mr. Biswas*:

> ... The organisation of the Tulsi house was simple. Mrs. Tulsi had only one servant, a negro woman who was called Blackie by Seth and Mrs. Tulsi, and Miss Blackie by everyone else. Miss Blackie's duties were vague. The daughters and their children swept and washed and cooked and served in the store. The husbands, under Seth's supervision, worked on the Tulsi land, looked after Tulsi animals, and served in the store. In return they were given food, shelter, and a little money; their children were looked after; and they were treated with respect by people outside because they were connected with the Tulsi family. Their names were forgotten; they became Tulsis.

> (*A House for Mr. Biswas*, pp. 87–8)

The quotation comes from the earlier section of a novel that covers a period of forty-six years—the span of Mr. Biswas's life. Over this fictional period, Naipaul chronicles the dissolution of Tulsi family life. The closing chapters are set in the city, Port of Spain, where

---

[1] Raymond T. Smith, *British Guiana* (1962), pp. 109–10.

in a crowded house owned by Mrs. Tulsi, the Tulsi daughters and their husbands coexist with one another as separate economic units, and the children are involved in the colonial scramble for education:

> In the house the crowding became worse. Basdai, the widow, who had occupied the servant room as a base for a financial assault on the city, gave up that plan and decided instead to take-in boarders and lodgers from Shorthills. The widows were now almost frantic to have their children educated. There was no longer a Hanuman House to protect them; everyone had to fight for himself in a new world, the world Owad and Shakhar had entered, where education was the only protection. As fast as the children graduated from the infant school at Shorthills they were sent to Port of Spain. Basdai boarded them.
>
> (*A House for Mr. Biswas*, p. 393)

A House for Mr. Biswas has resonances we would not expect in a sociologist's account. Basdai, for instance, is being satirized for the profit motive, and the throngs of children become functions of Mr. Biswas's agoraphobia; but the rapid disintegration of the Tulsi outpost following their momentous move from Arwacas to Shorthills corresponds to the break-up of Indian family life described by Naipaul himself in a non-fictional work:

> The family life I have been describing began to dissolve when I was six or seven; when I was fourteen it had ceased to exist. Between my brother, twelve years younger than myself and me there is more than a generation of difference. He can have no memory of that private world which survived with such apparent solidity up to only twenty-five years ago, a world which had lengthened out, its energy of inertia steadily weakening from the featureless area of darkness which was India.[1]

In the novel, we date the abandonment of Hanuman House as somewhere between 1941 and 1945: so close does the novel's calendar run to the factual one.

More important than this kind of accuracy is the way in which Naipaul uses the Tulsi cultural hulk in the creation of nightmare world for Mr. Biswas; but not to be aware that Hanuman House represents something in the Trinidad Indian past; and not to be

[1] V. S. Naipaul, *An Area of Darkness* (1964), pp. 37-8.

aware of the sense in which *A House for Mr. Biswas* is a historical novel is to follow Brathwaite (in the article already cited):

> . . . [I]n the world of Hanuman House, we have the first novel [f]rom the West Indies] whose basic theme is not rootlessness and the search for social identity; in *A House for Mr. Biswas* we have at last a novel whose central character is clearly defined and who is really trying to get *in* rather than get *out*.[1]

A House for Mr. Biswas I would suggest is the West Indian novel of rootlessness *par excellence*. We are in a better position to take this view if we recognize the novel's historicity. For convenience the case may be put like this: Mr. Biswas is an Indian who marries into an Indian enclave in Trinidad between the wars: he recognizes the blinkered insulation of this world from the outside, and he senses its imminent dissolution. He spends most of his life trying to escape its embrace, only to find that the future, the colonial society upon which he wishes to make his mark, is as yet uncreated. Mr. Biswas struggles between the tepid chaos of a decaying culture and the void of a colonial society. To put it like this is to gloss C. L. R. James's remark that 'after reading *A House for Mr. Biswas* many of our people have a deeper understanding of the West Indies than they did before'.[2] It is necessary to get our background information right in order to avoid misinterpreting novels like *A House for Mr. Biswas*. But I want to approach the work as an imaginative response to social phenomena, examining the texture of the fictional world in which Mr. Biswas toils, and his characteristic responses to it.

Before introducing the Tulsis, Naipaul establishes the insignificance of Mr. Biswas's birth and the lack of prospects before him. The author's chronicling voice relentlessly anticipates a visit by the adult Mr. Biswas to the place of his birth where he finds only 'oil derricks and grimy pumps, see-sawing, see-sawing, endlessly, surrounded by red No Smoking notices' (p. 38). Frustrated by a series of unsatisfactory jobs, and languishing in the back trace at Pagotes, Mr. Biswas discovers romance in the novels of Hall Caine and Marie Corelli, and becomes an addict of Samuel Smiles:

[1] L. E. Braithwaite in 'Roots', cited above.
[2] C. L. R. James, *Party Politics in the West Indies* (Vedic Enterprises Ltd., San Juan, Trinidad, 1962), p. 150.

... Samuel Smiles was as romantic and satisfying as any novelist, and Mr. Biswas saw himself in many Samuel Smiles heroes: he was young, he was poor, and he fancied he was struggling. But there always came a point when resemblance ceased. The heroes had rigid ambitions and lived in countries where ambitions could be pursued and had a meaning. He had no ambition, and in this hot land, apart from opening a shop or buying a motorbus, what could he do? What could he invent?

(*A House for Mr. Biswas*, p. 71)

Mr. Biswas differs in being literate, but his frustration is similar in conditioning to the frustration of the deprived characters in other West Indian novels like Roger Mais's *The Hills Were Joyful Together* (1953) and Austin Clarke's *Survivors of the Crossing* (1964). The difference between social comment and fictive generation begins to emerge, however, when we follow Mr. Biswas on his job-hunting walk along the main road of Pagotes:

... He passed dry goods shops—strange name: dry goods—and the rickety little rooms bulged with dry goods, things like pans and plates and bolts of cloth and cards of bright pins and boxes of thread and shirts on hangers and brand-new oil lamps and hammers and saws and clothes-pegs and everything else, the wreckage of a turbulent flood which appeared to have forced the doors of the shops open and left deposits of dry goods on tables and on the ground outside. The owners remained in their shops, lost in the gloom and wedged between dry goods. The assistants stood outside with pencils behind their ears or pencils tapping bill-pads with the funereally coloured carbon paper peeping out from under the first sheet. Grocers' shops, smelling damply of oil, sugar, and salted fish. Vegetable stalls, damp but fresh and smelling of earth. Grocers' wives and children stood oily and confident behind counters. The women behind the vegetable stalls were old and correct with thin mournful faces; or they were young and plump with challenging and quarrelsome stares; with a big-eyed child or two hanging about behind the purple sweet potatoes to which dirt still clung; and babies in the background lying in condensed milk boxes.

(*A House for Mr. Biswas*, p. 63)

Naipaul's intense observation of the superficies of things becomes the character's vision of a world that is dingy, overcrowded and smelly, with inconsequential objects and derelict human beings stranded in gloom and grease. Mr. Biswas's response to this world is nausea: '. . . Few persons now held him. Some feature always finally repelled, a tone of voice, a quality of skin, an over-sensuous hang of lip; one such lip had grown coarse and obscene in a dream which left him feeling unclean' (p. 71). But Naipaul also plants in Mr. Biswas an unquenchable hope: 'He had begun to wait, not only for love, but for the world to yield its sweetness and romance. He deferred all his pleasure in life until that day' (p. 73).

With the introduction of the Tulsis, Naipaul makes Mr. Biswas's world even more coarse-grained, chaotic, overcrowded and suffocating. Waiting for the appearance of Mrs. Tulsi, Mr. Biswas is assaulted by the disposition of the Tulsi furniture:

> The most important piece of furniture in the hall was a long *unvarnished* pitch-pine table, *hard-grained* and *chipped*. A hammock made from sugarsacks hung across one corner of the room. An old sewing machine, a baby chair and a black biscuit-drum occupied another corner. *Scattered* about were a number of *unrelated* chairs, stools and benches, one of which, low and carved with *rough ornamentation* from a *solid* block of cyp wood, still had the saffron colour which told that it *had been used* at a wedding ceremony. More elegant pieces—a dresser, a desk, a piano *so buried* among papers and baskets and other things that it was unlikely it was ever used— *choked* the staircase landing. On the other side of the hall there was a loft of curious construction. It was as if an enormous drawer had been pulled out of the top of the wall; the *vacated space, dark and dusty*, was *crammed* with all sorts of articles Mr. Biswas *couldn't distinguish*.
>
> (*A House for Mr. Biswas*, p. 79, my italics)

Earlier, he had noticed the Tulsi kitchen: 'It was lower than the hall and appeared to be completely without fight. The doorway gaped black; soot stained the wall about it and the ceiling just above, so that blackness seemed to fill the kitchen like a solid substance' (pp. 78–9). This world threatens to embrace and absorb Mr. Biswas, and Naipaul sets the stage with a highly suggestive description of Hanuman House:

> Among the tumbledown timber-and-corrugated-iron buildings in the High Street of Arwacas, Hanuman House stood like an alien white *fortress*. The *concrete walls* looked as *thick* as they were, and

when the *narrow* doors of the Tulsi Store on the ground floor were closed the House became *bulky, impregnable and blank*. The side walls were *windowless*, and on the upper two floors the windows were *mere slits* in the facade. The balustrade which *hedged* the flat roof was crowned with a concrete statue of the benevolent monkey-god Hanuman. From the ground his whitewashed features could scarcely be distinguished and were, if anything, slightly sinister, for dust had settled on projections and the effect was that of a face lit up from below.

(*A House for Mr. Biswas*, p. 73)

There is a great deal in this passage, but it is worth noting, especially, the way in which the description of Tulsi objects automatically suggests the Tulsi people ('thick . . . narrow . . . blank', and the rich 'hedged' which not only suggests their insulation but connects with the animal imagery Naipaul uses when establishing the Tulsis); next, the passage contains simultaneously both the protective ('fortress . . . impregnable . . . hedged') and the suffocating aspects of the Tulsi House ('thick . . . bulky . . . blank . . . windowless . . . mere slits'). The passage has relevance also to the Tulsis' out-of-date Hinduism: the explicit 'alien' is followed by a reference to the monkey-god Hanuman (in effect, a ridiculing reference) which identifies the alienness of the House as its Indian pretension. But that the features of the god should be 'whitewashed' and that 'dust had settled on projections' contribute to our sense of the Indian culture being already out of date. More broadly, the way in which the House stands out from 'among the tumble-down timber-and-corrugated-iron buildings'—the surrounding dereliction—suggests that it too cannot be far from decay. More impressionistically there seem to be suggestions of a huge bark, hatches closed, and becalmed. All these intimations of decay, it seems to me, are caught up in the ambiguity of the word 'facade'.

Into this specious world, Mr. Biswas is lured by the unlikely siren, Shama: 'She was of medium height, slender but firm, with fine features, and though he disliked her voice, he was enchanted by her smile' (pp. 74–5). But the rapid dismantling of illusion after illusion is another feature of the world Naipaul fashions for Mr. Biswas. Not even fantasy is safe from this process: Mr. Biswas's unfinished short stories of meetings with a slim, unkissed, barren

heroine go sour after a visit to Bhandat who has in fact deserted a
wife to live with the unknown in the person of a Chinese woman.
The couple of romance are found living in squalor, and 'Mr.
Biswas, thinking of deafness, dumbness, insanity, the horror of the
sexual act in that grimy room felt the yellow cake turn to a sweet
slippery paste in his mouth' (p. 40). Similarly, Mr. Biswas's excited
arrival in the city is swiftly succeeded by disillusion in a backwater:

> . . . Up to this time the city had been new and held an expectation
> which not even the deadest two o'clock sun could destroy. Any-
> thing could happen: he might meet his barren heroine, the past
> could be undone, he would be remade. But now not even the
> thought of the *Sentinel's* presses, rolling out at that moment reports
> of speeches, banquets, funerals (with all names and decorations
> carefully checked) could keep him from seeing that the city was no
> more than a repetition of this: this dark, dingy café, the chipped
> counter, the flies thick on the electric flex, the empty Coca Cola
> cases stacked in a corner, the cracked glasscase, the shopkeeper
> picking his teeth, waiting to close.
>
> (*A House for Mr. Biswas*, p. 341)

It is in keeping with the pattern of hope, illusion, disillusion and
nausea that even before the wedding to Shama, Mr. Biswas's swan
should turn into a Tulsi hen. But if Naipaul gives Mr. Biswas a
faith in life against all the evidence, so that he keeps coming back,
the author also endows his protagonist with a capacity for experiencing, for responding to the tiniest tremor as if it were a
cataclysm. Both these qualities operate to prevent Mr. Biswas from
being entirely the figure of pathos his author wants him to be, no
more so than in the Tulsi section of the novel. For when he is lured
into the Tulsi bog by their fairest flower, Mr. Biswas comes at last
within striking distance of an identifiable antagonist.

Although Chapter 3 'The Tulsis' and the next three chapters,
'The Chase', 'Green Vale' and 'A Departure' take up just over 200
pages of a 531-page novel, this section dominates most readers'
impressions of the work. It is not difficult to see why. It is in this
section that Naipaul establishes the Tulsis in their characteristic
attitudes: Mrs. Tulsi's dramatic faint, and her foxy intimacies; Seth
in bluchers and stained Khaki topee, a black notebook and ivory
cigarette holder sticking out of his khaki shirt pocket; the spoilt

Tulsi sons jerking into studious, stern, grave or querulous looks as occasion demands; Hari the household pundit posed enigmatically over his holy books; and Shama, Mr. Biswas's wife, sighing her Tulsi sigh and wearing her martyred look. In addition to these vivid shorthands for individuals, there are the group characterizations: 'the sisters', 'the eaters' at the communal table, 'the sleepers' unfolding beds in every available space, and 'the children' who turn up everywhere. Then there are the events in the Tulsi year— deaths, weddings, prayer-meetings and Christmas—at each of which there is a set pattern of behaviour. In this section of the novel, too, Naipaul renders characteristic Tulsi sounds (children being beaten, eaters chewing, sisters chit-chatting about husbands' illnesses) and smells (of Tulsi 'bad food', and Mrs. Tulsi's medicaments, 'bay rum, soft candles, Canadian Healing Oil, ammonia'). Since Naipaul's art relies heavily on repetition or allusion to something already established, each episode consolidates our first impression of the crowded, noisy, ritualized life and single-attribute people.

The most obvious danger for a novelist operating in this way is that his people may become cardboard figures, uninteresting with successive exposures, and may even be felt to be unfairly handled victims of an omniscient author. Naipaul does not seem to escape this dilemma altogether in *A House for Mr. Biswas*, but in the chapters under discussion several factors combine to animate the Tulsis. In the first place they are seen from the outside by a Mr. Biswas whose sensitivity converts them into sinister antagonists. The apparent Tulsi inaction after Mrs. Tulsi finds his love-letter to Shama is full of menace to Mr. Biswas, and when at last they move, Naipaul conveys the impression of secret doings in military chambers:

> Just before four, when the store closed and Mr. Biswas stopped work, Seth came, looking as though he had spent the day in the fields. He wore muddy bluchers and a stained khaki topee; in the pocket of his sweated khaki shirt he carried a black note book and an ivory cigarette holder. He went to Mr. Biswas and said in a tone of gruff authority, 'The old lady want to see you before you go.'

Mr. Biswas's response is that of a condemned man:

Mr. Biswas resented the tone, and was disturbed that Seth had spoken to him in English. Saying nothing, he came down the ladder and washed out his brushes, doing his soundless whistling while Seth stood over him. The front doors were bolted and barred and the Tulsi store became dark and warm and protected.

(*A House for Mr. Biswas*, p. 78)

The long silent walk through the Tulsi courtyard, past the black kitchen and into the furniture-crowded hall follows. And when a creak on the staircase almost melodramatically announces the entry of Mrs. Tulsi, things begin to move too fast for Mr. Biswas. Each of Mrs. Tulsi's question and statement sequences is followed by an increase of Tulsi background noises, or by the robot-like functioning of a Tulsi insider, until at the end Mr. Biswas feels faces of Tulsi women and Tulsi children closing in upon him.

Naipaul's strategy of presenting the first interview with the Tulsis in these terms, through Mr. Biswas's apprehensive and unaccustomed eyes is followed by the duelling that takes place between Mr. Biswas and the Tulsi high command. Mr. Biswas begins with name-calling that builds upon Naipaul's earlier disposition of the characters. As Mr. Biswas is too frightened at first to show his hand he carries on these name-calling sessions only when he is alone with his wife:[1]

> 'I got a name for another one of your brother-in-laws,' he told Shama that evening, lying on his blanket, his right foot on his left knee, peeling off a broken nail from his big toe. 'The constipated holy man.'
>
> 'Hari?' she said, and pulled herself up, *realising that she had begun to take part in the game.*
>
> He slapped his yellow, flabby calf and pushed his finger into the flesh. The calf yielded like sponge.
>
> *She pulled his hand away.* 'Don't do that. I can't bear to see you do that. You should be ashamed, a young man like you being so soft.'
>
> 'That is all the bad food I eating in this place.' *He was still holding her hand.* 'Well, as a matter of fact, I have quite a few names for him. The holy ghost. You like that?'
>
> 'Man!'
>
> 'And what about the two gods? It ever strike you that they look like two monkeys. So, you have one concrete monkey—god out-

---

[1] My italics. It is interesting to notice that Mr. Biswas is making love to his wife here—the only love scene in Naipaul's fiction.

side the house and two living ones inside. They could just call this place the monkey house and finish. Eh, monkey, bull, cow, hen. The place is like a blasted zoo, man.'

'And what about you? The barking puppy dog?'

'Man's best friend.' He flung up his legs and his thin slack calves shook. With a push of his finger he kept the calves swinging.

'Stop doing that!'

By now Shama's head was on his soft arm and they were lying side by side.

(*A House for Mr. Biswas*, p. 108)

But Mr. Biswas's sniping at the Tulsis is part of a contest. They can come back at him. He tells Govind that he wants to paddle his own canoe only to find himself being called 'the paddler', and his daughter Savi, 'the little paddler'. Seth who fills in the details on Savi's birth certificate knows just where Mr. Biswas is most vulnerable:

Suddenly he jumped up. 'What the hell is this?'

'Show me.'

He showed her the certificate. 'Look. Occupation of father. Labourer. Labourer! Me! Where your family get all this bad blood, girl?'

'I didn't see that?'

'Trust Seth. Look. Name of informant: R. N. Seth. Occupation: Estate Manager.'

'I wonder why he do that.'

(*A House for Mr. Biswas*, pp. 146–7)

This give and take between Mr. Biswas and the Tulsis provides much of the fun in *A House for Mr. Biswas*, and gives life to both contestants. It also provides a cover, and indeed a mood for Naipaul's animus, for the fierce authorial establishing and fixing of characters in terms of objects and animals is just held under control by the fetching and carrying that goes on between the omniscient author and the clowning, scurrilous character.

But it seems to me that when the Tulsi clan begins to disintegrate, and Hanuman House ceases to be a threat to Mr. Biswas, the author's attitudes begin to show too obtrusively as his own: instead of a duelling between Mr. Biswas and the Tulsis we have their routing by a biased omniscient author. Naipaul renders the apocalyptic sense of the Tulsi dissolution with skill, but chokes our response to it. A long paragraph of authorial reportage precedes the Tulsis' move from Arwacas to a new estate at Shorthills:

> . . . Shama heard its glories listed again and again. In the grounds of the estate house there was a cricket field and a swimming pool; the drive was lined with orange trees and gri-gri palms with slender white trunks, red berries and dark green leaves. The land itself was a wonder. The saman trees and lianas so strong and supple that one could swing on them. All day the immortelle trees dropped their red and yellow bird-shaped flowers through which one could whistle like a bird. Cocoa trees grew in the shade of the immortelles, coffee in the shade of the cocoa and the hills were covered with tonka bean. Fruit trees, mango, orange, avocado pear, were so plentiful as to seem wild. And there were nutmeg trees, as well as cedar, *poui* and the *bois-canot* which was so light yet so springy and strong it made you a better cricket bat than the willow.
>
> The sisters spoke of the hills, the sweet springs and hidden waterfalls with all the excitement of people who had known only the hot open plain, the flat acres of sugarcane and the muddy ricelands. Even if one did not have a way with land as they had, if you did nothing, life could be rich at Shorthills. There was talk of dairy farming, there was talk of growing grapefruit. More particularly, there was talk of rearing sheep, and of an idyllic project of giving one sheep to every child as his very own, the foundation it was made to appear, of fabulous wealth. And there were horses on the estate: the children would learn to ride.
>
> (*A House for Mr. Biswas*, pp. 353–4)

The passage begins insidiously with what looks like sympathetic infection, but ends with the most uncontaminated detachment. Naipaul works up the sisters' feverish excitement about the new estate only to mock their inflated expectations and degrade them with the money motive. (It is interesting to notice that all the trees over which the sisters are reportedly idyllic are useful.) How much more effective and balanced the deflation through Mr. Biswas is may be illustrated from the part of the novel where Mrs. Tulsi takes Mr. Biswas on a tour of the new property (pp. 356–60). In the following exchange at the beginning of the walking tour with Mrs. Tulsi, the anti-Tulsi points are scored lightly:

> Mr. Biswas waved at the forlorn little cemetery and the dirt lane

which, past a few tumbledown houses, disappeared behind bush and apparently led only to more bush and the mountain which rose at the end. 'Estate?' he asked.

Mrs. Tulsi smiled. 'And on this side.' She waved at the other side of the road.

Beyond a deep gully, whose sides were sheer, whose bed was strewn with boulders, stones and pebbles, perfectly graded, Mr. Biswas saw more bush, more mountains. 'A lot of bamboo,' he said. 'You could start a paper factory.'

(*A House for Mr. Biswas*, pp. 357–8)

More passages like this, and fewer in which the authorial voice becomes directly involved in deflating the Tulsis might have allowed the Tulsis' attempt to take the place of the departed French Creole estate owners to appear as what it is—the inadequate and pathetic fumblings of a group that has been turned inwards too long to be able to cope with changing conditions. But while elements of this may be discerned in the presentation, the emphasis is elsewhere.

How the Tulsi slide gathers momentum after the move to Short-hills is relentlessly conveyed. First, Mrs. Tulsi withdraws into congenial darkness, 'her window . . . closed, the room . . . sealed against light and air'; then three deaths in quick succession deprive the organization even further of its ancient figures of authority. With the high command broken, Tulsi husbands turn individualist and plunder the falling empire, while defenceless Tulsi widows cook up one blighted economic project after another. At this point it is clear that the object of Naipaul's satire is changing from a static communalism to the new colonial individualism. This gives a kind of back-flip of sympathy to the old Tulsi way of life (and this is supported by Mr. Biswas's recognition, at times of un-balancing stress, of the protectiveness even of Hanuman House), but Naipaul does not allow the mood to develop. The author turns the Tulsi retreat to Shorthills into an invasion (p. 368): the villagers band against them (pp. 368–9), and Tulsi mismanagement ravages and depletes the once fair land. At the climax, Naipaul directs our responses by reflecting the ruins of the Tulsi establishment in a surrounding dereliction we are persuaded they themselves are guilty of having created:

The canal at the side of the drive was at last completely silted over and the rain, which ran down the hillside in torrents after the briefest shower, flooded the flat land. The gully, no longer supported by the roots, began to be eaten away. The old man's beard was deprived of a footing; its thin tangled roots hung over the banks like a threadbare carpet. The gully bed, washed clean of black soil and the plants that grew on it, showed sandy, then pebbly, then rocky. It could no longer be forded by the car, and the car stayed on the road. The sisters were puzzled by the erosion, which seemed to them sudden; but they accepted it as part of their fate.

(*A House for Mr. Biswas*, p. 377)

Naipaul describes 'The Shorthills Adventure' as a climactic passage, but a climactic passage in what turns out to have been only a mock-saga: 'Bells were rung and gongs were struck, but the luck, the virtue, had gone out of the family' (p. 377). Out of the dissolution the second and third generations of Tulsis emerge into the wider colonial world. But in dealing with the individualism of the new Tulsis in Port of Spain, Naipaul turns them into vulgar materialists, and their children into half-baked readers and learners. Although we are dealing with the death of one way of life and the beginning of another, Naipaul does not permit us to imagine the Tulsis as capable either of shock or excitement.[1] To put it like this is perhaps to oversimplify and overstate the case. But if hostility to the Tulsi characters is in excess of, and prolonged beyond the rhetorical requirements of the novel, this is a blemish that *A House for Mr. Biswas* survives. To take notice of it, nevertheless, is to raise doubts about the satirist's imaginative ability to transcend his real life attitudes to the people upon whom the fictional characters are modelled.

There is another way in which the author's over-indulgence in a point of view initially attributed to the character threatens the balance of the novel. It is appropriate that Mr. Biswas should see his world as a sordid one, but the frequency with which he is made

[1] It is in keeping with what one might call the one-sided compassion of the novel that the struggles of Mr. Biswas and his brood should be presented as different in quality from those of their neighbours. It is interesting to notice, too, that in this section of the novel the point of view alternates between that of Mr. Biswas, and his son, Anand.

to do so lends emphasis to the novel's apparently gratuitous descriptions of decay, disease, squalor and blight. About Mr. Biswas's garden, we read: 'Untended, the rose trees grew straggly and hard. A blight made their stems white and gave them sickly, ill-formed leaves. The buds opened slowly to reveal blanched, tattered blooms covered with minute insects; other insects built bright brown domes on the stems. The lily-pond collapsed again and the lily-roots rose brown and shaggy out of the thick muddy water which was white with bubbles' (p. 340). And of Mr. Biswas's flesh we are told: 'His face grew puffy. His complexion grew dark; not the darkness of a naturally dark skin, not the darkness of sunburn: this was a darkness that seemed to come from within, as though the skin was a murky but transparent film and the flesh below it had been bruised and become diseased and its corruption was rising' (p. 529). To suggest that the author's obsession with decay seeps into the novel at too many crevices is not to be squeamish. It is rather to imply that in addition to dampeners already built into the structure of the novel, the work's affirmation has to be made against these local manifestations of Naipaul's temperament.

Very near the end of *A House for Mr. Biswas*, the protagonist acquires his house and gains land in a boundary dispute: 'In the extra space Mr. Biswas planted a laburnum tree. It grew rapidly. It gave the house a romantic aspect, softened the tall graceless lines and provided some shelter from the afternoon sun. Its flowers were sweet, and in the still hot evenings their smell filled the house' (p. 526). The Epilogue immediately following this triumphant moment restores a bleak perspective by describing Mr. Biswas's loss of status, his ageing, his sickness and his unremarked death. A similar delimiting function is served by the Prologue in which Mr. Biswas's achievement is rendered more effectively in negative terms—as an escape from the Tulsi realities:

He thought of the house as his own, though for years it had been irretrievably mortgaged. And during these months of illness and despair he was struck again and again by the wonder of being in his own house, the audacity of it: to walk in through his own front gate, to bar entry to whoever he wished, to close his doors and windows every night, to hear no noises except those of his family, to wander freely from room to room and about his yard instead of being condemned, as before, to retire the moment he got home to the crowded room in one or other of Mrs. Tulsi's houses, crowded with Shama's sisters, their husbands, their children. As a boy he had moved from one house of strangers to another; and since his marriage he felt he had lived nowhere but in the houses of the Tulsis, at Hanuman House in Arwacas, in the decaying wooden house at Shorthills in the clumsy concrete house in Port of Spain. And now at the end he found himself in his own house on his own half-lot of land, his own portion of the earth. That he should have been responsible for this seemed to him, in these last months, stupendous.

(A House for Mr. Biswas, p. 8)

In the story related to Mr. Biswas by an oyster man, the man's son puts a tin on a fence and shoots it down: ' "Pa", he say. "Look. I shoot work. I shoot ambition. They dead." ' And 'Escape' is the title of all the unfinished stories Mr. Biswas writes. One suspects that the world of *A House for Mr. Biswas* is one modelled upon a society from which the author has himself wished to escape, and that this attitude is the source of some of the over-emphasis in the fictional construct. But if Mr. Biswas finds his world a deterrent to ambition, as well as engulfing and repulsive, the faith in life with which his author endows him, his obstinate knowledge 'that below it all there was an excitement which was hidden but waiting to be grasped' (p. 341) is greater than the fictional character's impulse to escape. When Mr. Biswas acquires his house he does not so much create order as confirm its possibility. However wry the accompanying gestures, this is Naipaul's precarious achievement too.

XII

Novels of Childhood

Michael Anthony's novel, *The Year in San Fernando* (1965), records one year in the life of a twelve-year-old boy who leaves his native village, Mayaro, for the city, to go to school and work as a servant-companion in the house of an old lady, Mrs. Chandles. It is worth pointing out that the experiences of Francis in the novel have their real-life analogue in a year Michael Anthony himself spent in San Fernando, from after Christmas 1943 to just before Christmas 1944 when he himself was twelve years old. The novel was written in England in the late 1950's and early 1960's, but Anthony's art of memory is so vivid and his artistic control so tight that never once does the mature man impose an adult's perception on his adolescent narrating character; nor does the author at any point allow the older man he has become to break into the narrative, either directly or by anticipatory devices such as those used by the French Guinean Camara Laye in *The African Child* (1954), a book which in certain respects bears a resemblance to Michael Anthony's.

The Year in San Fernando is narrated in the first person, and from beginning to end the experiencing consciousness is that of the boy. People and places are seen 'objectively' through his eyes and subjectively in terms of his responses to them. This is the source of the novel's irony:

> We had heard only very little about Mr. Chandles. The little we had heard were whispers and we didn't gather much, but we saw him sometimes leaning over the banister of the Forestry Office and indeed he was as aristocratic as they said he was. He looked tidy and elegant and he always wore jacket and tie, unusual under the

blazing sun. These things confirmed that he was well off, and his manner and bearing, and the condescending look he gave everything about him, made us feel that he had gained high honours in life.

(The Year in San Fernando, p. 7)

But it would be a mistake to think of the work as one in which the boy is being used simply in the interests of social comment. There is indeed a vein of satire against the exploiting middle class, and some sweetly executed glances at the cultural and educational system:

> There came a fine break in the weather. For a spell we began having plenty of sun and little rain and people were saying the Indian Summer was here. But it could not be. Mr. Langley said this. Mr. Langley said the time of the Indian Summer was long past. But the rains held up, anyhow. It was as if the clouds had drained themselves out and hung there sadly because they could not rain any more.

(The Year in San Fernando, p. 144)

So much for the bookish teacher Langley. Yet this aspect of the novel appears only intermittently and in the most unobtrusive manner, never getting in the way of our illusion of living through the boy's consciousness. The same cannot be said about Austin Clarke's *Amongst Thistles and Thorns* (1965), another West Indian novel of childhood. The eye of this work is nine-year-old Milton Sobers. In the quotation below, the scene is a classroom in a colony. It is a state occasion and the children are singing 'Rule Britannia':

> . . . The headmaster was soaked in glee. And I imagined all the glories of Britannia, our Motherland, Britannia so dear to us all, and so free; Britannia who, or what or which, had brought us out of the ships crossing over from the terrible seas from Africa, and had placed us on this island, and had given us such good headmasters and assistant masters, and such a nice vicar to teach us how to pray to God—and he had come from England; and such nice white people who lived on the island with us, and who gave us jobs watering their gardens and taking out their garbage, most of which we found delicious enough to eat. . . .

(Amongst Thistles and Thorns, p. 12)

In Clarke's novel of childhood, the boy is used only as a different point of view from which to make social protest.

The Year in San Fernando differs from another West Indian novel of childhood, this time a much better known one. George Lamming's *In the Castle of My Skin* (1953) evokes the boy's world, but Lamming's intention is to suggest the essential outlines of typical boyhood in a West Indian community that is growing painfully—like the four boys in the novel—into political self-awareness; and his concern to suggest the complex shiftings in the community at large, at times, takes precedence over any notion of fidelity to the boys' consciousness. Michael Anthony's novel, set in the penultimate year of the Second World War, registers neither that event nor the political stirrings in Trinidad of that period.

A third West Indian novel of childhood, *Christopher* (1959) by Geoffrey Drayton, invests, like *The Year in San Fernando*, in the very particular consciousness of an isolated boy; and again like Anthony's novel it does not have an explicit social or political drive. But *Christopher* concentrates on a crucial period in the life of a boy, the pattern of the novel being insisted upon in the final paragraph when Christopher fails to suppress his desolation at the funeral of his nurse Gip. He tries to leap into the grave, but is caught and taken to his anxious mother:

> . . . Then as the high wail went up, she held him against her. And her body shook and she did not know if she was weeping for Gip or weeping because he was again the child that Gip had nursed—a child . . . for a few minutes more as he clung to her, he was a child—a few minutes more that were the last of his childhood.
>
> (*Christopher*, p. 192)

This is the most contrived paragraph in the novel, but what it attempts to underline is a theme implicit in Drayton's organization of the work. In the final paragraph of *The Year in San Fernando* in contrast, we find Francis on a bus taking him back to Mayaro:

> I closed the window because the rains were almost pouring down now. I sat down cosily and there was a lot of talking inside the bus. It was cosy to sit with the windows closed and the rains pouring and the bus speeding along the wet road. The talking was very cheerful. I remembered the mountain and suddenly I looked

back but all the windows were closed because of the rains. The bus roared on and my mind went on Mrs. Chandles, who was dying, and Mr. Chandles—so strange of late, and now homeless; and I thought also of Mrs. Princet, and I thought of Edwin and that dollar—I thought of all the mixed-up things, of all the funny things in fact, which made the year at Romaine Street.

(*The Year in San Fernando*, pp. 189–90)

Michael Anthony's novel does not have any such identifiable themes as 'the passing of childhood', and it seems to end without any kind of resolution. Although its language is not limp like the language in 'Lauchmonen's' (i.e. Peter Kempodoo's) pointlessly pseudonymous account of estate life in Guiana, *Guiana Boy* (1960), it has been described in terms better suited to that vulgarly exotic novel of West Indian childhood:

> . . . [*The Year in San Fernando*] is an apparently meaningless chronicle with no foundation in any strong or profound philosophy. It moves along unrelieved and at the end signifies little.

The reviewer, in *Bim*, continues patronizingly:

> I feel too that there is a brave attempt at profundity somewhere in the conception of the book, but all that comes off the page is a very weak suggestion of an unreal something. If Michael Anthony had wanted to chronicle the profundities latent in a loss of innocence— which would have called for an essentially much more dynamic mind—it would have been more effective in this case, I think, to have made a passionate concentrate of what he now offers us. Seventy-five poignant pages, perhaps, might have made a master-piece.[1]

As in Barbados, so in Jamaica—*The Year in San Fernando*'s freedom from easily recognizable theme or social message has made it seem to be without significance. A review in *The Sunday Gleaner* (Jamaica) of Anthony's most recent novel[2] returns to a previous judgement:

> Just as was said of *The Year in San Fernando* the author is extremely accurate in portrayal of each incident so that each and every one sounds authentic so that one is forced to ask the question 'so what?' or 'was the story worth telling?'.

Although *The Year in San Fernando* does not have such a clear-cut

[1] Kevyn Arthur in *Bim* 41, June–December 1965.
[2] *Green Days by the River*, 1967.

theme as *Christopher*, and although it does not refer to the West
Indian political and social scene as obviously as the other West
Indian novels of childhood already mentioned, I want to suggest
that in it Michael Anthony is practising an art of fiction of a very
subtle kind. The elucidation which follows will try to answer
implicitly some of the criticisms of the novel which have been
raised.

In the opening pages, Michael Anthony follows an economical
set of conventions for suggesting community, in terms of a land-
mark (the Forestry Office fenced off with spiky tiger-wire), out-
standing people (the high-stepping Marva, and the elegant Mr.
Chandles leaning over the Forestry Office banister), routine activity
(playing cricket, throwing stones at guavas), and gossip ('Everybody knew what time of night Mr. Chandles arrived in the village
and how Marva went down to the bus-stop to meet him, and how
they walked up the road hugging up in the dark. Ma said as far as
she knew Mr. Chandles had never arrived in the night. Anyway that
did not stop the gossips, and whenever the women went to the
Forestry Office they looked at Marva in a very knowing way' p. 9).
As we shall see, these conventions become more than conventions
as the novel develops, but the point to be emphasized now is that
Anthony does not idealize the community; on the other hand, the
social divisions which become obvious to the reader are unobtru-
sively suggested, and Mrs. Samuels's economic exploitation of
Francis's widowed mother is brought to the fore through gossip
('They said she would run her blood to water'), and then siphoned
off through the boy's literal consciousness ('Hearing this often I
seriously feared it would happen. I always thought, if it *could*
happen, would it happen one of these days?'). Anthony is neither
setting the novel towards social protest nor preparing for the
conventional contrast between integrated village and alienating
city. This is not to say that there is no comparison between the
village and the city; only that when the comparison is made it is
not in exposition of an authorially held thesis about the relative
merits of town and country. Anthony wishes primarily to establish
our faith in the pure experiencing quality of the boy's mind; and
the village is sensuously presented as the known and loved place,

soon to become the place in memory. When Francis's mother announces that the boy is to live in San Fernando with Mr. Chandles's mother, Francis's disturbance, and his sudden nostalgia which he does not understand, are expressed simultaneously in a correspondent Wordsworthian landscape:

> . . . Somehow, the knowledge that I was going away made Mayaro look very strange. The lime trees looked greener for one thing, and the sudden down-sweep of the land towards the ravine, rising again at the far grassy hills seemed to make the place unusual this morning and rare.
> I did not know why this was so. I was sure it was I who was unusual for I was feeling that way inside me. Nearby, close to our pear trees stood the giant guava tree, just on the other side of the tiger-wire. A great many of its branches hung over to our side, and they were laden with ripe fruit and it was these that I often stoned, standing almost concealed between the pear trees.
> I just did not feel like stoning the guavas this morning. I saw them and they meant little to me. . . .
>
> (*The Year in San Fernando*, pp. 12–13)

Instead of lengthening out this listless mood, Anthony tactfully allows Francis's mind to take the course of natural recovery; nostalgia begins to give way to anticipation of San Fernando, and the boy's contrary states are fused and intensified in a shock image of the promise and the menace of Mr. Chandles:

> And now, slowly, my thoughts shifted to the big house in San Fernando. I wished I had some idea of what it looked like. I wondered if it was as fine a building as this Forestry Office here. This was really a huge, great building. Terrific. As I turned my head to take in again the vastness of the Forestry Office, my heart almost leaped to my mouth. Just on the other side of the tiger-wire was Mr. Chandles. He smiled with me.
>
> (*The Year in San Fernando*, p. 13)

This movement of mind is reversed on Francis's journey by bus to the town. Through the boy's alert senses, Michael Anthony re-creates the sights and sounds of the journey so that the passing scene is evoked in an 'objective' way. But Anthony's purpose is not to decorate the novel with a tourist description (in contrast, read

pp. 120–2 of *The African Child*). We are made to enter the bewildered consciousness of the boy and the groping efforts of his
mind to find a familiar resting place:

> The night was cool and it was pitch black over the far houses. All
> around, cafes and rum-shops were open. The noises of people
> talking and the noises of cars and trucks and buses rose and fell but
> never died away. There was no silence here. At this hour, in
> Mayaro, most people would have settled in for the night. Then,
> all that could be heard was the barking of dogs or the cry of a
> cigale or the wind in the trees. Here, life was not settling down for
> the night. Life was teeming. The night seemed to make no differ-
> ence. Every moment I was blinded by the headlamp of some
> vehicle. The vehicles came roaring from the wide road ahead—the
> San Fernando road. The noises of the town rose and fell like waves
> running up and down a beach in the night. There were many
> people in our bus now. I was feeling tired. Just across the road
> there was a cafe full of people. Some were eating things and some
> had bottles of soft drinks held up to their heads. I was feeling
> thirsty for a drink. The noises rose and fell and the feeling was
> very similar to what it was when you were on Mayaro beach in
> the night.
>
> (*The Year in San Fernando*, p. 17)

The short sentences, the boy's shifting attention, and his nostalgic
comparisons with the seaside village where he has always lived,
contribute to the expression of bewilderment, imaged in the blinding lights of the vehicles speeding out of the darkness ahead. But
what is most remarkable in this passage is Anthony's gift of stealthy
simile, creeping upon the reader from the '*rose and fell* but never
died away' of confused sounds in the second sentence, through the
'*roaring*' of the vehicles from the wide road ahead, to the overwhelming noises of the town which 'rose and fell like waves running up and down a beach in the night'. Here, the tide turns as it
were. For once having become explicit, the simile shifts direction
and purpose to become at the end of the passage the agent by which
the new bewildering life around is absorbed in an image of past
experience: 'The noises rose and fell and the feeling was very
similar to what it was when you were on Mayaro beach in the
night.' By such a complex linguistic manœuvre and clear awareness
of function does Anthony use the difference between the old and

new worlds of Francis. Instead of drawing out a contrast, he unites them in the experiencing consciousness of the boy.

The boy's vision suffuses elements of experience which we are habituated to seeing as disparate or indeed as belonging to opposed categories, like nostalgia–anticipation, town–country, pure–sordid. Further examples will occur later, and it will be necessary to draw some conclusions from all this. But enough has been quoted so far to suggest that Anthony is committed in *The Year in San Fernando* to involving us in the feel of a peculiarly open state of consciousness; that this is achieved by a scrupulous adherence to the boy's point of view, in a deceptively easy style that carries the necessary sensuous burden as well as sustaining the illusion of adolescent reportage. The kind of participation invited in this way seems to me to be of a more experiential kind than that which V. S. Naipaul suggests may be achieved in another way: 'A literature can grow only out of a strong framework of social convention. And the only convention the West Indian knows is his involvement with the white world. This deprives his world of universal appeal. The situation is too special. The reader is excluded; he is invited to witness and not to participate. It is easier to enter any strong framework of social convention, however alien. It is easier to enter the tribal world of an African writer like Camara Laye.'[1] The reader's sensuous involvement in Anthony's fiction will be illustrated in further quotations below, but there is another element, not restricted to the question of involvement, to be traced in Naipaul's remark. The West Indian hankering after something like a tribal past or coherent social present as an organizing principle for fiction, only latent in Naipaul's comment, appears more distinctly in *Bim* of July–December 1963 where Edward Brathwaite's praise for *A House for Mr. Biswas* is followed by this conclusion: 'The Negro West Indian cannot really expect novels like *Biswas* until he has a strong enough framework of social convention from which to operate and until his own technique is flexible and subtle enough to take advantage of it.' Novels do indeed reflect the society out of which they have been created, but coherence in the world of the novel is one thing and an external

[1] *The Middle Passage* (1962), p. 70.

framework of social convention is another. It is naïve to confuse life with fiction at this level to the extent of implying that you cannot write a well-organized novel if you do not live in a well-organized society.

The boy's experiencing consciousness is both the means of securing the reader's involvement and of giving unity to the world of the novel, but before examining this, it is necessary to look at some other features that are used to suggest a framework of convention within which the boy's way of feeling and seeing operates. In the first place, there is a nearly classical observance of the unities: there is one action (what happens to the boy), one place (where the boy is), one time (the year), and one agent (the active and passive boy). Next, Francis's physical world is clearly defined in terms of a house (the Chandles house), places at prescribed distances from the house (the market, the wharf), and objects and persons (the girl Julia and Mt. Naparima) seen on journeys to and from the house. Within this physically framed world, Francis's behaviour is regulated by a number of routine or repetitive activities which serve as social conventions in the social world of the novel: going to market, sweeping the house, watering the plants and rubbing Mrs. Chandles's legs with Sacrool, 'The Indian Sacred Oil'; or, looking at the growing cane and the cane fires in the distant fields, sitting still in the hideaway among the concrete pillars of the tall house, listening to the sounds—passing traffic, distant music, voices upstairs—and thinking of the things and people in his life.

Since the novel covers a full year in the boy's life, Anthony is able to use a cycle of natural change and progression as a larger reference against which the novel's structural conventions are not only built up as conventions but absorbed in a more enduring pattern of growth. All the novel's repetitive activities are varied by, and become increasingly integrated with, the progress of the changing year. The daily round of the market changes subtly as the fruits of different seasons appear on the stalls; at the end of the dry season, Mrs. Chandles's legs do not have to be rubbed, and the listening boy's ears pick up the swish-swish of tyres on the wet road announcing the arrival of the rainy season. In the dry season, the cane fires are seen drawing closer and closer from the distant fields as the crop draws to an end; and at the same time the plant-watering routine is modified to twice a day, and to different hours, to cope with the aridity and heat. These repetitive activities are registered primarily in terms of the boy's consciousness, the physical impact on him of the world he is growing into; they are not placed in the novel in a mechanical or rigidly systematic way as symbolic or thematic.

All the more remarkable then is the following extended passage. After half a year in San Fernando, Francis receives a visit from his mother. The meeting promises much, but the ingratiating behaviour of Mrs. Chandles comes between the boy and his mother, and she leaves again after having been within touching distance. As her bus speeds away, the son is conscious that his chance to escape is receding too:

> I thought of the bus speeding away and I walked slowly back to the house. The pavement along Romaine Street rose very prominently from the road and I was just slightly eased of my sadness and I stepped up onto the pavement then down to the pitch again and I walked right down the street like that. In the little spaces between the houses I could see red flickers. They were 'burning-out'—the estate people were. I stood up to watch the fire whenever I came to a little space, and I could hear the crackle and the way the flames roared in the wind. This was the last of the cane-fires, for the crop was nearly ended. Watching the fires had been a great attraction for me through all these months. They had started from far away in that great expanse of green. Now the fires were blazing out the last patch, near the town. I stood up at the big gap between the school and our house, and the fire I could see here stretched over some distance, and the flame-tongues licked the air, and they reddened a large part of the sky between the houses. Away over the brown open field I could see the dusk coming.
>
> I stood up for a while looking at the cane-fire and at the dusk but my mind was wandering and I was thinking of the speeding bus. I wondered how far was she now. I tried to think of sugarcane. Tomorrow the cutters would come with their cutlasses, and the field, having been scorched of vermin and needless leaves, would be quickly cut down. The mills at the Usine Ste Madeleine would still be grinding, and the three chimneys would still be puffing smoke, but really, the crop would be over. Tomorrow when I got home from school I would see brown earth where the

last patch of green used to be. And perhaps the ploughs would come to this little part soon. I had often seen them working in the parts already cleared. Owen, my friend, who had been to all places, said the ploughs made long mounds and furrows as they went along. He said their work was to turn up the earth and to manure it and then the whole place was left alone until planting time. I did not know about all this. I could not see the mounds from here, nor the manure which the ploughs put on. But I had seen the planting at the beginning of the year, and then what looked like endless green fields, and lately, the fires every night. And with the fires, the three chimneys of the Usine Ste Madeleine had started puffing smoke. For they were grinding the cane. When Owen explained it, it seemed very simple for him. But for me there was always a little mystery about the cane. I left off looking at the fires and I went home again. The thoughts of the cane had held off the feelings of dejection. Now I felt it coming like a storm.

(The Year in San Fernando, pp. 95–6)

There is a great deal in these paragraphs: the meeting of 'speeding away' and 'walked slowly' at the co-ordinating conjunction, which in fact turns out to be the point of separation, the structure of the sentence compelling us to enact its meaning kinetically; the way in which the boy's up and down movement between road and pavement expresses his agitation, yet rhythmically soothes it; how the literal approaching dusk at the end of the first paragraph becomes the metaphorical storm of dejection in the last two sentences of the second paragraph; but there is another feature to be noticed particularly.

The fires which catch Francis's eyes and offer temporary distraction from his sense of loss are in fact signs of the end of the cane season: at the beginning of the year he had seen 'what looked like endless green fields', and later the start of the firing process, until now, the last field was being burnt out. To put it like this is to suggest the way in which the cane fields become an image of the progression of the boy's year in San Fernando; the elucidation almost inevitably makes the whole episode sound contrived, but a re-reading should confirm that Anthony's art allows of our discovering the pattern without the slightest authorial urging. It is implicit in Anthony's narrative design that the reader should be aware of more at some points than Francis is; and here, the boy's depression is intensified as he turns from the cane fields, while the reader who is both inside and outside of the boy's consciousness recognizes the cycle of natural regeneration within which the boy's harrowing period is absorbed. It is being suggested then, that in an apparently spontaneous way, what might so easily have been exotic information about the planting and harvesting of cane comes to serve an archetypal function in the novel. Francis, *told* by Owen about the ploughing and furrowing and the period of lying fallow, 'did not know about all this'. Yet two paragraphs later when he has arrived in the Chandles house, so subtly is Anthony's art possessed of both literalness and a natural symbolic germ, the fires migrate, and the furrowing is understood and accepted by the boy as a phase in his particular growth:

> . . . My eyes looked out on Celesta Street but it was not the lit-up panes I was seeing now. Dejection swept upon me. Now at this hour I was suffering for the need of home. Now I felt a prisoner in this giddy town. My heart was burning for home. For a moment I felt like crying out, but at the moment of greatest pain my mother's voice came back to me. It was as if she was here and talking. She had said, Stay and take in education, boy. Take it in. That's the main thing.
>
> That was about the last thing she had said to me. I heard it now as plain as ever.
>
> (*The Year in San Fernando*, p. 96)

Built-in with the structuring of the novel is a pattern of growth, but not simply in a finite sense. When Francis first arrives in the town, with its neon signs flashing, its teeming crowds, and its tall strange buildings towering high above the streets, he is more than bewildered: 'Mr. Chandles had said one could get lost here so easily. Already I could see myself getting lost. I could see myself wandering hopelessly about this maze of streets. Listening to him, without considering the words themselves, I had the feeling things would be very mixed up when I went out' (p. 20). It is part of the spontaneous metaphorical design of the book that Francis's bewilderment, and his process of groping towards an understanding of the town, the Chandles house, and the people who strike him as mysterious, should appear to the reader as part of a process of coming to learn about life:

Novels of Childhood

... We were still approaching the school and I was still looking at the weird empty yard when Mr. Chandles spoke.

'You'll have to watch this school,' he said. 'This house here is yours.'

The House just before the school was journey's end.

(*The Year in San Fernando*, p. 22)

This quality in the novel may be illustrated with reference to Francis's mastery of marketing skills, a finite process by which the boy can measure his own growth, but a metaphoric one through which the reader is made aware of a more open-ended journeying. Francis's initial bewilderment at the market is expressed in terms that remind us of his first responses to the town, both episodes suggesting the bewilderment of a sensitive confrontation with life:

> The vastness of this interior bewildered me, and also I was amazed by the great mass of people and by the steady roar of human voices which startled you because you saw no one screaming. The roof was all slate, half-transparent, and you could see the brightness of the sun filtering through. When there was a little room to turn round in, Brinetta looked at me and grinned. 'Well, this is the market,' she said.

(*The Year in San Fernando*, p. 39)

Although the boy's initial confusion steadily gives way to an increasing confidence and pride in his marketing skills, and to his becoming in a sense a member of the market community, these developments are coloured for the reader by another complication. The boy's visits to the market echo his need to belong somewhere, against a background feeling (not so much *recognized by* as *felt through* the boy) for mankind's vulnerability in the face of time. Francis had first visited the market with Brinetta, an elderly woman already passing out of the story and out of life. It is around the memory of Brinetta that the new feeling begins to form:

> The vendors knew me well by now, and they could almost tell what things I came for, and how much I wanted, and the things Mrs. Chandles liked best. It astonished me and pleased me very much that they should know this. . . . They laughed all the time and they talked in Hindi to one another and they looked very nice in their saris and muslin veils. And mostly there would be gold

217

plated teeth in their mouths and heavy gold bracelets on their
wrists and ankles. They were very pleasant to buy from.

When ever they spoke in English it would be to ask me about
Brinetta and I would say I did not know where Brinetta was.
'Where she garn,' they would press, 'you don't know where she
garn?' And when I said no, they would shake their heads and look
at each other as if to say it was very strange I did not know. They
had never forgotten Brinetta.

(*The Year in San Fernando*, p. 143)

And at the end of the novel when the characters are moving apart,
with Mrs. Chandles dying ('she travelling home') and Francis about
to get his bus back to the village, Brinetta and the market become
the means by which the boy knows, yet scarcely knows that he
knows, that death is part of the streaming life he is still to enter:

Thinking of the market I remembered Brinetta and I was glad for
remembering her now. For she had slipped entirely from my mind.
I thought, look how Brinetta has gone away forever, and how I
was leaving for good now and she wouldn't know, and she might
never know Mrs. Chandles died this year.

(*The Year in San Fernando*, p. 186)

At the end of the novel, Francis has come to understand a certain
section of San Fernando, an area of experience has been sounded.
But there is no attempt on the novelist's part to suggest that the
boy has now 'reached maturity' or lost his innocence. What is
equally evident is that the boy is unable to pass judgement on the
events and people that impinged upon his consciousness during the
year in San Fernando: 'The bus roared on and my mind went on
Mrs. Chandles, who was dying, and Mr. Chandles—so strange of
late, and now homeless; and I thought also of Mrs. Princet, and
I thought of Edwin and that dollar. I thought of all the mixed-up
things, of all the funny things, in fact, which made the year at
Romaine Street' (pp. 189–90). But if the argument so far tends to
suggest the superiority of the reader's vision to that of Francis, it
is necessary now to modify that impression.

It was suggested earlier that in *The Year in San Fernando* Anthony
is committed to involving us in the feel of a peculiarly open state
of consciousness. The consciousness is open in several senses. In
the first place it is a fluid condition, in which different times,

different events and different places coexist. This is implicit in the structure of the novel (one time, one action—what the boy endures —and one place—where the boy is) and it expresses itself again and again in the boy's capacity for simultaneous recall and experience. It is the source of the spontaneous metaphorical activity in the novel. Examples of this have already been seen, and will occur later in this discussion. But one small instance in which a curious resonance is suggested may be looked at here. During the dry season, much of Francis's time is spent watering the dried-up plants. When, late in the novel, Mr. Chandles is kind to the boy, we read: 'Joy had flowed like water through me and filled me up' (p. 141). It is worth insisting that while the correspondence between Francis's arid life and that of the plants strikes us forcibly at this point, and spreads backwards to invest the watering activity with a wishful mirroring function, there is no sign at all of a mechanical author fixing a symbol.

The boy's consciousness is further open in the sense that it is void of conventional associations between object and experience, or person and attribute:

> . . . Mrs. Chandles thought I was smiling with her. She looked strangely pleased. Her smile had big pleats on the cheeks and under the chin, and the flabby skin round her eyes were now a thousand tiny folds. Her gums showed pink and I could see the sockets and her eyes shone out like two jumbie-beads. It was strange because she looked spooky somehow, and yet she looked so sincere. I believed in her. We smiled broadly.
>
> (*The Year in San Fernando*, p. 98)

These two senses of 'open' have to be seen in relation to a third: the open consciousness responds to each experience in an immediate, excitable way. This extreme susceptibility leads the boy away from judgement, into conflicting responses to the same thing or person from situation to situation, but its most prominent mark on the novel is in the number of occasions when Francis experiences shock. The structure of the novel lends itself to this recurrent aspect of the boy's behaviour. What goes on away from the house is outside his consciousness, but those who are involved in these actions (notably Mr. Chandles) are in periodic contact with Francis.

For this reason in the novel, Mr. Chandles's return from Mayaro at midday on Saturday is a source of dread to the boy; his departure, listened for, brings great release: 'From where I was I could hear him brushing his teeth very forcibly, and I could hear the tap water running and being sucked down the drain. Then the water stopped running and I did not hear him for a little while. Then came his footsteps, and when the front door opened and shut again, my heart was pounding. The next moment the gate slammed. I was wildly glad' (p. 57). On one occasion Anthony uses Francis's unusually long absence from the house to great effect. The boy returns from his stolen visit to the sea to a terrific row between Mrs. Chandles and her son, about Marva, the woman in Mayaro. Francis disturbs his routine and keeps busy, unnecessarily watering the plants on the veranda, until the smell of the flowers makes him think about Julia:

> I stopped a little and laughed at my silly thinking and then I jumped because the front door was pushed open. Then I heard Mr. Chandles in the veranda. His footsteps were sounding double, and when he came to the steps I straightened up and stood on the side, allowing him to pass. And then, turning round with the can, my heart gave a violent thump. Mr. Chandles and Marva were going out through the gate.
>
> (*The Year in San Fernando*, p. 138)

In so far as Anthony is able to involve us in the feel of a consciousness open in the senses described, we are made to live in a world emptied of complacent existence, so that we grope with Francis towards a 'meaning' for his experiences. It is also part of the novel's technique that the reader should be able to 'recognise' some of these experiences over Francis's head. But Anthony is not interested in an ironic contrast between innocent vision and experienced interpretation. The story itself is a sordid one—a protracted squabble for the house between Mrs. Chandles and Mr. Chandles who wishes to take it away from his brother Edwin; a double love affair being conducted by Mr. Chandles, with Marva the girl in Mayaro and Julia the girl in San Fernando; and the callous treatment of the little boy in the Chandles's household. How little Anthony is concerned with a moral judgement or indignant

protest or other forms of opposition may be illustrated by the boy's
changing perspectives on Mrs. Chandles.

He first hears of her as 'old and lonely' and wanting someone
to stay with her (p. 10); his first experience of her is as a remote
voice (p. 23) and when he first sees her she is aloof and somewhat
frightening: 'Mrs. Chandles had stood up for a moment as if in-
specting me. She was very old and wrinkled and small. The next
moment she hobbled away through the door through which Mr.
Chandles had gone' (p. 24). As the novel progresses, Mrs. Chandles
emerges as demanding, cunning and nasty. After a row with Mr.
Chandles she locks herself in for the day and leaves Francis stranded
(. . . 'I wondered to myself what sort of human being this old lady
could be. She hadn't cooked. She couldn't expect that I had eaten.
She had left me to starve and like Mr. Chandles she did not care
a damn' (p. 69). Yet Francis tries to please her, and when Mrs.
Princet arrives to visit her girlhood friend, Francis enjoys Mrs.
Chandles's good humour as if her previous manner did not matter;
'My heart was light and as open as the skies in a way I had hardly
known it before. This was an Easter Day beautiful in itself and
beautiful because of Mrs. Princet, and because of the strange kind-
ness of Mrs. Chandles. I thought I should never forget it' (p. 77).
Later, when the rains come, Francis feels himself bound to an
extraordinarily winning Mrs. Chandles (pp. 111–28) who is now
like a relative. When Mrs. Chandles becomes ill and is dying, the
boy neither sentimentalizes her nor is vindictively joyful at her
imminent death, but becomes the agent of the novel's compassion.
The open consciousness of the boy allows him each time to make
an appropriate response to the Mrs. Chandles of the moment.

Putting this as a statement about character in novels, we might
say that *The Year in San Fernando* continuously leads us away from
a settled notion of the person to a more liberal view of latent and
only sporadically realized possibilities. As on the level of character,
so with respect to object and event: one of the effects of Anthony's
narrative technique in *The Year in San Fernando* is to promote a
vision for the reader in which each 'known' factor in experience
is restored to a more primordial condition of latency.

It is here I think that the astonishing originality of *The Year in*

San Fernando lies. The image of Francis, deprived, and tethered to the Chandles house (even to having a lair below the house), in a circumscribed world of which he is trying to make sense, is an image of the condition of the modern West Indian.[1] But out of this distress, Anthony has created an archetypal situation. On the one hand, there is the pattern of growth and natural progression suggested by the spontaneous metaphorical activity of the novel's language. On the other, there is the narrator's extreme openness to the possibilities of experience, marked by Francis's capacity for shock. Through the boy's consciousness Anthony induces us to make the confession of weakness, of unknowing, by which an unstable world is transformed into the flux of re-creation:

> I remembered walking through the short-cut in the heat of the dry season when the tall trees among the houses had been stricken and barren-looking and had not caught my eye at all. I remembered seeing the mango—so sensitive to heat—and their leaves had been shrivelled up and their barks peeled, as if they had surrendered and could take no more. I remembered the cedar, too, one of the giant cedars, and I had even looked at it and thought how much firewood there was here. But all those trees had sprung to life again, with the rains, and were so rich in leaf now it was unbelievable. But I had seen this myself. And now I watched the great cedars sending even more branches into the sky of the town.
>
> (*The Year in San Fernando*, p. 147)

[1] From another point of view, it may be seen as the technical problem of the West Indian artist operating in the shadow of the British nineteenth-century novel. Anthony's unpretentious jettisoning of omniscient authorial conventions is a feature left implicit in the argument.

XIII

Terrified Consciousness

The publication in 1966 of Jean Rhys's *Wide Sargasso Sea* directs attention to at least three other novels[1] by people of European origin who were born or who grew up in the islands. The four writers belong to a minority group called White West Indians. 'The English of these islands are melting away,' wrote Froude. 'Every year the census renews its warning. The rate may vary; sometimes for a year or two there may seem to be a pause in the movement, but it begins again, and is always in the same direction. The white is relatively disappearing, the black is growing; this is the fact with which we have to deal.'[2] Emancipation laid bare the spiritual failures of the planter class in the West Indies and hastened the financial ruin of many. As Froude indignantly foresaw, it portended Black majority rule: 'Were it worthwhile, one might draw a picture of the position of an English governor, with a black parliament and a black ministry. . . . No Englishman, not even a bankrupt peer, would consent to occupy such a position.'

Brown Sugar (1967), written by a West Indian of the old planter type, expresses in the form of political lampoon the extremist white reaction to the kind of situation pictured by Froude. Emtage's bitterness at the rise of the new colonial politicians prevents him from following the fortunes of Hoggy Cumberbatch with the artistic detachment that Naipaul shows in the management of Ganesh Ramsumair in *The Mystic Masseur*; and the White West Indian's reactionary political stance interferes too often, either in

[1] P. Shand Allfrey, *The Orchid House* (1953); Geoffrey Drayton, *Christopher* (1959); and J. B. Emtage, *Brown Sugar* (1966).

[2] This and the two succeeding quotations come from James Anthony Froude, *The English in the West Indies* (1887), pp. 284-5, p. 285 and p. 287.

authorial comment or in the reflections of authorially approved characters, to allow *Brown Sugar* to be a valid satire on the West Indian political situation today. It is to Froude, indeed, that we might conveniently turn for an epigraph to the bludgeonings of *Brown Sugar*: 'Their education, such as it may be, is but skin deep, and the old African superstitions lie undisturbed at the bottom of their souls. Give them independence, and in a few generations they will peel off such civilisation as they have learnt as easily and as willingly as their coats and trousers.'

The other novels by White West Indians relate to West Indian society in more interesting ways. *The Orchid House*, *Christopher* and *Wide Sargasso Sea* differ in narrative technique and theme, and while the first two are set in the twentieth century, Jean Rhys's work is located in the immediate post-Emancipation period. But the elements of continuity between them are remarkable: attitudes of the White characters to landscape and to the other side represented by the Negro masses; the functional presence of long-serving Negro nurses, and of obeah-women; the occurrence of dreams, nightmares and other heightened states of consciousness; and references to an outer socio-economic situation that is recognizable as the fall of the planter class. These elements of continuity arise not from the authors' knowledge of one another or of one another's work, but involuntarily from the natural stance of the White West Indian. With differing degrees of intensity, the three novels reflect a significant, but in these days forgotten aspect of West Indian experience:

> . . . [D]ecolonisation is always a violent phenomenon. . . . Its unusual importance is that it constitutes, from the very first day, the minimum demands of the colonised. To tell the truth, the proof of success lies in a whole social structure being changed from the bottom up. The extraordinary importance of this change is that it is willed, called for demanded. The need for this change exists in its crude state, impetuous and compelling, in the consciousness and in the lives of the men and women who are colonised. *But the possibility of this change is equally experienced in the form of a terrifying future in the consciousness of another 'species' of men and women: the colonisers.*[1]

[1] Frantz Fanon, *The Wretched of the Earth*, p. 29. My italics.

Adapting from Fanon we might use the phrase 'terrified consciousness' to suggest the White minority's sensations of shock and disorientation as a massive and smouldering Black population is released into an awareness of its power. To consider the three novels in this light is to insist upon their social relevance. To consider them at all is to bring forward some imaginative works that tend to be neglected in the demanding contexts of Black nationalism.

The Orchid House is narrated in the first person by a peripheral character, Lally—the long-serving Negro nurse of a White family in a fictional island modelled upon the actual island of Dominica. Lally's memory spans three generations. It is part of the author's purpose to convey a particular sense of the decline of the class to which the planter family belong, and to comment on the emergence of the new economic and ruling forces: the novel satirizes the power complex of Church and business in the island and it expresses, and places, the hot-house life of the White characters.

Mrs. Allfrey uses the experience of the First World War as the immediate cause of the present Master's state of shock and dope-addiction, but that this is only an intensification of something pervasive is readily apparent: Lally describes the Old Master's habit of insulating himself for 'hours and hours' in the strange shapes, scents and colours of his orchid house at L'Aromatique; and Andrew, the cousin of the Master's three daughters, is given as dying slowly of consumption, without the will to live, in a retreat called Petit Cul-de-Sac. The *malaise* in the novel thus spreads from the time of the Old Master to his grandchildren's day.

When the three sisters, Stella, Joan and Natalie, return after many years abroad, to visit their parents and their native land, they find that a strange *entente* has been established between the elderly virgin Mamselle Bosquet and their mother, both of whom love and are ministering to the Master; and as the three sisters visit Andrew, who lives in concubinage with their coloured cousin Cornelie, the reader discovers that each of the girls is in love with Andrew, as he is with them. To the sense of withdrawal we must add sexual inbreeding (a feature of enclave life which appears fleetingly in *Wide*

Sargasso Sea, and in *Christopher*, where the boy's aunt turns out to be in love with her sister's husband). The effect of the land on all this is more than implicit.

Just as their father on his return from the war expresses his sensuous feel for the native place, so each sister indulges nostalgically in the sounds and sights of a clinging land: 'In Stella's sick dreams of home the island had been a vision so exquisite that she was now almost afraid to open her eyes wide, lest she might be undeceived and cast down, or lest confirmation would stab through her like a shock. Treading the black damp earth of the bridle-path, brushed by ferns and wild begonias, experiencing the fleet glimpse of a ramier flying from the forest floor through the branches into the Prussian Blue sky, it was impossible not to look and look and drink it in like one who had long been thirsty. *It is more beautiful than a dream, for in dreams you cannot smell this divine spiciness, you can't stand in a mist of aromatic warmth and stare through jungle twigs to a spread of distant town, so distant that people seem to have no significance: you cannot drown your eyes in a cobalt sea, a sea with the blinding gold of the sun for a boundary!*' (p. 64, novelist's italics). This attitude to the West Indian landscape occurs in different moods in the three novels under consideration. In *The Orchid House*, the sensuously felt land is a function of the characters' nostalgia (and incidentally that of the author) but nostalgia is only one component of the authorial view made explicit at another point: 'Beauty and disease, beauty and sickness, beauty and horror: that was the island. A quartering breeze hurried eastward, over cotton clouds; the air was soft and hot; colour drenched everything, liquid turquoise melted into sapphire and then into emerald' (p. 75).

It is a weakness of *The Orchid House* that Mrs. Allfrey's language is not equal to the sensuous task she sets it: there are too many laboured passages of passionate declaration and too few which involve us dramatically. But the 'beauty and sickness' view of the island is the source of the novel's peculiar difference from *Wide Sargasso Sea* and *Christopher*. Reflecting on her period of service with the family, Lally (the embodiment of the traditionally devoted Negro servant) contrasts her past with her present outlook: 'When I was nurse to the little girls, I had no time to fall ill or to see how beautiful everything was. And anyhow, when you are working for white people whom you love, you can only think of those people and their wants, you hardly notice anything else. I did not even pay any attention to my own people, the black people, in those days, but now I am observing them and seeing what is happening to them. I am seeing how poor they are, and how the little babies have stomachs swollen with arrowroot and arms and legs spotted with disease' (p. 9). An awareness of the deprivation of the Black masses is used to create a shock experience for *Christopher* when the boy is confronted by a desperate beggar, and it is used to create a sense of menace and persecution in *Wide Sargasso Sea*. The politically conscious author of *The Orchid House*, however (Mrs. Allfrey was a minister in the short-lived West Indian Federation), brings opposing sides together in a political association between the educated liberal Joan, and Baptiste the Negro labour organizer. Mrs. Allfrey is tough-minded enough to allow Lally to ridicule Joan for her abstract conception of the people, and to give point to that ridicule by letting Joan's and Baptiste's first meeting with 'those vagabonds' end with some looting of the family's livestock. But it is obvious that Joan's stance is an authorially approved one. At the close of the novel, the Master dies on the air journey to a foreign hospital; Andrew, on the same flight, is heading for a sanitorium in Canada; Stella who has murdered the drug peddlar Mr. Lilipoulala hovers in New York, disaffected from her husband; Natalie continues to parade a self-protecting cynicism; the Madam and Mamselle Bosquet are left desolate; Lally turns to the holy book; but Joan, blackmailed by the Church into refraining from political activity herself, prepares for the arrival of her husband who will take her place in the front line of the struggle beside Baptiste.

The way in which Mrs. Allfrey critically combines her dirge for a decadent past with hope for a political future in the bewitching land, may be illustrated by the episode in which the ailing Andrew comes to visit Joan. The meeting takes place in the symbolic orchid house. Andrew's wish to smother himself against Joan's breasts is seen as an escapist impulse and is contrasted with Joan's desire to make him look out of the window and breathe freely. When Andrew challenges Joan with not caring for him her reply suggests the enlarged sympathy of the committed character. The whole episode is witnessed by the eavesdropping nurse:

> 'You are a poor spoilt boy,' Miss Joan said, with a sigh.
> 'A dying man', he said. 'And if you were Stella, you would cry out in protest, "Live for me!" But you don't care.'
> 'I care, but differently,' she said. I could hear the tears springing up in her throat. Some came into my own foolish old eyes then. When I wiped them away I myself gazed outwards at the scene around me, trying to see what there was in this common everyday outlook of mountains and blueness which filled my girls with passionate admiration. All I could see was a riot of gold and purple and crimson (Madam's flowering bushes) and the two huge mango trees, the shining silver from against a damp wall, and the purple shadows on far hills. Nothing unusual, except to those who had lived like exiles in grey shadows.
>
> (*The Orchid House*, p. 170)

The scene ends with the arrival of the priest, Brother Peregrine, who tears Andrew away from the girl and announces the disapproving interest of Father Toussaint in Joan's and Baptiste's political activities.

If Mrs. Allfrey's awareness of the exploitation of the people by the new merchant class and by their allies in the Church provides her White character with an antagonist and a possibility of belonging to people and place, Geoffrey Drayton turns the social situation inwards. *Christopher* draws on a time 'when all the planters went poor—and the merchants rich' (p. 48), but Drayton criticizes the new class only by implication. Ralph Stevens's disappointment at his ruined finances turns to resentment of the new rich from among whom his wife comes. The socio-economic situation, however, lies in the background as an unobtrusive source of the estrangement between Ralph Stevens and Mrs. Stevens. The novel's emphasis is on the consequences of this estrangement upon a particularly sensitive boy in an already isolated household.

Christopher is narrated in the third person by an omniscient author but narrated from the boy's point of view. Christopher lives in the isolated Great House of his unsuccessful father, and we are made to look in upon the boy's thoughts and feelings as he prowls silently about the grounds, extracting lonely pleasures from his observation of plants and trees and insects, birds and fish: 'He played God to them: it was night when his shadow fell across the pool and day when he leant away again. The insignificant fish, sand-coloured and black, easily camouflaged themselves. He did not care about them. But there were others, angel fish with yellow moons about them and spotted porgies' (p. 192). Over the course of the novel, Drayton conveys an impression of loneliness, nervous excitability and suppressed spirits. The natural surroundings are used to reflect Christopher's hot-house existence and to afford him relief. But as the following quotation from the description of Christopher's walk in his grandfather's orchid-house shows, the sensuously felt land is turned to further account: 'In beds around a small goldfish pool were more varieties of terrestrial orchid than he had ever imagined existed. Pink, purple, and bright orange, they exploded at eye-level into shapes as strange as fireworks on Guy Fawkes's day. But the orchids that hung from the roof in wire baskets, or clung to cradles of charcoal and coconut fibre, were even more startling. *Some wore long sepals that dropped below their chins like Chinamen's moustaches. Others had eyes on tall stilts and grimaced with protruding tongues'* (p. 177, my italics). The landscape is used to intensify Christopher's terror, appearing in his nightmares (see pp. 186–8) and in his day-time delirium (pp. 40–1). The troubled consciousness of the child is the substance of Drayton's novel, but *Christopher* resembles *The Orchid House* in that the distress situation is placed within an ameliorating design.

Drayton's story of a boy's growth in awareness is also an account of a White boy's growing involvement with and understanding of his Black countrymen. At first, Negroes and the Negro drumming and singing from the village are part of Christopher's nightmares: 'In the sudden silence between hymns he grew limp and cold. The shadows fell away from his bed and stood in shapeless waiting, then gathered again as he tensed once more with the drums. At some point if he were not still as death, they would close right in upon him, and at their touch he would shrivel into nothingness' (p. 29). After being taken into his parents' bed, 'he lay close to his mother and did not look up, because staring over the bottom rail of the bed were black faces with wide eyes and mouths that grinned'

(p. 31). Christopher's initial sense of the menace and mystery of his countrymen is reflected in his attitude to obeah. But his growing up and his increasing familiarity with the Negro world around him are charted by his changing attitudes to this phenomenon—from mystification and fear to childish participation and finally to an understanding of obeah in psychological terms. Drayton's use of obeah in the novel's process is more integral than the uses made by either Mrs. Allfrey or Jean Rhys; so too is his use of the Negro nurse. The novel's essaying towards *rapprochement* in the stratified society is symbolically fulfilled in the presentation of Gip as mother to the constricted White boy. When she dies at the end, the reader is left to imagine that the experience of her love will assist Christopher in finding an orientation and in developing resources to cope with the problems to come.

Wide Sargasso Sea, which is set in the 1830's, opens with the girl Antoinette and her mother living on a derelict plantation. They are avoided by the rest of the Whites and derided by the Negroes in the neighbourhood. Antoinette's mother is then saved by her marriage with a rich Englishman, Mr. Mason, only to be plunged into madness after a Negro rising. Later it is a letter from an embittered mulatto that destroys Antoinette's marriage and leads to her removal and confinement in an attic in England. It is not difficult to recognize in *Wide Sargasso Sea* the plight of some White Creoles at Emancipation, caught up between social forces and with nowhere to belong to, as the Creole Antoinette explains to her English husband when they hear the Negroes' taunting song: ' "It was a song about a white cockroach. That's me. That's what they call all of us who were here before their own people in Africa sold them to the slave traders. And I've heard English women call us white niggers. So between you I often wonder who I am and why I was ever born at all" ' (p. 102). But *Wide Sargasso Sea* is only incidentally about the dilemma of a class. Nor does it have the political drive of *The Orchid House* or the concern for *rapprochement* in the society noticeable in *Christopher*. Although the novel is much more 'historical' than *The Orchid House* or *Christopher* it creates out of its raw material an experience that we like to think of as essentially modern.

Terrified Consciousness

The Emancipation Act functions as a root of insecurity and the cause of despair. In a scene of throwaway violence, Antoinette, the torpid Creole narrator of Part I recounts the death of a ruined planter: 'One calm evening he shot his dog, swam out to sea and was gone for always. No agent came from England to look after his property—Nelson's Rest it was called—and strangers from Spanish Town rode up to gossip and discuss the tragedy' (p. 17). The new speculators and the English in the islands are presented as alien invaders, like Antoinette's husband, out of sympathy with people and place: 'Everything is too much, I felt as I rode wearily after her. Too much blue, too much purple, too much green. The flowers too red, the mountains too high, the hills too near. And the woman is a stranger' (Antoinette's husband, p. 70). The smouldering Negroes become a nightmare avenging force: '... We could not move for they pressed too close round us. Some of them were laughing and waving sticks, some of the ones at the back were carrying flambeaux and it was light as day. Aunt Cora held my hand very tightly and her lips moved but I could not hear because of the noise. And I was afraid, because I knew that the ones who laughed would be the worst. I shut my eyes and waited' (p. 42).

In *The Orchid House*, the Madam's increasing apathy, and in *Christopher*, Mrs. Stevens's constriction and sense of being at bay both suggest the dramatic possibilities of the female character as a suffering, vulnerable agent. In *Wide Sargasso Sea*, these possibilities are exploited to their limits. Through the singular narrating consciousness of Antoinette Cosway as girl and as married woman, Jean Rhys creates a pattern of alienation within alienation, distress multiplied upon distress, as first mother and then daughter are pushed towards madness and despair:

> It was too hot that afternoon. I could see the beads of perspiration on her upper lip and the dark circles under her eyes. I started to fan her, but she turned her head away. She might rest if I left her alone, she said.
> Once I would have gone back quietly to watch her asleep on the blue sofa—once I made excuses to be near her when she brushed her hair, a soft black cloak to cover me, hide me, keep me safe. But not any longer. Not any more.

> (*Wide Sargasso Sea*, p. 22)

The novel's peculiar quality lies in this, that the emotional intensities in which Jean Rhys involves us are being explored for their own sakes, and are, as in *King Lear*, in excess of any given determinant.

A sense of being menaced, literally established in relation to the rising Black population, is rendered again and again in oppressive tactile detail: 'Then the girl grinned and began to crack the knuckles of her fingers. At each crack I jumped and my hands began to sweat. I was holding some school books in my right hand and I shifted them to under my arm, but it was too late, there was a mark on the palm of my hand and a stain on the cover of the book. The girl began to laugh, very quietly . . .' (p. 49). A childhood episode when the Great House is ablaze and the Cosways about to take to flight, suggests not only Antoinette's hopeless identification with her native place and the loss of individual choice when violent socio-historical forces are at work, but also the dark image of the self that broods over the novel:

> Then, not so far off, I saw Tia and her mother and I ran to her, for she was all that was left of my life as it had been. We had eaten the same food, slept side by side, bathed by the same river. As I ran, I thought, I will live with Tia and I will be like her. Not to leave Coulibri. Not to go. Not. When I was close I saw the jagged stone in her hand but I did not see her throw it. I did not feel it either, only something wet, running down my face. I looked at her and I saw her face crumple up as she began to cry. We stared at each other, blood on my face, tears on hers. It was as if I saw myself. Like in a looking-glass.
>
> (*Wide Sargasso Sea*, p. 45)

Antoinette's childhood alienation comes over strongly in the novel as a recoil from a lush absorbent landscape suddenly gone rank and threatening:

> Our garden was large and beautiful as that garden in the Bible—the tree of life grew there. But it had gone wild. The paths were overgrown and a smell of dead flowers mixed with the fresh living smell. Underneath the tree ferns, the light was green. Orchids flourished out of reach or for some reason not to be touched. One was snaky looking, another like an octopus with long thin brown tentacles bare of leaves hanging from a twisted root. Twice a year

the octopus orchid flowered, then not an inch of tentacle showed.
It was a bell-shaped mass of white, mauve, deep purples, wonderful
to see. The scent was very sweet and strong. I never went near it.

(Wide Sargasso Sea, p. 19)

Over against this sense of recoil, however, is a revulsion from
people that turns into self-mutilation and a desire for annihilation
or transcendence:

> I took another road, past the old sugar works and the water
> wheel that had not turned for years. I went to parts of Coulibri
> that I had not seen, where there was no road, no path, no track.
> And if the razor grass cut my legs and arms I would think 'it's
> better than people'. Black ants or red ones, tall nests swarming
> with white ants, rain that soaked me to the skin—once I saw a
> snake. All better than people.
> Better. Better, better than people.
> Watching the red and yellow flowers in the sun thinking of
> nothing it was as if a door opened and I was somewhere else,
> something else. Not myself any longer.

(Wide Sargasso Sea, p. 28)

The terms in which Antoinette's childhood alienation is expressed,
and the sensuous immediacy with which it is done make it clear
that history and place, however accurately evoked, are being used
only to lend initial credibility to a mood that establishes itself in
the novel as a way of experiencing the world. In Antoinette's
nightmares at the convent school, a desire for annihilation, or death
wish, becomes associated (as in the relationship between Gerald
and Gudrun in *Women in Love*) with a magnetized anticipation of
sexual experience:

> . . . I am wearing a long dress and thin slippers, so I walk with
> difficulty, following the man who is with me and holding up the
> skirt of my dress. It is white and beautiful and I don't wish to get
> it soiled. I follow him, sick with fear but I make no effort to save
> myself; if anyone were to try to save me, I would refuse. This must
> happen. We are under the tall dark trees and there is no wind.
> 'Here?' He turns and looks at me, his face black with hatred, and
> when I see this I begin to cry. He smiles slyly. 'Not here, not yet'
> he says and I follow him weeping. Now I do not try to hold up
> my dress, it trails in the dirt, my beautiful dress.

(Wide Sargasso Sea, pp. 59–60)

Approaches

The nightmare in Jean Rhys's novel is used to point the work towards the relationship between Antoinette and her husband that is the baffling substance of Part II. For if the troubled consciousness of *Christopher* is the main subject of Drayton's novel, a distressed childhood is only the background for an even more shattering experience in *Wide Sargasso Sea*.

Having established Antoinette's desolation, Miss Rhys proceeds to marry her in Part II to the embittered younger son of an English gentleman: '... Dear Father. The thirty thousand pounds have been paid to me without question or condition. . . . I have a modest competence now. I will never be a disgrace to you or to my dear brother the son you love. No begging letters, no mean requests. None of the furtive shabby manœuvres of a younger son' (p. 70). Once again it is obvious that the novelist is building upon a type situation in island history—the marrying of Creole heiresses for their dowry by indigent younger sons—but this is used merely as a credible background 'explanation' of the twistings and turnings of love that the fiction now begins to explore. It is in this section of the novel that Jean Rhys makes maximum use of the chemical properties of a sensuous correspondent land. On the simplest level, we and the husband (with whose narration Part II opens) are made to see Antoinette's 'blank face' and protective indifference giving way to animation as they move on the long journey through virgin land to the cool remote estate in the hills, farther and farther away from the scenes of her earlier distress. At the 'sweet honeymoon house', a drugging sexuality associated with the sensuous land brings happiness at last to Antoinette (see p. 92). From the point of view of Christopher, and it is also the point of view of an obeah woman (so cleverly does Jean Rhys combine two elements seen in the novels discussed earlier), the husband has bewitched the vulnerable girl: '. . . You make love to her till she drunk with it, no rum could make her drunk like that, till she can't do without it. It's she can't see the sun any more. Only you she see' (p. 155). But although this is true, it is only one side of the author's design.

Cruel and bitter though the young man may be, the novelist's purpose is not to lead us into an easy moral judgement. It is, rather, to explore the depths of his longing and frustrations too. This is

234

reflected in the dividing of the narrative in Part II between Antoinette and the husband. But it is largely done through his changing attitudes to a seemingly changing land. At first it is menacing ('Those hills would close in on you', p. 69); then it is 'too much'; then sensuously overpowering; then charged with 'a music I had never heard before', sounding intimations of a wished-for unknown: 'It was a beautiful place—wild, untouched, above all untouched, with an alien disturbing, secret loveliness. And it kept its secret. I'd find myself thinking "What I see is nothing. I want what it *hides*—that is not nothing" ' (p. 87). By allowing the husband to identify Antoinette with the secret land in this movement of the novel, the author invests love or the sensual relationship between the characters with supreme possibilities. The husband's disappointment at the end issues in hate for Antoinette and the land:

> I hated the mountains and the hills, the rivers and the rain. I hated the sunsets of whatever colour, I hated its beauty and its magic and the secret I would never know. I hated its indifference and the cruelty which was part of its loveliness. Above all I hated her. For she belonged to the magic and the loveliness. She had left me thirsty and all my life would be thirst and longing for what I had lost before I found it.
>
> (*Wide Sargasso Sea*, p. 172)

Since for Antoinette too the land becomes a hated place, to correspond with her unhappiness and her hate for her husband, it is possible to see that the author is less interested in a specific view of the place itself than in using it as a highly subjective landscape ('It has nothing to do with either of us'), upon which the impersonal and obscure forces at work in the characters of love may be projected.

Unlike Lawrence, Jean Rhys does not see the fierce sexuality between the characters as destructive. It is, indeed, the means by which each of the broken characters can abandon defensive postures: 'If I have forgotten caution, she has forgotten silence and coldness' (p. 91). It is, however, part of the unsentimentality with which the author explores the terrified consciousness, and her fidelity to the facts of her fictional world, that the young man's extreme self-consciousness and his susceptibility to intrusions from outside love's retreat should frustrate his yearning to possess and be possessed.

In the husband's long period of vacillation following Daniel Cosway's accusations against Antoinette (pp. 162–73), Jean Rhys conveys the buffeting feel of love's uncertainties, and it is worth noting that when the decision to hate is taken it is love's tyranny rather than its absorbing power of which we are reminded: 'Even if she had wept like Magdalene it would have made no difference. I was exhausted. All the mad conflicting emotions had gone and left me wearied and empty. Sane' (p. 172). Yet, in the 'sweet honeymoon house' episodes Jean Rhys is driven to posit the value of even an annihilating love; and with less emphasis, but never beyond the characters' consciousness, a visionary love that promises to disclose itself only upon the surrender of our conventional premises in an increasingly materialistic world. The placing of these only fleeting realized possibilities within the characters' reach intensifies the pattern of deprivation, insecurity and longing Miss Rhys sees in our own time and recognizes in the historical period in which the novel is set. The kind of transference or concurrency achieved in this way is reflected in the history of the person when Antoinette's resentful firing of her tyrannical husband's house is made to parallel the Negro burning of the Great House which had lodged in her childhood memory. In *Wide Sargasso Sea* at last, the terrified consciousness of the historical White West Indian is revealed to be a universal heritage.

PART III

Precursor

XIV

The Road to *Banana Bottom*

(i) *Precursors*

It may be inferred from earlier chapters that H. G. de Lisser (1878–1944) is the type of the West Indian writer who has little to express, but plenty of sociological and historical raw material for documentary purposes. And it has been argued that the art of Tom Redcam (1870–1933) was not equal to his energetic efforts at the beginning of this century to launch in *The All Jamaica Library* a literature 'dealing directly with Jamaica and Jamaicans and written by Jamaicans'. Nevertheless, these early novelists were precursors in other senses than just a simple chronological one. Although neither used dialect for other purposes than vulgar realism and for sketches of the comic Negro, their inwardness with the folk speech and the zest with which they introduced it in their fiction mark them off from users of the lame Negro English of British convention, and place them at the beginnings of an inventive use of dialect (whose increasing stylistic flexibility and enriching contextualizations have already been illustrated).

Redcam and de Lisser are precursors in other ways. If the dilemmas Redcam poses for his fictional heroines, and his attitudes to them anticipate developments in the work of Claude McKay (especially *Banana Bottom*, 1933), and George Lamming (especially *Season of Adventure*, 1960), de Lisser's *Jane's Career* (1913) is the first novel by a West Indian to be handled by a British publisher, and the first in which the Black character is at the novel's centre.

Redcam and de Lisser in no way constituted a school or a partnership. More closely related in this manner were the Trinidadians Alfred Mendes (b. 1897) and C. L. R. James (b. 1901) who were at the centre of literary activity in Trinidad in the late 1920's and early 1930's. The tradition of social realism and compassionate protest in which they worked is a persistent feature of West Indian writing: Mendes's first novel, *Pitch Lake* (1934), which expresses the deracination of a Portuguese youth, in revulsion against the gross shop-keeping world of his father, and ill at ease in the second-generation world of rich and urban Portuguese into which he breaks, is a staggering intimation of the more polished *A House for Mr. Biswas* (1961).

Another group of precursors may be made up from among the large numbers of West Indians who emigrated to the United States in the Harlem era and before the immigration laws of the 1920's. It is difficult to assess the number of emigrants, since there was such rapid absorption in American Negro life. It is just as difficult to work out who are the lost West Indian writers. In the bibliography to *The Negro Novel in America* (revised edition, N.Y., 1965) Robert Bone writes:

> The problem of national origin arises chiefly in regard to West Indian authors. On the grounds of national consciousness I have excluded Eric Rasmussen, who was born in the Virgin Islands, who has lived sporadically in New York, but who writes of Caribbean life in *The First Night* (1951). For similar reasons I have excluded R. Archer Tracy, who was born in the British West Indies, who practised medicine for a time in Georgia, but who writes of island life in *The Sword of Nemesis* (1919). Also excluded are Thomas E. Roach and W. Adolphe Roberts, two authors of West Indian origin whose inept fantasies and historical extravaganzas reflect little knowledge of American life. Included, however, are Nella Larsen, born in the Virgin Islands and Claude McKay, born in Jamaica, because they participated actively in the Negro Renaissance and write primarily of the American scene.

To the names listed by Bone we must add: Joel Augustus Rogers, author of *From Superman to Man* (Chicago, A. Donohue and Co., printers, 1917)—the thinnest imaginable fictional excuse for a tract on the Negro race; and the more imposing name of the Guyanese, Eric Walrond (1898–1966). Walrond's collection of stories set in Panama and in the islands, *Tropic Death* (New York, Boni and Liveright, 1926), is a work of blistering imaginative power and compassion. Walrond's life of exile, journalism and vagabondage, his promise and his strange failure to produce must form an important chapter in West Indian literary history, but it is with the career of a more emblematic figure in West Indian writings that it is proposed to deal here.

Claude McKay (1890–1948) was the first Negro novelist from the West Indies, and the first of the exiles. The two facts are inseparable. Redcam and de Lisser could earn their living in Jamaica by journalism and business, and write as amateurs. McKay, a Black man, was obliged to emigrate and become a professional. This was in 1912. In the 1950's, the social situation was substantially the same in the West Indies. Although the chosen direction of the later *émigré* writers was England not the United States, McKay was the first in a long line. McKay seems to anticipate patterns in West Indian writing in another way. His early involvement with race and colour problems, and his participation in or witnessing of the international Negro movements of the early twentieth century leave their mark on his fictions: to follow his life and work in relation to one another, and in chronological order, is to raise precisely those questions of technique and significance which we have to raise in dealing with the usually committed, and personally involved West Indian writer of the present time.

(ii) *Claude McKay: Life and Poetry*

Shortly after the publication of his *Constab Ballads* (1912), McKay left Jamaica to study at Booker T. Washington's Tuskegee Institute. Once in America, however, he felt that Tuskegee was too claustrophobic and too disciplined. All that he did over the next two years (1913–14) is not known, but he took courses in Agriculture and English at Kansas State College where his English teacher introduced him to W. E. B. Du Bois's *The Souls of Black Folk*. 'The book shook me like an earthquake,'[1] he declares in his autobiography *A Long Way from Home*. After two years, according to McKay himself, 'I was gripped by the lust to wander and wonder. The spirit of the vagabond, the daemon of some poets had

[1] Claude McKay, *A Long Way from Home* (New York, 1937), p. 110. Further quotations will be followed by page references in the text.

got hold of me. I quit college' (p. 4). An unsuccessful venture at running a restaurant in a tough New York district in 1914 was followed by several years (up to 1919) as a dining-car waiter on the Pennsylvania railroad. Giving a shape to these years of vaga-bondage, McKay in his autobiography describes them as years of preparation: 'I wandered through the muck and the scum with the one objective dominating my mind. I took my menial tasks like a student who is working his way through a university. My leisure was divided between the experiment of daily living and the experi-ment of essays in writing. If I would not graduate as a bachelor of arts or science I would graduate as a poet' (p. 4). Three of the basic constituents in McKay's life may be extracted from all this: an involvement with the Negro question, vagabondage, the urge to be a writer. The first appears again and again in his poems, and dominates his first two novels. The second expressed itself as a profound *malaise* in all his work and in the roving heroes Jake and Ray in *Home to Harlem* (1928), and Banjo and Ray in *Banjo* (1929). The third, he introduced explicitly in Ray's discussions about the writer's craft and raw material in the same two novels:

> Dreams of making something with words. What could he make . . . and fashion? Could he ever create Art? Art around which vague, incomprehensible words and phrases stormed? What was art, any-way? Was it more than a clear-cut presentation of a vivid im-pression of life? Only the Russians of the late era seemed to stand up like giants in the new. Gogol, Dostoievski, Tolstoy, Chekhov, Turgeniev. When he read them now he thought: Here were ele-ments that the grand carnage swept over and touched not. The soil of life saved their roots from the fire. They were so saturated, so deep-down rooted in it.
>
> (*Home to Harlem*, p. 229)

We will have to ask the same questions about McKay himself later, but I would like to carry on with the short sketch of his life.

McKay's first opportunity as a writer came in the winter of 1918 when Frank Harris imperiously summoned him to a private inter-view at his home in Waverley Place. In an all-night session, the boastful, patronizing but appreciative Harris overwhelmed and inspired the Negro poet. The opening chapter of *A Long Way from*

Home, 'A Great Editor' (pp. 3–25), pays sincere tribute to the man who published McKay's poems in 1918. But the chapter is full of ironies:

> Suddenly he said something like this: 'I am wondering whether your sensitivity is hereditary or acquired.' I said that I didn't know, that perhaps it was just human. . . .
>
> 'Don't misunderstand me,' he said. 'Your sensitivity is the quality of your work. . . . What I mean is, the stock from which you stem—your people—are not sensitive. I saw them at close range, you know, in West Africa and the Sudan. They have plenty of the instinct of the senses, much of which we have lost. But the attitude toward life is different; they are not sensitive about human life as we are. Life is cheap in Africa. . . .'

No sooner had Harris published his exceptional Negro in *Pearson's Magazine* (September 1918) than another radical magazine took notice of McKay. It was in the pages of *The Liberator*, much to the jealous annoyance of Frank Harris, that the following sonnet first appeared in July 1919. It was McKay's response to the race riots of the same year:

> *If we must die, let it not be like hogs*
> *Hunted and penned in an inglorious spot,*
> *While round us bark the mad and hungry dogs,*
> *Making their mock at our accursed lot.*
> *If we must die, O let us nobly die,*
> *So that our precious blood may not be shed*
> *In vain; then even the monsters we defy*
> *Shall be constrained to honor us though dead!*
> *O kinsmen! we must meet the common foe!*
> *Though far outnumbered let us show us brave,*
> *And for their thousand blows deal one deathblow!*
> *What though before us lies the open grave?*
> *Like men we'll face the murderous, cowardly pack,*
> *Pressed to the wall, dying but fighting back!*[1]

The piece was reprinted in almost every pro-Negro magazine and newspaper in America. It illustrates the directness of emotion that

[1] *Selected Poems of Claude McKay*, intr. John Dewey (New York, 1953), p. 36. Other poems quoted are to be found in this edition.

is a characteristic of all McKay's verse. It was well timed and it was excellent rhetoric. Years later it was quoted by an orator, Winston Churchill, to the House of Commons when Britain feared a German invasion.[1]

Financed by a bizarre idealist named Gray (he was 'lank and limp and strangely gray-eyed and there was a grayness in his personality like the sensation of dry sponge') McKay himself travelled to England in late 1919 and remained there suffering, by his account, until late 1920. For a short period he was a reporter on Sylvia Pankhurst's the *Workers Dreadnought*,[2] but the visit to the Mother Country was a disappointment to the Black Briton. The 'fog of London was like a heavy suffocating shroud. It not only wrapped you around but entered into your throat like a strangling nightmare'. Not only the climate, '. . . the English as a whole were a strangely unsympathetic people, as coldly chilling as their English fog' (pp. 66–7).

Meanwhile, McKay the poet was still in training. In London he wrote the nostalgic 'Flame-heart' ('So much have I forgotten in ten years'), and had several poems published in C. K. Ogden's the *Cambridge Magazine*.[3] Through Ogden, his first collection since *Constab Ballads* (1912) was published with a hypocritical preface by I. A. Richards.[4] The poems in *Spring in New Hampshire* (1920) reveal nostalgia for the Jamaican homeland ('The Tropics in New York' and 'I shall Return'), nostalgia for a vague ancestral place ('Outcast'), protest on the racial level, and love poems expressing a sense of loss ('A Memory of June'). But McKay didn't remain in London to read the reviews. In the middle of Pankhurst's

[1] Mentioned by Stephen H. Bronz in *Roots of Negro Racial Consciousness* (New York, 1964), p. 74.

[2] Published between 28th July 1917 and 14th June 1924. Pankhurst had previously run the *Woman's Dreadnought* as part of her suffragette activities.

[3] 'Spring in New Hampshire' and 'The Tired Worker' were reprinted (from *The Liberator*) in the *Cambridge Magazine* (6th September 1919), p. 962. A letter from F. Marwick the following week gave biographical information and quoted poems from McKay's first volume *Songs of Jamaica* (1912). Further poems by McKay appeared in the *Cambridge Magazine* in 1920 after McKay himself had arrived in England.

[4] Published by Grant Richards Ltd. There does not seem in fact to have been an American edition advertised as to be published simultaneously by Alfred A. Knopf. But most of the poems were reprinted in the United States in *Harlem Shadows* (1922).

troubles with the police, the poet took off for the United States. On the returning ship he read what *The Spectator* had to say about *Spring in New Hampshire*. The reviewer was not only misinformed about McKay's identity, he was prejudiced in the usual way: 'Perhaps the ordinary reader's first impulse in realising that the book is by an American Negro is to inquire into its good taste. Not until we are satisfied that his work does not overstep the barriers which a not quite explicable but deep instinct in us is ever alive to maintain can we judge it with genuine fairness. Mr. Claude McKay never offends our sensibilities. His love of poetry is clear of the hint which would put our racial instinct against him, whether we would or not.'[1] McKay passed the test, but even in a favourable review the Negro poet was less poet than Negro.

In America, he could be nothing else. As an associate editor of *The Liberator* during the next two years he mixed with White radicals and the Harlem intelligentsia. But after a brief attempt with some Negro leaders in 1921 to influence Marcus Garvey to make his flourishing movement as much part of the class struggle, as of the race struggle, McKay seems to have cooled towards institutionalized protest of any kind. *Harlem Shadows* (N.Y., 1922), his first American collection, reveals that his concern for the Negro in America, and for the race, were as personally felt as ever.

In *Harlem Shadows*, McKay is a poet of social and racial protest, but he is above all the romantic, the poet of nostalgia and yearning. Protest and nostalgia mingle in the troubled sonnet 'Outcast', which swings from the moving Wordsworthian simplicity of 'Something in me is lost, forever lost/Some vital thing has gone out of my heart' to the self-pitying pose of a Byronic figure: 'And I must walk the way of life a ghost/Among the sons of earth a thing apart'. In the final couplet, protest, nostalgia for the 'pays natal', and the personal *malaise* which is the fundamental McKay experience all come together,

> For I was born, far from my native clime
> Under the white man's menace, out of time.

[1] *The Spectator*, 23rd October 1920.

'For I was born . . . out of time' is the feeling which McKay objectifies brilliantly in his finest poem 'The Harlem Dancer':

> *Applauding youths laughed with young prostitutes*
> *And watched her perfect, half-clothed body sway;*
> *Her voice was like the sound of blended flutes*
> *Blown by black players upon a picnic day.*
> *She sang and danced on gracefully and calm,*
> *The light gauze hanging loose about her form;*
> *To me she seemed a proudly-swaying palm*
> *Grown lovelier for passing through a storm.*
> *Upon her swarthy neck black shiny curls*
> *Profusely fell; and, tossing coins in praise*
> *The wine flushed, bold-eyed boys and even the girls,*
> *Devoured her with eager, passionate gaze:*
> *But looking at her falsely-smiling face,*
> *I knew herself was not in that strange place.*

The well-selected details are the observations of the appreciative *habitué* of Harlem. The objectified dancer is an image of McKay's own condition, an identification for which we are prepared by lines 7 and 8, and of which we are convinced in the final rhyming couplet. As we will see in the account of the novels, the sense of being born out of time never allowed McKay or his heroes to rest.

The year of the publication of *Harlem Shadows* (1922) was the year he resigned from *The Liberator*, the year when the sudden re-entry of 'a woman to whom I had been married seven years before' turned McKay's desire to be footloose and wandering again into a necessity. Attending the Fourth Congress of the Communist International (Moscow, 1922) the Negro poet enjoyed the wondering friendliness of the folk and the calculated lionization of the Bolsheviks. He didn't object to any of it: 'Never in my life did I feel prouder of being an African . . . I was carried along on a crest of sweet excitement . . . I was the first Negro to arrive in Russia since the revolution . . . I was like a black ikon' (p. 168). He made the most of it, but it did not go to his head. The fabulous pilgrimage over, McKay spent the ten years between 1923 and 1934 working and wandering in the varied worlds of France, Spain and Morocco. In these restless years were produced three novels, a collection of stories[1] and very probably part of the autobiographical *A Long Way from Home.*

(iii) *The Novels of Claude McKay*

Home to Harlem (1928) is set in the group life of the American Black Belt; *Banjo* (1929), more loosely constructed, assembles a pan-Negro cast on the Marseilles waterfront called the Ditch. In both novels, McKay's preoccupation with the place of the Negro in white civilization takes the form of a celebration of Negro qualities on the one hand, and attacks upon the civilized white world on the other:

> For civilisation had gone out among these native, earthy people, had despoiled them of their primitive soil, had uprooted, en-chained, transported and transformed them to labor under its laws, and yet lacked the spirit to tolerate them within its walls.
>
> That this primitive child, this kinky-headed, big-laughing black boy of the world, did not go down and disappear under the serried crush of trampling white feet; that he managed to remain on the scene, not worldly wise, not 'getting there', yet not machine-made nor poor-in-spirit like the regimented creatures of civilisation, was baffling to civilised understanding. Before the grim, pale rider-down of souls he went his careless way with a primitive hoofing and a grin.
>
> *(Banjo*, p. 314)

The cultural dualism towards which McKay developed raises problems of three kinds for the artist. Characterization of the primitive Negro would run close to the White man's stereotype; the polemic novelist might be tempted into passionate statement at the expense of imaginative rendering; and the celebration of one race in exclusive terms could harden into a denial of the possibilities of life and of our common humanity.

Home to Harlem and *Banjo* are not exempt from weaknesses along these lines. But the novels are more dramatic and more tentative than they are usually held to be. In a significant passage in his

---

[1] *Home to Harlem* (1928); *Banjo* (1929); *Gingertown* (stories, 1932) and *Banana Bottom* (1933). All were published by Harper and Brothers, New York and London.

autobiography, McKay wrote that it was impossible for him to take D. H. Lawrence seriously as a social thinker. Yet Lawrence was the modern writer he preferred above any: 'In D. H. Lawrence I found confusion—all of the ferment and torment and turmoil, the hesitation and hate and alarm . . . and the incertitude of this age, and the psychic and romantic groping for a way out.'[1] I take this as an unconscious declaration of affinity, and I wish to see *Home to Harlem* and *Banjo* as part of a 'romantic groping for a way out'. The life was to end in disillusion, poverty and despair, with a pathetic conversion to a scavenging Roman Catholicism in 1944: the art was to achieve a splendid resolution in the serene pages of *Banana Bottom* (1933), where a surer grasp of technique matches a sudden access to understanding.

Disillusioned by the 'white folks' war', and seized by loneliness after two years in England, Jake Brown of *Home to Harlem* (1928) returns to the joyful place where he immediately strikes it up with Felice a 'little brown girl' at a cabaret called the Baltimore. His exultation at being back in sweet-sweet Harlem where there are such 'pippins for the pappies' (p. 14) carries over into authorial amplification: 'Oh to be in Harlem again after two years away. The deep-dyed colour, the thickness, the closeness of it. The noises of Harlem. The sugared laughter. The honey-talk on its streets. And all night long, ragtime and "blues" playing somewhere . . . singing somewhere, dancing somewhere! Oh the contagious fever of Harlem. Burning everywhere in dark-eyed Harlem. . . . Burning in Jake's sweet blood . . .' (p. 15). The disappearance of Felice is the device by which McKay gives the novel the appearance of a plot, allowing Jake to taste other joys in Harlem while he looks for the missing girl:

> . . . The pianist was a slight-built, long-headed fellow. His face shone like anthracite, his eyes were arresting, intense, deep yellow slits. He seemed in a continual state of swaying excitement, whether or not he was playing.
> They were ready, Rose and the dancer-boy. The pianist began, his eyes towards the ceiling in a sort of ecstatic dream. Fiddler, saxophonist, drummer and cymbalist seemed to catch their inspiration from him. . . .

[1] *A Long Way from Home*, p. 247.

The Road to 'Banana Bottom'

They danced, Rose and the boy. Oh they danced! *An exercise of rhythmical exactness for two. There was no motion she made that he did not imitate.* They reared and pranced together, smacking palm against palm, working knee against knee, grinning with real joy. They shimmied, breast to breast, bent themselves far back and shimmied again. Lifting high her short skirt and showing her green bloomers, Rose kicked. . . .

And the pianist! At intervals his yellow eyes, almost bloodshot swept the cabaret with a triumphant glow, gave the dancers a caressing look, and returned to the ceiling. *Lean, smart fingers beating barbaric beauty out of a white frame.* Brown bodies, caught up in the wild rhythm, wiggling and swaying in their seats.

(*Home to Harlem*, pp. 92–4)

In the first of the italicized phrases, McKay's power of expression flags, and in the second there is a self-conscious straining for a polemic effect. But there is something to be said for this passage. Impressionistic syntax creates a rhythmic quality; the vividly seen pianist's transport is all the more intense for being confined by the ceiling; and McKay's tactic of shifting the focus from pianist to dance and back to the inspired medium communicates the infectious quality of the music. The description is not an exotic *tour de force*: the capacity for joy and life which McKay projects as Harlem's priceless instinctive possession is the novel's central value. McKay is not always as tactful as this in his presentation of Harlem's and the Negro's rhythmic qualities. Sometimes indeed there is no presentation, only authorial romanticizing, as in the following passage from another point in the novel:

The piano-player had wandered off into some dim, far-away ancestral source of music. Far, far away from music-hall syncopation and jazz, he was lost in some sensual dream of his own. No tortures, banal shrieks and agonies. Tum-tum . . . tum-tum . . . tum-tum. The notes were naked, acute, alert. Like black youth burning naked in the bush. Love in the deep heart of the jungle. . . . The sharp spring of a leopard from a leafy limb, the snarl of a jackal, green lizards in amorous play, the flight of a plumed bird, and the sudden laughter of mischievous monkeys in their green homes. Tum-tum . . . tum-tum . . . tum-tum . . . tum-tum. . . . Simple-clear and quivering. Like a primitive dance of war or of love . . . the marshalling of spears or the sacred frenzy of a phallic celebration.

(*Home to Harlem*, pp. 196–7)

249

And in another jazz passage, from *Banjo*, McKay loses all artistic instinct to make his point against civilization:

> Shake to the loud music of life playing to the primeval round of life. Rough rhythm of darkly-carnal life. Strong surging flux of profound currents forced into shallow channels. Play that thing! One movement of the thousand movements of the eternal life-flow. Shake that thing! In the face of the shadow of Death. Treacherous hand of murderous Death, lurking in sinister alleys, where the shadows of life dance, nevertheless to their music of life. Death over there! Life over here! Shake down Death and forget his commerce, his purpose, his haunting presence in a great shaking orgy. Dance down the Death of these days, the Death of these ways in shaking that thing. Jungle jazzing, Orient wriggling, civilised stepping. Shake that thing! Sweet dancing thing of primitive joy, perverse pleasure, prostitute ways, many-colored variations of the rhythm, savage, barbaric, refined—eternal rhythm of the mysterious, magical, magnificent—the dance divine of life. . . . Oh, Shake That Thing!
>
> (*Banjo*, pp. 57–8)

Jake, like Banjo, is an exponent of values McKay sometimes artlessly propagandizes. So I would like to turn for a while from problems of the authorial voice to problems of characterization.

'*Home to Harlem* for the most part nauseates me, and after the dirtier parts of its filth I feel distinctly like taking a bath. . . . It looks as though McKay has set out to cater for that prurient demand on the part of white folk for a portrayal in Negroes of that utter licentiousness which conventional civilisation holds white folk back from enjoying—if enjoyment it can be called.'[1] So wrote the high-minded W. E. B. du Bois. Reviewing *Banjo*, another Coloured conservative advised: 'If you like filth, obscenity, pimpery, prostitution, pan-handling and more filth you ought to be enthusiastic about *Banjo*.'[2] Although he celebrates the unfettered joy that lower-class Negro life has to offer, McKay does not sentimentalize either the Ditch or Harlem. This is implicit in the characterization of Jake. Jake's capacity for a life of sensations is his uncorrupted legacy, but McKay also makes him a romantic spirit yearning for

[1] W. E. B. du Bois in *Crisis Magazine*. Quoted by Stephen Bronz in *Roots of Negro Consciousness*, p. 84.

[2] Dewey Jones in the Chicago *Defender*, quoted by Bronz, p. 84.

transcendence. 'I love you. I ain't got no man,' says Congo Rose, and Jake yields like Tom Jones. But the affair proves unsatisfactory because 'her spirit lacked that charm and verve, the infectious joy of his little lost brown. He sometimes felt that she had no spirit at all—that strange elusive something that he felt in himself, some-times here, sometimes there, roaming away from him . . . wandering to some unknown new port, caught a moment by some romantic rhythm, color, face, passing through cabarets, saloons, speakeasies, and then returning to him. . . . The little brown had something of that in her, too. That night he had felt a reaching out and a marriage of spirits' (pp. 41–2). Jake stands for the best that Harlem has to offer—he is its natural exponent, but by the end of Part I his need for relief has been established: 'Jake had taken the job on the railroad just to break the hold that Harlem had upon him. When he quitted Rose he felt that he ought to get right out of the atmo-sphere. If I don't get away from it for a while it'll sure git me he mused' (p. 125).

In Part II of *Home to Harlem*, McKay introduces Ray, a Haitian intellectual with literary ambitions, a man exiled from his native island by the American occupation. Two processes begin at this point. The first is the education of Jake. When Ray honours both Wordsworth and Toussaint by quoting the sonnet on the great revolutionary:

> Jake felt like one passing through a dream, vivid in rich, varied colors. It was revelation beautiful in his mind. That brief account of an island of savage black people, who fought for collective liberty and were struggling to create a culture of their own. A romance of his race, just down there by Panama. How strange!
>
> Jake was very American in spirit and shared a little of that comfortable Yankee contempt for poor foreigners. And as an American Negro he looked askance at foreign niggers. Africa was a jungle and Africans bushniggers, cannibals. And West Indians were monkey-chasers. But now he felt like a boy who stands with the map of the world in colors before him, and feels the wonder of the world.
>
> (*Home to Harlem*, p. 134)

Although McKay does not develop Jake's educative process farther than race consciousness, the character remains conscious of a deficiency to the end, and becomes critical of his way of living. In the mainly North American criticism of McKay's work, it is customary to blur the circumstantial distinctions between Jake and Banjo as fictional characters and concentrate on their identical symbolic functions. Bone,[1] for instance, describes Jake as 'the typical McKay protagonist—the primitive Negro untouched by the decay of Occidental civilisation . . . Jake represents pure instinct'. This implies a simple-minded view of the connection between authorial philosophy and characterization, especially hazardous in a case like McKay's where the philosophy is changing, and changing so often as a result of clarifications achieved through fictional airing. But the mistaken view begins with and depends on misreading. After meeting Ray's girl Agatha and admiring her poise and her simple charm, Jake becomes reflective. The passage is explicit:

> His thoughts wandered away back to his mysterious little brown of the Baltimore. She was not elegant and educated, but she was nice. Maybe if he found her again—it would be better than just running wild around like that! Thinking honestly about it, after all, he was never satisfied, flopping here and sleeping there. It gave him a little cocky pleasure to brag of his conquests to the fellows around the bar. But after all the swilling and boasting, it would be a thousand times nicer to have a little brown woman of his own to whom he could go home and be his simple self with. Lay his curly head between her brown breasts and be fondled and be the spoiled child that every man loves sometimes to be when he is all alone with a woman. *That* he could never be with the Madame Lauras. They expected him always to be a prancing he-man. Maybe it was the lack of a steady girl that kept him running crazy round. Boozing and poking and rooting around, jolly enough all right, but not altogether contented.
>
> (*Home to Harlem*, p. 212)

Although Jake is easy-living, it is in the novel *Banjo* that we meet the complete insulated vagabond hero, the folk artist linked by his instrument to the improvising unconventional world of jazz. The meeting with Agatha inspires Jake to articulate his discontent with the vagabonding life. It is in reaction to the same girl, however, that Ray recognizes the menace of respectability: 'He was afraid

[1] Robert A. Bone, *The Negro Novel in America* (N.Y., 1965), p. 69.

that some day the urge of the flesh and the mind's hankering after the pattern of respectable comfort might chase his high dreams out of him and deflate him to the contented animal that was a Harlem nigger strutting his stuff. "No happy-nigger strut for me" he would mutter when the feeling for Agatha worked like a fever in his flesh. *He saw destiny working in her large, dream-sad eyes, filling them with the passive softness of resignation to life, and seeking to encompass and yoke him down as just one of the thousand niggers of Harlem. And he hated Agatha and, for escape, wrapped himself darkly in self-love'* (p. 264).

Ray's quest for a *modus vivendi* is the second process that begins with the meeting of Ray and Jake. Ray in *Home to Harlem* and in *Banjo* is a portrait of the Negro intellectual in western civilization. He is a figure of *malaise*, and through his tortured consciousness, a set of social and racial dilemmas are expressed. There can be little doubt that the discomfort and dilemmas of McKay himself inform the presentation of the fictional character in direct ways. But there are still distinctions to be made. A look at the chapter 'Snowstorm in Pittsburgh' from *Home to Harlem* will facilitate matters. Jake and Ray have just returned from an all-night bar:

> Jake fell asleep as soon as his head touched the dirty pillow. Below him Ray lay in his bunk, tormented by bugs and the snoring cooks. The low-burning gaslight flickered and flared upon the shadows. The young man lay under the untellable horror of a dead-tired man who wills to sleep and cannot.
>
> In other sections of the big barn building the faint chink of coins touched his ears. Those men gambling the hopeless Pittsburgh night away did not disturb him. They were so quiet. It would have been better, perhaps, if they were noisy.
>
> (*Home to Harlem*, pp. 151–2)

This is a precisely rendered description of sleeplessness, and from it we move into the troubled consciousness of the character counting up to a million, thinking of love and then thinking about home:

> ... There was the quiet, chalky-dusty street and, jutting out over it, the front of the house that he had lived in. The high staircase built on the outside, and pots of begonias and ferns on the landing. ... All the flowering things he loved, red and white and pink hibiscus, mimosas, rhododendrons, a thousand glowing creepers,

climbing and spilling their vivid petals everywhere, and bright-buzzing humming-birds and butterflies. . ..

(Home to Harlem, pp. 152–3)

It is not difficult to recognize that McKay's own nostalgia is being expressed here, but it is relevant as part of the character's mental effort to induce sleep. The author's sense of the dramatic situation is strong, moreover, so there is no question of this plausible nostalgia getting out of hand:

> . . . Intermittently the cooks broke their snoring with masticating noises of their fat lips, like animals eating. Ray fixed his eyes on the offensive bug-bitten bulk of the chef. These men claimed kinship with him. They were black like him. Man and nature put them in the same race. . . . Yet he loathed every soul in that great barrack-room except Jake. Race. . . . Why should he have and love a race? Races and nations were things like skunks, whose smells poisoned the air of life.

(Home to Harlem, pp. 153–4)

Thus smoothly do we move with the character, and with the implied author, from particular sleeplessness and particular reactions to people, to larger questions of race and nation. But even at this point, McKay's sense of Ray as a particular character with a particular past, and his awareness of his fictional creature as a troubled being remain in tactical control. Ray's thoughts about race and nation dart back and forth, with his own island always in his mind. The American occupation has thrown him into being one with the 'poor African natives' and 'Yankee "coons"', but he agitatedly slips out of such an affinity only to be faced again by the returning thought:

> . . . Some day Uncle Sam might let go of his island and he would escape from the clutches of that magnificent monster of civilisation and retire behind the natural defenses of his island, where the steam-roller of progress could not reach him. Escape he would. He had faith. He had hope. But, oh, what would become of that great mass of black swine. . . . Sleep! Oh, sleep! . . . But all his senses were burning wide awake. Thought was not a beautiful and re-assuring angel. . . . No. It was suffering. . . .

(Home to Harlem, pp. 155–6)

McKay does not hesitate to use Ray as a means of grinding the authorial axe, but the grinding is done by a character convincingly presented as a man aggrieved, and as a man debating with himself.

The effect of such a dramatic presentation may be felt in the well-known chapter 15. Here, Ray thinks like McKay about the art and raw material of fiction, supplies what is virtually a bibliography of intellectual influences upon McKay, and then registers the two events that shook McKay's life—'the great mass carnage in Europe' and 'the great mass revolution in Russia'. Ray, we are told, realized that he had lived through an era:

> And also he realised that his spiritual masters had not crossed with him into the new. He felt alone, hurt, neglected, cheated, almost naked. But he was a savage, even though he was a sensitive one, and did not mind nakedness. What had happened? Had they re-fused to come or had he left them behind? Something had hap-pened. But it was not desertion nor young insurgency. It was death. Even as the last scion of a famous line prances out his day and dies and is set aside with his ancestors in their cold whited sepulcher, so had his masters marched with flags and banners flying all their wonderful, trenchant, critical satirical, mind-sharpening, pity-evoking constructive ideas of ultimate social righteousness into the vast international cemetery of the century.
>
> (*Home to Harlem*, pp. 226–7)

A reading of McKay's autobiography *A Long Way from Home* might indeed suggest that Ray is nothing but the author's mouth-piece, but here it is necessary to make a theoretical distinction of some consequence. We have to discriminate between, on the one hand, a character who is simply an author's mouthpiece or embodi-ment of a consciously held theory, and on the other, an independent fictional character who happens to be modelled upon an author's own life. Ray in *Home to Harlem* is modelled upon McKay. Because Ray's dilemmas are presented, crucially, in dramatic terms in the novel itself, the authorial urgency intensifies that of the character. It is like hitting with the spin. There is a loss of concentration in the next novel.

Banjo has even less of a plot than *Home to Harlem*: the sub-title declares it to be 'a story without a plot'. The setting on the Mar-seilles waterfront is less cohesive than the Harlem of the previous novel. The group of international Negroes McKay assembles hardly live together—they meet like delegates at a conference for the Negro stateless. Long stretches of the novel are turned over to debating and discussing Negro questions: Senghor is mentioned a few times, and Garvey haunts the conversations, but every shade of Negro and every shade of Negro opinion is represented. The loss of concentration on characters is met by a heavy reliance upon speech-making.

When a Martiniquan student refuses to accompany Ray to a bar on the grounds that there are likely to be too many Senegalese there, Ray attacks him for despising his racial roots:

> . . . 'In the modern race of life we're merely beginners. If this Renaissance we're talking about is going to be more than a sporadic and scabby thing, we'll have to get down to our racial roots to create it.'
>
> 'I believe in a racial renaissance', said the student, 'but not in going back to savagery.'
>
> 'Getting down to our native roots and building up from our own people', said Ray, 'is not savagery. It is culture.'
>
> 'I can't see that,' said the student.
>
> 'You are like many Negro intellectuals who are belly-aching about race,' said Ray. 'What's wrong with you all is your education. You get a white man's education and learn to despise your own people. You read biased history of the whites conquering the colored and primitive peoples, and it thrills you just as it does a white boy belonging to a great white nation.'
>
> (*Banjo*, pp. 200–1)

There are another two hundred and eighty words in Ray's speech, in which he advises the Martiniquan to read Russian novels, to learn about Gandhi, and to be humble before the simple beauty of the African dialects instead of despising them. This does not bring about a change in the Martiniquan's life. But he does not appear in the novel again.

There are easier examples to discredit, where Ray's views are more controversial, and where there is not even the pretence of a living situation. This seems to be a fair selection, however, and I want to argue from it that even when we agree with what McKay wishes to declare, and when we share the author's passion, it is still difficult for us as readers of fiction to accept such blatant manipulating of character and event as occurs in the novel. It is a central weakness that McKay uses Ray to state authoritatively points of view which do not strictly arise out of the presented life of the novel.

Another weakness becomes apparent when we consider the passages in which McKay takes us into the consciousness of the fictional character. A good example comes at the end of the novel when Ray's attitude to Banjo's method of raising funds becomes the occasion of a two-thousand-word authorial reportage of Ray's thoughts, culminating in McKay's theory of cultural dualism or legitimate difference:

> The more Ray mixed in the rude anarchy of the lives of the black boys—loafing, singing, bumming, playing, dancing, loving, working—and came to a realisation of how close-linked he was to them in spirit, the more he felt that they represented more than he or the cultured minority the irrepressible exuberance and legendary vitality of the black race. And the thought kept him wondering how that race would fare under the ever tightening mechanical organisation of modern life. . . .
>
> The grand mechanical march of civilisation had levelled the world down to the point where it seemed treasonable for an advanced thinker to doubt that what was good for one nation or people was also good for another. But as he was never afraid of testing ideas, so he was not afraid of doubting. All peoples must struggle to live, but just as what was helpful for one man might be injurious to another, so it might be with whole communities of peoples.
>
> (*Banjo*, pp. 324–5)

The reverie is only slightly motivated, and is so prolonged that it loses sight of the immediate situation (Banjo waiting for a reply to a question), but what really matters here is that Ray's consciousness is entered into not for the sake of creating a sense of that consciousness but only as a variation on speech-making. McKay's view of himself as a misfit in White civilization had lent itself in *Home to Harlem* to the presentation of a tortured, uncertain mind. The key to the novel's dramatic interest lay in the sensed need for something more than what the life of the boys had to offer: 'Life burned in Ray perhaps more intensely than in Jake. Ray felt more and more and his range was wider, and he could not be satisfied with the easy, simple things that sufficed for Jake' (p. 265). By the time that *Banjo* comes to be written, McKay's position has changed: the life of vagabondage is desperately held to be the only preservative value in a decadent White world.

The belief is successfully embodied in the presentation of Banjo, the protagonist. He dominates the all too brief first part of the novel in which McKay sets the scene and introduces the tramps of the sea-front: 'It was as if all the derelicts of all the seas had drifted up here to sprawl out the days in the sun' (p. 18). From the mimetically impressive opening sentence, however, McKay asserts life: 'Heaving along from side to side, like a sailor on the unsteady deck of a ship, Lincoln Agrippa Daily, familiarly known as Banjo, patrolled the magnificent length of the great breakwater of Marseilles, a banjo in his hand' (p. 3). Through the spontaneity, improvisation, and unconventionality of Banjo and his beach boys, McKay suggests the rhythmic quality of unquenchable life. But Banjo the folk artist of the jazz world is presented circumstantially as a person, and it is this which allows us to accept him as standing for a way of life. The supremacy of the new faith is made evangelically clear when Jake is reintroduced to spell out his allegiance. He is married to Felice but has taken a seaman's job: ' "I soon finds out . . . that it was no joymaking business for a fellah like you' same old Jake, chappie, to go to work reg'lar ehvery day and come home ehvery night to the same old pillow. Not to say that Felice hadn't kep' it freshin' up and sweet-smelling all along. . . . But it was too much home stuff, chappie" ' (pp. 292–3).

The new faith obviously turns Ray into a zealous preacher. But at one moment, the character affirms to himself that 'civilisation would not take the love of color, joy, beauty, vitality and nobility out of *his* life and make him like one of the poor mass of its pale creatures. . . . Rather than lose his soul, let intellect go to hell' (pp. 164–5). And at another point the same character is represented thus in authorial reportage: 'From these boys he could learn how to live—how to exist as a black boy in a white world and rid his conscience of the used-up hussy of white morality. He could not scrap his intellectual life and be entirely like them. He did not want

or feel any urge to "go back" that way . . . Ray wanted to hold on
to his intellectual acquirements without losing his instinctive gifts.
The black gifts of laughter and melody and simple sensuous feelings and responses' (pp. 322–3). These two statements suggest that
McKay is still in doubt. But none of this uncertainty informs the
characterization. Ray comes over as a learned interpreter of Negro
values, and a critic of Babylon. The author's unresolved tension,
and his unhappiness with the authoritative figure he has created are
allowed to break in at the end of the novel, however, when Ray
and Banjo set off together on a life of vagabondage. ' "Youse a book
fellah . . . and you' mind might tell you to do one thing and them
books persweahs you to do another." ' There is fulfilment in every
sense in the new world of *Banana Bottom*.

Home to Harlem and *Banjo* had ended with the departures of
exiles. *Banana Bottom* begins with the return of a native. The
characters of the first two novels extracted a living on the edges
of society, the characters of the third are rooted in a landscape. The
violent debates of the earlier works, in which there is only a thin
line between author and character are now succeeded by the con-
trolled idyllic tone of a distanced narrator. The central character
is not a figure of *malaise* like Ray of the preceding novels, nor does
McKay find it necessary to externalize *malaise* in the form of a
complementary but separated pair such as Jake and Ray or Banjo
and Ray. The polarized pair of heroes of the first two novels are
replaced by a single heroine. Bita Plant, the daughter of a Jamaican
peasant, is brought up by the Reverend Malcolm Craig and his wife
Priscilla. After seven years abroad at an English University and on
the Continent, Bita returns to her native land. *Banana Bottom* tells
the story of how she gradually strips away what is irrelevant in her
English upbringing, and how she marries Jubban the strong silent
drayman in her father's employ. To put it in this way is to make
it clear at once that McKay's theme is still cultural dualism. The
differences between *Banana Bottom* and the other novels are differences in art. Bita Plant is the first achieved West Indian heroine and
Banana Bottom is the first classic of West Indian prose.

The action of the novel alternates between the village of Banana

Precursor

Bottom where Bita spends her early years, and the adjoining town of Jubilee where she is groomed by the Craigs; and McKay makes unobtrusive use of the nominal difference between the two in order to symbolize Bita's final liberation and embrace of the folk. But our first impression is of the community:

> *That* Sunday when Bita Plant played *the* old straight piano to the singing of *the* coloured Choristers in the beflowered school-room was the most exciting in the history of Jubilee.
>
> Bita's homecoming was an eventful week for the folk of the tiny country town of Jubilee and the mountain village of Banana Bottom. For she was the only native Negro girl they had ever known or heard of who had been brought up abroad. Perhaps the only one in the island. Educated in England—the mother country as it was referred to by the Press and official persons.
>
> (*Banana Bottom*, p. 1)

The communal memory is of specific times and specific events: '*That* Sunday when Bita played'; it has its landmarks, its familiar items and its own institutions—'*the* . . . schoolroom . . . *the* . . . piano' and 'the Coloured Choristers'. The private experience 'Bita's homecoming' is also an event for the folk. In the second paragraph the authorial voice glides mimetically into the communal voice. From these opening moments of the novel, McKay steadily builds up a sense of a way of life. Its constitutive elements are tea-meeting, picnic, market, harvest festival, pimento picking, house-parties and ballad-making. Its people range themselves across an ordered spectrum of swiftly and vividly drawn individuals: Squire Gensir the Englishman in exile; Reverend and Mrs. Craig, the missionaries with a civilizing purpose; Belle Black, the village free-living maid, and her friend Yoni Legge; Tack Tally and Hopping Dick, the village dandies; Kojo Jeems and Nias Black, drummers; Phibby Patroll the roving gossip; Herald Newton Day the pompous theological student, local boy being groomed by the Craigs for stardom with Bita; Crazy Bow the wandering flute boy; the Lambert brood on the weary road to whiteness; the mulatto Glengleys, and Wumba the obeah man.

The main action takes place against a background buzzing with life and implication. But it is more than this. Bita belongs to a sustaining community just as a Naipaul character sticks incongruously out of a crowded depressing canvas. It is because Bita belongs, and because the community is realized as having spontaneous values of its own that we can credit her fictional process. The incident with Crazy Bow which leads to Bita's adoption by the Craigs illustrates how McKay enriches the background life of the community by drawing out one of the background characters to perform a specific significant function and then letting him slip back into his independent life again. The incident also illustrates how McKay at last integrates music (a recurrent vitalizing element in the other novels) into the action and meaning of the novel without signs of straining.

In what looked at first only like a charming anecdote in the novel, McKay establishes Crazy Bow as the village's wandering musician: 'Unheralded he would thrust his head into the doorway of a house where any interesting new piece of music was being played' (p. 6). Breaking into the village choir rehearsals, he would not be induced 'to participate in a regular manner . . . but no one wanted to stop him, everybody listened with rapture' (p. 6). The account continues:

> He was more tractable at the tea meetings, the unique social events of the peasantry, when dancing and drinking and courting were kept up from nightfall till daybreak. Then Crazy Bow would accept and guzzle pint after pint of orange wine. And he would wheedle that fiddle till it whined and whined out the wildest notes, with the dancers ecstatically moving their bodies together to follow every twist of the sound. And often when all was keyed high with the music and the liquor and the singing and dancing Crazy Bow would suddenly drop the fiddle and go.
>
> (*Banana Bottom*, p. 7)

To be noted here is that McKay has dispensed with the hyphenated words, the impressionistic dots, and the ancestral transports of dancers and players which characterized music passages in the earlier novels. But it is difficult to resist the rhythmic re-creation in the passage. It is difficult to resist not only because of the mimetic quality of the language, but because McKay's description is firmly attached to the scene and the participants. In another passage,

McKay's tact is even more impressive. Crazy Bow is a frequent visitor to the home of Jordan Plant:

> And whenever Crazy Bow was *in the mood* he would take the fiddle down from the wall and play. And sometimes he did play in a way that moved Jordan Plant inside and made tears come into his eyes —tears of sweet memories when he was younger down at Jubilee and fiddled, too, and was a gay guy at tea-meetings. Before the death of his father. Before he became a sober member and leader of the church.
>
> (*Banana Bottom*, p. 8)

Because the community has replaced a vague ancestral land, like that evoked in *Banjo*, and because each character in it has a specific past to which to refer, McKay's rendering of the moving power of the music needs no authorial insistence. It is not in keeping with the spirit of the passage to indicate too strongly that McKay has stealthily infiltrated a polemic point about the deadening weight of civilization represented by the church, for our responsive gaze is fixed on the dissolving character.

Relating Crazy Bow to the earlier novels we might note that he combines vagabondage with music. A brilliant student at school, he shoots 'right off the straight line' after the first year 'and nothing could bring him back' (p. 5). The school piano turns him 'right crazy. . . . It knocked everything else out of his head. Composition and mathematics and the ambition to enter the Civil Service. All the efforts of the headmaster were of no avail' (p. 6). Crazy Bow represents the same kind of protest against civilization as the guitar-playing Banjo, but McKay's well-proportioned world does not admit of that protest being over-insistent nor of the protesting character being central. The value that Crazy Bow represents is a real one which the society must assimilate. But it does not set itself up as the only value. Where Matthew Arnold fails, McKay triumphs sweetly.

It is with all this insinuated, the ravishing power of Crazy Bow's music and the tenseness of the fiddler, that the crucial incident takes place. Crazy Bow, the harmless idiot, often frisks with Bita by the riverside. As they do one Saturday:

> As they romped, Bita got upon Crazy Bow's breast and began

rubbing her head against his face. Crazy Bow suddenly drew himself up and rather roughly he pushed Bita away and she rolled off a little down the slope.

Crazy Bow took up his fiddle, and sitting under a low and shady guava tree he began to play. He played a sweet tea-meeting love song. And as he played Bita went creeping upon her hands and feet up the slope to him and listened in the attitude of a bewitched being.

And when he had finished she clambered upon him again and began kissing his face. Crazy Bow tried to push her off. But Bita hugged and clung to him passionately. Crazy Bow was blinded by temptation and lost control of himself and the deed was done.

(*Banana Bottom*, p. 10)

The setting is idyllic. Bita is drawn like a natural creature 'creeping upon her hands and feet up the slope to him' and Crazy Bow is involuntarily possessed. The incident does not call for a moralizing gloss. The ballad-makers put it into 'a sugary ditty' (p. 14). The stabilizing community absorbs and transforms the deed 'and soon the countryside was ringing' with songs:

> You may wrap her up in silk,
> You may trim her up with gold,
> And the prince may come after
> To ask for your daughter,
> But Crazy Bow was first.
>
> (*Banana Bottom*, p. 15)

This is one of the ways in which McKay suggests the distinctive value of the Banana Bottom society but there is an attempt to use the incident in a more explicit way. We are returning to the question of how presented life in fiction relates to authorial theory.

Burning to deliver herself of the news, Sister Phibby Patroll travels the fifteen miles from Banana Bottom to Jubilee by foot. Her overnight trek gives her a decisive lead:

> So Sister Phibby told the tale to Priscilla Craig. And although she thought it was a sad thing as a good Christian should, her wide brown face betrayed a kind of primitive satisfaction as in a good thing done early. Not so that of Priscilla Craig's. It was a *face full of high-class anxiety a face that generations upon generations of Northern training in reserve, restraint, and Christian righteousness have gone to cultivate, a face fascinating in its thin benevolent austerity.*
>
> (*Banana Bottom*, pp. 15–16)

For much of *Banana Bottom*, McKay expresses cultural dualism not by setting up explicit contrasts but by celebrating the *Banana Bottom* community. This is why it is possible to read the work as a serene evocation of the loved place. In this passage, however, McKay does not resist the temptation to make an easy hit. It is plausible enough that Sister Phibby should show the kind of satisfaction McKay describes—and the satisfaction derives from Sister Phibby's understanding of what is likely to be Mrs. Craig's view on the subject. But in the section I have italicized McKay seems to be stating his case according to an authorial preconception or prejudice about a type, and not in relation to the individual character in the interview. The whole is re-done with much less self-consciousness and with great effect a few lines later:

> 'Poor child,' said Priscilla Craig.
> 'Yes, poor child,' echoed Sister Phibby. . . . 'But she was oberwormanish ob a ways the folkses them say.'
> 'That's no reason she should have been abused,' said Priscilla Craig.
> 'Temptation, Missis,' sighed Sister Phibby, 'and the poor fool was mad! What kyan a poah body do ag'inst a great big temptation?'
> 'Pray to God, of course, Sister Phibby,' said Mrs. Craig.
> (*Banana Bottom*, p. 16)

The conversation comes close to the truth of the presented incident. And the Banana Bottom ethic proves to be a more flexible one than that represented by Mrs. Craig. It does so simply by being itself.

The Crazy Bow incident establishes Bita's natural connection with the Banana Bottom world. Her transference to Jubilee and tutelage under the Craigs is an artificial thing. When Bita returns after her seven years abroad she is still herself. The character who is a returned native presents McKay with a plausible medium for the nostalgia expressed in his poems and in the earlier novels. Bita goes to the market. McKay describes the wealth of the land collected in one place and records the sounds and sights of the higgling scene. Then:

> Bita mingled in the crowd, responsive to the feeling, the colour, the smell, the swell and press of it. It gave her the sensation of a

reservoir of familiar kindred humanity into which she had descended for baptism. She had never had that big moving feeling as a girl when she visited the native market. And she thought that if she had never gone abroad for a period so long, from which she had become accustomed to viewing her native life in perspective, she might never have had that experience. . . .

The noises of the market were sweeter in her ears than a symphony. Accents and rhythms, movements and colours, nuances that might have passed unnoticed if she had never gone away, were now revealed to her in all their striking detail. And of the foodstuff on view she felt an impulse to touch and fondle a thousand times more than she wanted to buy.

(Banana Bottom, p. 41)

But this is not simply plausible nostalgia, it is part of a dramatic process that is to end with the marriage of Bita to her father's drayman. I shall return to this process later. After her experience at the market, Bita meets the dandy Hopping Dick.

In *Banana Bottom*, McKay reveals a comic talent for the first time. ' "Such hands like yours, Miss Plant, were trained for finer work than to carry common things like pineapples." ' Thus gallantly begins the courtship of Bita by the village dandy, grogshop customer, horse-gambler and notorious feminine heart-breaker. ' "There's more big-foot country gals fit to carry pines than donkeys in Jamaica. Please give me the pleasure to relieve you, as I am walking your way" ' (p. 42). With the swelling disapproval of big-foot Rosyanna, servant of the mission and sister in the church, the trio pursue their way:

Hopping Dick turned on his dandiest strut walking up the main street with Bita. Out of the corner of his eye he saw a group of his set in the door of the grogshop watching him open-mouthed; but apparently unseeing he strutted more ornamentally, ostentatiously absorbed in conversation with Bita. . . . After the first compliments Hopping Dick was stumped of what to say. He was very ready-tongued with the local girls in the market and at the tea-meetings, but he felt he could not use the same talk upon a person like Bita, and he wanted to shine. So the few minutes between the market and the mission were mostly spent in perfecting his strut.

(Banana Bottom, p. 43)

The ungodly set are treated to the spectacle of Hopping Dick

Precursor

attending church and helping at choir-practice, and the grog-shop gossipers of Jubilee provide a running commentary. The latest ballad is about the fall of Gracie Hall and one of the boys sitting on top of a cracker barrel has just been whistling the tune:

> 'Well, dat was one to fall down,' said a little-sized brown drinker. 'Wonder who be the next?'
> 'De nex' is you,' said the barkeeper. 'You habent call for a roun' yet.'
> 'Set him up, set him up deah,' said the little one. 'Dis is one way a falling, but de way Gracie fall is anodder. . . .'
> 'To fin' out de nex' you mus' ask Hopping Dick,' said a tall black.
> 'Hoppin' Dick ain't nuttin',' said the little one contemptuously. 'Him get a look in on the miss in de mission, though. . . .'
>
> (*Banana Bottom*, p. 106)

Matters reach a dramatic head when Mrs. Craig sends the following telegram to Jordan Plant:

> 'Bita ruining her reputation with worthless man. Please come at once.' (p. 219)

For McKay has more than a comic use for Hopping Dick. Bita's association with the strutting young man is the occasion for a conflict between Mrs. Craig and Bita:

> 'He's not a fit person for you to be seen in the street with, Bita. And he had no right to take advantage of your ignorance and force his company upon you. He is a brazen bad young man.'
> 'He didn't force himself on me. He asked me if he could come and I said all right.'
> '. . . You know there are certain things we just can't do, simply because they reflect on the mission.'
> 'But I don't think walking and talking a little with Mr. Delgado could have anything to do with the mission. Even if he's not a person of the best character.'
> 'Bita, my child! Don't try to be ridiculous. A mere child even could see the right thing to do. You have received an education to do the correct thing almost automatically. Even Rosyanna feels a certain responsibility because she is connected with the mission. . . .'
>
> (*Banana Bottom*, p. 45)

The clash between Bita and Mrs. Craig is successfully dramatized as a particular one between two incompatible people. From this

266

sound beginning it develops into a confrontation between two ways of life. Instead of the rhetoric of an authorial voice, we move into the consciousness of a character seeking a *modus vivendi*:

> Bita retired to her bed. And the more she thought of the incident the more resentful she became. She wondered now that she had come home to it after all the years of training, if she would be able to adjust herself to the life of the mission.
>
> (*Banana Bottom*, p. 45)

With matters thus poised, the scene shifts from the town of Jubilee to the lush village of Banana Bottom for the week of festivities beginning with the celebration of Emancipation Day. It is thirty years before Great Gort and Jack O'Lantern and before the march to Independence square in *Season of Adventure*, so we have to make do with Nias Black, and Kojo Jeems:

> ... Kojo Jeems, the drummer, had a fine set of drums and he was loved for his wonderful rattling of the battle-drum. His son beat the big drum. They went playing down the hill followed by a few ragged kiddies, to the hub of the village. There they were joined by the fiddler and the flute-blower and played and played, with the sun mounting higher and hotter, until there was gathered together a great crowd. And all marched swaying to the music, over the hill, and picking up marchers marking time along the wayside, up to the playground.
>
> (*Banana Bottom*, p. 63)

At the picnic on Table Top Plateau, McKay's feel for the dialect and his vivid sense of people swiftly contribute to our impression of a known and bounded world. 'First among the rum-shop fellows was Tack Tally, proudly wearing his decorations from Panama: gold watch and chain of three strands, and a foreign gold coin attached to it as large as a florin, a gold stick-pin with a huge blue stone, and five gold rings flashing from his fingers. He had on a fine bottle-green tweed suit with the well-creased and deep-turned pantaloons called peg-top, the coat of long points and lapels known as American style. And wherever he went he was accompanied by an admiring gang' (p. 66). Contained in the Banana Bottom world too are the 'Misses Felicia, Elvira and Lucinda Lambert ... cashew-brown daughters of the ebony parson. They were prim of manners, precise and halting of speech as if they were always thinking, while talking, that they were the minister's daughters' (p. 65). It is a world of gossip and ballad and anecdote. But it is a world whose laws are framed from the outside.

Bita explains to the exiled Englishman Squire Gensir that her function at the mission prevents her from dancing and from attending tea-meetings. Gensir nevertheless persuades her to attend Kojo Jeems's tea-meeting. Under this unofficial teacher's tutelage, Bita's rebellion begins. At Kojo's tea-party, Bita looks at the dancers and declares 'I'm going to join them'; about possible disapproval 'Oh, I don't care anyhow'. Wilfully she begins:

> . . . And Bita danced freely released, danced as she had never danced since she was a girl at a picnic at Tabletop, wiggling and swaying and sliding along, the memories of her tomboyish girlhood rushing sparkling over her like water cascading over one bathing upon a hot summer's day.
>
> The crowd rejoiced to see her dance and some girls stood clapping and stamping to her measure and crying: 'Dance, Miss Bita, dance you' step! Dance, Miss Bita, dance away!' And she danced forgetting herself, forgetting even Jubilee, dancing down the barrier between high breeding and common pleasures under her light stamping foot until she was one with the crowd.
>
> (*Banana Bottom*, p. 84)

The roving reporter Phibby Patroll takes the news to Jubilee, and Bita's second clash with Mrs. Craig occurs. The consequences are softened by Bita's use of Gensir's chaperoning name but the Craigs decide to speed up their plans for Bita's marriage with Herald Newton Day.

McKay's presentation of Herald Newton Day is enhanced by the new sense of characterization and human relationships that we see in *Banana Bottom*, and by the newly discovered comic resources. Because Day poses a threat to the heroine we can enjoy his deflation —in the way it is not always possible to do when Naipaul deflates a peripheral character even in *A House for Mr. Biswas*. McKay lets Day's own pompous language do the work, and he allows Bita and Gensir to patronize him. Gensir tells Bita and Herald Newton that he had fruitlessly spent much of the previous day hunting for a rare flower about which Jubban had informed him:

'I think I'll try again tomorrow,' the Squire said.

'By God's help you'll succeed in finding it, sir,' said Herald Newton.

Bita was shaking from suppressed laughter and Herald Newton, remarking a humorous expression on the squire's face wondered what he might have done. . . .

'I wish I could be sure God will help me to find that flower,' said the Squire, his eyes twinkling. 'Do you think he could help me, really?'

'I am sure He will if you ask him in faith,' replied Herald Newton.

'Let us play,' said Bita, turning to the piano.

(*Banana Bottom*, pp. 171–2)

Since Day is the willing protégé of the Craigs, McKay can satirize him plausibly as a Negro who gets a white man's education and learns to despise his own people. When Day proposes marriage ' "Everybody would be happy if we both get married" ' and Bita feels bound to accept ' "I suppose we might as well do it and please everybody" ', Herald is gratified and insensitive:

'. . . You know at first when I began studying for the ministry and thinking of the great work before me, I thought that perhaps only a white woman could help me. One having a pure mind and lofty ideals like Mrs. Craig. For purity is my ideal of the married state. With clean hearts thinking and living purely and bearing children under the benediction of God.

'I know you will understand,' . . . Herald squeezed Bita's hand, but she felt that it was not she herself that inspired the impulse, but perhaps his thought . . . 'just as Mrs. Craig would. For you have been trained like a pure-minded white lady.'

'I don't know about that,' said Bita. 'But whatever I was trained like or to be, I know one thing. And that is that I am myself.'

(*Banana Bottom*, p. 100)

Herald Newton Day is the same type as the Martiniquan attacked by Ray in the novel *Banjo*, but it is only within the regulating structure of *Banana Bottom* and with McKay's sense of Day as an individual in the fictional world that the satiric effect can be achieved without signs of authorial straining. But the art of *Banana Bottom* is not free from impurities: it seems to be an indication of a loss of control in the novelist as well that, by the most violent irony, 'Herald Newton . . . suddenly turned crazy and defiled himself with a nanny goat. Consternation fell upon that sweet rustic scene like a lightning ball of destruction. And there was confusion among these hill folk, which no ray of understanding could penetrate' (p. 175). The plot demands that Herald Newton should be removed from the scene but one cannot help feeling that the author is indulging a spiteful impulse. The spite in this account may be compared with the humour and tolerance with which in a later section, McKay presents the scandal discovered by Sister Phibby Patroll, at the height of a religious revival, that Sister-in-Christ Yoni Legge is pregnant by a fellow convert Hopping Dick (see pp. 270–2).

Bita's conflicts with Mrs. Craig and her antagonism to Herald Newton Day are associated with her alienation from the town of Jubilee, and with her increasing preference for the village of *Banana Bottom* where she had spent her early childhood. She spends more and more time in the village. 'It was so much pleasanter and freer at Banana Bottom' (p. 161). A number of images of immersion associated with constitutive elements of village life or with the landscape impress her belonging to Banana Bottom. An example of the first is her dance at Kojo Jeems's tea-meeting. The following example of the second illustrates incidentally the way in which McKay is able to make maximum dramatic use of the nostalgia felt by some West Indian writers who are abroad. On a visit to Banana Bottom, Bita wanders through her childhood haunts:

> All of her body was tingling sweet with affectionate feeling for the place. For here she had lived some of the happiest moments of her girlhood, with her schoolmates and alone. Here she had learned to swim, beginning in the shallow water of the lower end with a stout length of bamboo. She remembered how she screamed with delight with her schoolmates cheering and clapping their hands that day when she swam from one bank to the other.
>
> She slipped off her slight clothes and plunged into the water and swam round and round the hole. Then she turned on her back to enjoy the water cooling on her breasts. Now she could bear the sun above burning down.

(*Banana Bottom*, p. 117)

The unpretentious manner in which this passage suggests Bita's belonging and her exultation is best brought out by a comparison with the poverty of declaration in the closing sentences of Neville Dawes's *The Last Enchantment* (1960): 'I was a god again, drunk on the mead of the land, and massive with the sun chanting in my veins. And so, flooded with the bright clarity of my acceptance, I held this lovely wayward island, starkly, in my arms' (p. 288).

Bita's increasing sense of her rootedness in the Banana Bottom community is reflected in her deliberate flouting of Mrs. Craig's wishes. A climax of a kind is reached when with Herald Newton long banished, the two women clash over Hopping Dick's coming to the mission to escort Bita to a dance. Mrs. Craig wants to know if Bita loves Dick. Bita says she could love him:

> 'A low peacock,' said Mrs. Craig, 'who murders his h's and altogether speaks in such a vile manner—and you an educated girl—highly educated.'
> 'My parents also speak broken English,' said Bita.
> Anger again swept Mrs. Craig and a sharp rebuke came to her lips, but it was checked when her eyes noted Bita toying enigmatically and ostentatiously with Herald Newton's engagement ring on her finger.
>
> (*Banana Bottom*, p. 210)

Moving from this particular show of antagonism between the two characters, and with the weight of similar demonstrations in earlier episodes behind him, McKay enters the consciousness of Bita:

> Bita was certain now that the time had arrived for her to face the fact of leaving Jubilee. It would be impossible for her to stay when she felt not only resentment, but a natural opposition against Mrs. Craig. A latent hostility would make her always want to do anything of which Mrs. Craig disapproved. Bita could not quite explain this strong feeling to herself. It was just there, going much deeper than the Hopping Dick affair. Maybe it was an old unconscious thing now manifesting itself, because it was to Mrs. Craig, a woman whose attitude to life was alien to her, and not to her parents, she owed the entire shaping of her career.
>
> (*Banana Bottom*, p. 211)

The passage is a crucial one in the sense that the doctrine it contains plays a part in the conception of the novel, but it is also crucial in terms of Bita's growing self-awareness. The flat declaration of an attitude which we have just seen in action is followed by the tentative 'could not quite explain', 'maybe', groping for an explanation, and then a resolution repeated—'Bita knew that she was going to go'—which leads into a wave of disgust and an assertive action:

> She became contemptuous of everything—the plan of her education and the way of existence at the mission, and her eye wandering to the photograph of her English college over her bed, she suddenly took and ripped it from its frame, tore the thing up and trampled the pieces under her feet. . . .
>
> (*Banana Bottom*, p. 212)

It is a much more convincing and suggestive process than Ray's generalization in *Home to Harlem* that 'civilisation is rotten'. The difference is one between understanding through art, and becoming constricted through polemics.

Bita's return to the folk is confirmed when she witnesses a religious ceremony held by a drumming cult during a period of drought: 'Magnetized by the spell of it Bita was drawn nearer and nearer into the inner circle until with a shriek she fell down. A mighty shout went up and the leading woman shot out prancing around Bita with uplifted twirling supple-jack, but a man rushed in and snatched her away before she could strike' (p. 250). It is interesting to notice that George Lamming uses a religious ceremony in a similar scene in *Season of Adventure* (1960). But whereas Fola's season of adventure into her true self *begins* at the ceremony of the souls Bita's mesmerization occurs at the end of her particular process. Fola is involved by Lamming in a process of self-discovery. McKay's heroine, it is possible to see more clearly by comparison, is involved in a process of self-assertion. By the end of the novel, Bita has married Jubban, her rescuer at the ceremony, and the land has prospered under his hand. Bita herself is in full bloom: 'Her music, her reading, her thinking were the flowers of her intelligence, and he the root in the earth upon which she was grafted, both nourished by the same soil' (p. 313). In the final scene, Aunty Nommy rejoices over the child of the marriage:

> 'What a pickney, though! What a pickney!' Aunty Nommy was saying and playfully slapping little Jordan's bottom.

'Showin' you' strength a'ready mi li't' man. Soon you'll be l'arnin' for square you' fist them off at me.'

In the world of *Banana Bottom*, life is going on. The recurrent McKay experience of *malaise*, of being born 'out of time', lies behind *Banana Bottom*. But the achievement of the artist in this work is the creation of a world that disperses *malaise*. The episode at Bita's childhood pool is only one example of the novel's characteristic imaging of the act of immersion:

> She slipped off her slight clothes and plunged into the water and swam round and round the hole. Then she turned on her back to enjoy the water cooling on her breasts. Now she could bear the sun above burning down. How delicious was the feeling of floating! To feel that one can suspend oneself upon a yawning depth and drift, drifting in perfect confidence without the slightest intruding thought of danger.
>
> (*Banana Bottom*, p. 117)

Art reveals possibilities. Mr. Naipaul's observed Tulsi world is a copy of a society from which it is necessary to escape. In *Banana Bottom*, Claude McKay imagined a community to which it is possible to belong.

Author Bibliography

Aarons, Rudolph L. C., *The Cow that Laughed and Other Stories*, Kingston, printed by Printers Ltd., 194?, 93 pp.

Allfrey, Phyllis Shand, *The Orchid House*, London, Constable, 1953, 223 pp.

Anthony, Michael, *The Games were Coming*, London, André Deutsch, 1963, 223 pp.

The Year in San Fernando, London, André Deutsch, 1965, 190 pp.

Green Days by the River, London, André Deutsch, 1967, 192 pp.

Bennett, Alvin, *Because They Know Not*, London, Phoenix Press, n.d. [1961?], 160 pp.

God the Stonebreaker, London, Heinemann, 1964, 248 pp.

Black, Clinton, *Tales of Old Jamaica*, London, Pioneer Press, 1952, 121 pp.

Braithwaite, E. R., *Choice of Straws*, London, The Bodley Head, 1965, 198 pp.

Campbell, W. A., *Marguerite: A Story of the Earthquake*, Kingston, The Times Printery, 1907, 69 pp.

Carew, Jan, *Black Midas*, London, Secker and Warburg, 1958, 288 pp.

The Wild Coast, London, Secker and Warburg, 1958, 256 pp.

The Last Barbarian, London, Secker and Warburg, 1961, 286 pp.

Clarke, Austin C., *The Survivors of the Crossing*, London, Heinemann, 1964, 202 pp.

Amongst Thistles and Thorns, London, Heinemann, 1965, 183 pp.

The Meeting Point, London, Heinemann, 1967, 250 pp.

Dathorne, Oscar R., *Dumplings in the Soup*, London, Cassell, 1963, 192 pp.

The Scholar-man, London, Cassell, 1964, 180 pp.

Dawes, Neville, *The Last Enchantment*, London, MacGibbon and Kee, 1960, 288 pp.

De Boissiere, Ralph, *Crown Jewel*, Melbourne, Australasian Book Society, 1952, 432 pp.

Rum and Coca Cola, Melbourne, Australasian Book Society, 1956, 313 pp.

De Lisser, Herbert G., *Jane: a Story of Jamaica*, Kingston, Jamaica, Gleaner Co., 1913.

Jane's Career: a Story of Jamaica, [First British Reprint of a West Indian novel], London, Methuen, 1914, 156 pp.

Susan Proudleigh, London, Methuen, 1915, 309 pp.

Triumphant Squalitone: a tropical extravaganza, Kingston, Jamaica, The Gleaner Co. Ltd., Printers, 1917, 137 pp.

Revenge: a Tale of Old Jamaica, Kingston, Jamaica, The Gleaner Co. Ltd., 1919, 103 pp.

The White Witch of Rosehall, London, E. Benn, 1929, 286 pp.

Under the Sun: A Jamaican Comedy, London, E. Benn, 1937, 269 pp.

Psyche, London, E. Benn, 1952, 224 pp.

Morgan's Daughter, London, E. Benn, 1953, 220 pp.

The Cup and the Lip, London, E. Benn, 1956, 256 pp.

The Arawak Girl, Kingston, Jamaica, Pioneer Press, 1958, 91 pp.

Donaldson, Robert N., *Heart's Triumph*, Trinidad, Printed for the Author, 1944 [Revised edition printed at Rahaman Printery Ltd., 1963, 175 pp.].

Drayton, Geoffrey, *Christopher*, [a novel of childhood in the West Indies], London, Collins, 1959, 191 pp.

Zohara, London, Secker and Warburg, 1961, 185 pp.

DuQuesnay, Frederick J. Le Mercier, *A Princess for Port Royal: a romantic novel*, Ilfracombe, N. Devon, A. H. Stockwell, 1960, 158 pp.

Durie, Alice, *One Jamaica Gal*, Kingston, The Jamaica Times, 1939, 80 pp.

Emtage, James B., *Brown Sugar: A Vestigial Tale*, London, Collins, 1966, 128 pp.

Author Bibliography

Ferguson, Merril, *Village of Love*, London, MacGibbon and Kee, 1960, 270 pp.

Fraser, Fitzroy, *Wounds in the Flesh*, London, New Authors, 1962, 189 pp.

Harris, Wilson, *Palace of the Peacock*, London, Faber and Faber, 1960, 152 pp.

    The Far Journey of Oudin, London, Faber and Faber, 1961, 136 pp.

    The Whole Armour, London, Faber and Faber, 1962, 128 pp.

    The Secret Ladder, London, Faber and Faber, 1963, 127 pp.

    Heartland, London, Faber and Faber, 1964, 96 pp.

    The Eye of the Scarecrow, London, Faber and Faber, 1965, 108 pp.

    The Waiting Room, London, Faber and Faber, 1967, 80 pp.

Hearne, John, *Voices under the Window*, London, Faber and Faber, 1955, 164 pp.

    Stranger at the Gate, London, Faber and Faber, 1956, 304 pp.

    The Faces of Love, London, Faber and Faber, 1957, 267 pp.

    The Autumn Equinox, London, Faber and Faber, 1959, 272 pp.

    The Land of the Living, London, Faber and Faber, 1961, 280 pp.

Hercules, Frank, *Where the Humming-bird Flies*, New York, Harcourt, Brace, 1961, 212 pp.

    I Want a Black Doll, London, Collins, 1967.

Holder, Geoffrey, *Black Gods, Green Islands*, by Geoffrey Holder with Tom Harshman, New York, Doubleday, 1959, 235 pp.

James, Alexander MacG., *The Cacique's Treasure and Other Tales*, Kingston, Jamaica, The Gleaner Co., 1920, 44 pp.

James, Cyril L. R., *Minty Alley*, London, Secker and Warburg, 1936, 320 pp.

Kempadoo, Peter [pseud. Lauchmonen], *Guiana Boy*, New Literature (Publishing) Ltd., 1960, 172 pp.

    Old Thom's Harvest, London, Eyre and Spottiswoode, 1965, 195 pp.

Khan, Ismith, *The Jumbie Bird*, London, MacGibbon and Kee, 1961, 224 pp.

    The Obeah Man, London, Hutchinson, 1964, 191 pp.

Lamming, George, *In the Castle of My Skin*, London, Michael Joseph, 1953, 303 pp.

    The Emigrants, London, Michael Joseph, 1954, 271 pp.

Of Age and Innocence, London, Michael Joseph, 1958, 412 pp.
Season of Adventure, London, Michael Joseph, 1960, 366 pp.
Lindo, Archie, *Bronze*: short stories, articles, a poem and a play, Mandeville, Jamaica, Printed by the College Press, 1944, 80pp.
My Heart was Singing: poems and short stories, Mandeville, Jamaica, Printed by the College Press, 1945, 60 pp.
Lovelace, Earl, *While Gods are Falling*, London, Collins, 1965, 254 pp.
McKay, Claude, *Home to Harlem*, New York, London, Harper and Brothers, 1928, 340 pp.
Banjo: a Story without a Plot, New York, London, Harper and Brothers, 1929, 326 pp.
Gingertown, New York, London, Harper and Brothers, 1932, 274 pp.
Banana Bottom, New York, London, Harper and Brothers, 1933, 317 pp.
McLellan, G. H. H., *Old Time Story*; some old Guianese yarns re-spun by 'Pugagee Puncuss' (G. H. McLellan), ed. Vincent Roth, Georgetown, British Guiana, 'Daily Chronicle', 1943, 266 pp.
Mais, Roger, *Face and Other Stories*, Kingston, Jamaica, Universal Printery, 194?, 109 pp.
And Most of All Man, Kingston, Jamaica, City Printery, 194?, 84 pp.
The Hills were Joyful Together, London, Jonathan Cape, 1953, 288 pp.
Brother Man, London, Jonathan Cape, 1954, 191 pp.
Black Lightning, London, Jonathan Cape, 1955, 222 pp.
Mendes, Alfred H., *Pitch Lake*, London, Duckworth, 1934, 352 pp.
Black Fauns, London, Duckworth, 1935, 328 pp.
Mittelholzer, Edgar, *Corentyne Thunder*, London, Secker and Warburg, 1941, 320 pp.
A Morning at the Office, London, Hogarth Press, 1950, 246 pp.
Shadows Move Among Them, London, Peter Nevill, 1952, 334 pp.
Children of Kaywana, London, Secker and Warburg, 1952, 515 pp.
The Weather in Middenshot, London, Secker and Warburg, 1952, 238 pp.

Author Bibliography

The Life and Death of Sylvia, London, Secker and Warburg, 1953, 287 pp.

The Harrowing of Hubertus, London, Secker and Warburg, 1954, 303 pp. [issued as *Kaywana Stock* in 1959].

The Adding Machine; a fable for capitalists and commercialists, Kingston, Jamaica, Pioneer Press, 1954, 102 pp.

My Bones and My Flute, London, Secker and Warburg, 1955, 222 pp.

Of Trees and the Sea, London, Secker and Warburg, 1956, 256 pp.

A Tale of Three Places, London, Secker and Warburg, 1957, 347 pp.

Kaywana Blood, London, Secker and Warburg, 1958, 523 pp.

The Weather Family, London, Secker and Warburg, 1958, 339 pp.

The Mad MacMullochs, London, Peter Owen, Ltd., 1959, 234 pp.

A Tinkling in the Twilight, London, Secker and Warburg, 1959, 269 pp.

Latticed Echoes, London, Secker and Warburg, 1960, 254 pp.

Eltonsbrody, London, Secker and Warburg, 1960, 191 pp.

The Piling of Clouds, London, Putnam and Co., 1961, 262 pp.

Thunder Returning, London, Secker and Warburg, 1961, 240 pp.

The Wounded and the Worried, London, Putnam and Co., 1962, 223 pp.

Uncle Paul, London, Macdonald and Co., 1963, 222 pp.

The Aloneness of Mrs. Chatham, London, Library 33, 1965, 224 pp.

The Jilkington Drama, London, New York, Toronto, 1965.

Naipaul, Vidiadhar Surajprasad, *The Mystic Masseur*, London, André Deutsch, 1957, 215 pp.

The Suffrage of Elvira, London, André Deutsch, 1958, 240 pp.

Miguel Street, London, André Deutsch, 1959, 222 pp.

A House for Mr. Biswas, London, André Deutsch, 1961, 531 pp.

Mr. Stone and the Knights Companion, London, André Deutsch, 1963, 159 pp.

The Mimic Men, London, André Deutsch, 1967, 301 pp.

Nicole, Christopher, *Off-White*, London, Jarrolds, 1959, 223 pp.

Shadows in the Jungle, London, Jarrolds, 1961, 223 pp.

Ratoon, London, Jarrolds, 1962, 256 pp.

Dark Noon, London, Jarrolds, 1963, 240 pp.

Blood Amyot, London, Jarrolds, 1964, 256 pp.

Amyot's Cay, London, Jarrolds, 1964, 256 pp.

The Amyot Crime, London, Jarrolds, 1965, 240 pp.

White Boy, London, Hutchinson, 1966, 286 pp.

Ogilvie, William G., *Cactus Village*, Kingston, Jamaica, Pioneer Press, 1953, 171 pp.

The Ghost Bank, Kingston, Jamaica, Pioneer Press, 1953, 124 pp.

Palmer, C. Everard, *A Broken Vessel*, Kingston, Jamaica, Pioneer Press, 1960, 112 pp.

The Adventures of Jimmy Maxwell, Jamaica, Ministry of Education, Publications Branch, 1962, 122 pp. [children's novel].

A Taste of Danger, Jamaica, Ministry of Education, Publications Branch, 1963, 62 pp. [children's novel].

The Cloud with the Silver Lining, London, André Deutsch, 1966, 159 pp.

Patterson, H. Orlando, *The Children of Sisyphus*, London, New Authors, Ltd., 1964, 206 pp.

An Absence of Ruins, London, Hutchinson, 1966, 160 pp.

Quayle, Ada, *The Mistress*, London, MacGibbon and Kee, 1957, 303 pp.

Redcam, Tom [pseud. for Thomas H. MacDermot], *Becka's Buckra Baby*, Kingston, Jamaica Times' Printery, 1903, 68 pp.

One Brown Girl and—, Kingston, Jamaica Times' Printery, 1909, 122 pp.

Reid, Victor Stafford, *New Day*, New York, Knopf, 1949, 374 pp.

The Leopard, London, Heinemann, 1958, 185 pp.

Sixty-Five, London, Longmans, 1960, 110 pp. [children's novel].

Rhys, Jean, *Wide Sargasso Sea*, London, André Deutsch, 1966, 190 pp.

Roberts, W. Adolphe, *The Haunting Hand*, London, Hutchinson, 1926.

The Mind Reader, New York, Macaulay Co., 1929, 277 pp.

The Moralist, New York, Mohawk Press, 1931, 300 pp.

The Pomegranate, Indianapolis, New York, Bobbs-Merrill Co., 1941, 313 pp.

Royal Street, Indianapolis, New York, Bobbs-Merrill Co., 1944, 378 pp.

Brave Mardi Gras, Indianapolis, New York, Bobbs-Merrill Co., 1946, 318 pp.

Creole Dusk, Indianapolis, Bobbs-Merrill Co., 1948, 325 pp.

The Single Star, Indianapolis, Bobbs-Merrill Co., 1949, 378 pp.

Rogers, Joel Augustus, *From Superman to Man*, Chicago, A. Donohue and Co., Printers, 1917, 128 pp.

Roy, Namba, *Black Albino*, London, New Literature, 1961, 196 pp.

Salkey, Andrew, *A Quality of Violence*, London, New Authors, Ltd., 1959, 205 pp.

Escape to an Autumn Pavement, London, Hutchinson, 1960, 208 pp.

Hurricane, London, O.U.P., 1964, 118 pp. [children's novel].

Earthquake, London, O.U.P., 1965, 123 pp. [children's novel].

Drought, London, O.U.P., 1966, 144 pp. [children's novel].

The Shark Hunters, London, Nelson, 1966, 74 pp. [children's novel].

Riot, London, O.U.P., 1966, 198 pp. [children's novel].

Selvon, Samuel, *A Brighter Sun*, London, Allan Wingate, 1952, 236 pp.

An Island is a World, London, Allan Wingate, 1955, 288 pp.

The Lonely Londoners, London, Allan Wingate, 1956, 171 pp.

Ways of Sunlight, London, MacGibbon and Kee, 1957, 188 pp.

Turn Again Tiger, London, MacGibbon and Kee, 1958, 219 pp.

I Hear Thunder, London, MacGibbon and Kee, 1963, 192 pp.

The Housing Lark, London, MacGibbon and Kee, 1965, 155 pp.

Snod, E. [E. A. Dodd], *Maroon Medicine* [and three other stories], Kingston, Times' Printery, 1905, 88 pp.

St. Omer, Garth, 'Syrop', in Introduction 2: Stories by New Writers, London, Faber and Faber, 1964, pp. 139–87.

Taylor, Stanley A. G., *The Capture of Jamaica*, Kingston, Jamaica, Pioneer Press, 1956, 164 pp.

Buccaneer Bay, Kingston, Jamaica, Pioneer Press, 1952, 243 pp.

Pages from our Past, Kingston, Jamaica, Pioneer Press, 1954, 183 pp.

Thompson, Claude, *These My People*, Kingston, Jamaica, The Herald Ltd., Printers, 1943, 78 pp.

Author Bibliography

Tomlinson, F. C., *The Helions or The Deeds of Rio*, London, Simpkin, Marshall, 1903, 343 pp.

Waite-Smith, Cicely [Howland], *Rain for the Plains and other Stories*, Kingston, Jamaica, printed by the Gleaner Co., 1943, 139 pp.

Walrond, Eric, *Tropic Death*, New York, Boni and Liveright, 1926, 282 pp.

Webber, A. R. F., *Those That Be in Bondage*, Georgetown, The Daily Chronicle Printing Press, 1917, 236 pp.

Williams, Denis, *Other Leopards*, London, New Authors, Ltd., 1963, 221 pp.

Wynter, Sylvia, *The Hills of Hebron*, London, Jonathan Cape, 1962, 283 pp.

Year by Year Bibliography

Places of Publication are given in brackets
U.K. = United Kingdom; U.S. = America
G = Guyana; J = Jamaica; T = Trinidad

1903	Redcam:	*Becka's Buckra Baby*	(J)
	Tomlinson:	*The Helions or the Deeds of Rio*	(J)
1905	Snod:	*Maroon Medicine*	(J)
1907	Campbell:	*Marguerite: A Story of the Earthquake*	(J)
1909	Redcam:	*One Brown Girl And—*	(J)
1913	De Lisser:	*Jane: A Story of Jamaica*	(J)
1914	De Lisser:	*Jane's Career*	(U.K.)
1915	De Lisser:	*Susan Proudleigh*	(U.K.)
1917	De Lisser:	*Triumphant Squalitone*	(J)
	Rogers:	*From Superman to Man*	(U.S.)
	Webber:	*Those that be in Bondage*	(G)
1919	De Lisser:	*Revenge*	(J)
1920	James:	*The Cacique's Treasure and Other Tales*	(J)
1926	Roberts:	*The Haunting Hand*	(U.S.)
	Walrond:	*Tropic Death*	(U.S.)
1928	McKay:	*Home to Harlem*	(U.S.)
1929	De Lisser:	*The White Witch of Rosehall*	(U.K.)
	McKay:	*Banjo*	(U.S.)
	Roberts:	*The Mind Reader*	(U.S.)
1931	Roberts:	*The Moralist*	(U.S.)
1932	McKay:	*Gingertown*	(U.S.)
1933	McKay:	*Banana Bottom*	(U.S.)
1934	Mendes:	*Pitch Lake*	(U.K.)
1935	Mendes:	*Black Fauns*	(U.K.)

1936	James:	*Minty Alley*	(U.K.)
1937	De Lisser:	*Under the Sun*	(U.K.)
	McKay:	*A Long Way from Home*	(U.S.)
1939	Durie:	*One Jamaica Gal*	(J)
1941	Mittelholzer:	*Corentyne Thunder*	(U.K.)
	Roberts:	*The Pomegranate*	(U.S.)
1943	McLellan:	*Old Time Story*	(G)
	Waite-Smith:	*Rain for the Plains and other Stories*	(J)
1944	Aarons:	*The Cow that Laughed*	(J)
	Donaldson:	*Heart's Triumph*	(T)
	Lindo:	*Bronze*	(J)
	Roberts:	*Royal Street*	(U.S.)
1945	Lindo:	*My Heart was Singing*	(J)
	Mais:	*And Most of all Man*	(J)
1946	Mais:	*Face and Other Stories*	(J)
	Roberts:	*Brave Mardi Gras*	(U.S.)
1948	Roberts:	*Creole Dusk*	(U.S.)
1949	Reid:	*New Day*	(U.S.)
	Roberts:	*The Single Star*	(U.S.)
1950	Mittelholzer:	*A Morning at the Office*	(U.K.)
1951	Taylor:	*The Capture of Jamaica*	(J)
1952	Black:	*Tales of Old Jamaica*	(J)
	De Boissiere:	*Crown Jewel*	(Austr)
	De Lisser:	*Psyche*	(U.K.)
	Mittelholzer:	*Shadows Move Among Them*	(U.K.)
	Mittelholzer:	*Children of Kaywana*	(U.K.)
	Mittelholzer:	*The Weather in Middenshot*	(U.K.)
	Selvon:	*A Brighter Sun*	(U.K.)
	Taylor:	*Buccaneer Bay*	(J)
1953	Allfrey:	*The Orchid House*	(U.K.)
	De Lisser:	*Morgan's Daughter*	(U.K.)
	Lamming:	*In the Castle of My Skin*	(U.K.)
	Mais:	*The Hills Were Joyful Together*	(U.K.)
	Mittelholzer:	*The Life and Death of Sylvia*	(U.K.)
	Ogilvie:	*Cactus Village*	(J)
	Ogilvie:	*The Ghost Bank*	(J)

Year by Year Bibliography

1954	Lamming:	*The Emigrants*	(U.K.)
	Mais:	*Brother Man*	(U.K.)
	Mittelholzer:	*The Harrowing of Hubertus*	(U.K.)
	Mittelholzer:	*The Adding Machine*	(J)
	Taylor:	*Pages from Our Past*	(J)
1955	Hearne:	*Voices Under the Window*	(U.K.)
	Mais:	*Black Lightning*	(U.K.)
	Mittelholzer:	*My Bones and My Flute*	(U.K.)
	Selvon:	*An Island is a World*	(U.K.)
1956	De Boissiere:	*Rum and Coca Cola*	(Austr.)
	De Lisser:	*The Cup and the Lip*	(U.K.)
	Hearne:	*Stranger at the Gate*	(U.K.)
	Mittelholzer:	*Of Trees and the Sea*	(U.K.)
	Selvon:	*The Lonely Londoners*	(U.K.)
1957	Hearne:	*The Faces of Love*	(U.K.)
	Mittelholzer:	*A Tale of Three Places*	(U.K.)
	Naipaul:	*The Mystic Masseur*	(U.K.)
	Quayle:	*The Mistress*	(U.K.)
	Selvon:	*Ways of Sunlight*	(U.K.)
1958	Carew:	*Black Midas*	(U.K.)
	Carew:	*The Wild Coast*	(U.K.)
	De Lisser:	*The Arawak Girl*	(U.K.)
	Lamming:	*Of Age and Innocence*	(U.K.)
	Mittelholzer:	*Kaywana Blood*	(U.K.)
	Mittelholzer:	*The Weather Family*	(U.K.)
	Naipaul:	*The Suffrage of Elvira*	(U.K.)
	Reid:	*The Leopard*	(U.K.)
	Selvon:	*Turn Again Tiger*	(U.K.)
1959	Drayton:	*Christopher*	(U.K.)
	Hearne:	*The Autumn Equinox*	(U.K.)
	Holder:	*Black Gods, Green Islands*	(U.S.)
	Mittelholzer:	*A Tinkling in the Twilight*	(U.K.)
	Mittelholzer:	*The Mad MacMullochs*	(U.K.)
	Naipaul:	*Miguel Street*	(U.K.)
	Nicole:	*Off White*	(U.K.)
	Salkey:	*A Quality of Violence*	(U.K.)
1960	Dawes:	*The Last Enchantment*	(U.K.)

	Du Quesnay:	*A Princess for Port Royal*	(U.K.)
	Ferguson:	*Village of Love*	(U.K.)
	Harris:	*Palace of the Peacock*	(U.K.)
	Kempadoo:	*Guiana Boy*	(U.K.)
	Lamming:	*Season of Adventure*	(U.K.)
	Mittelholzer:	*Latticed Echoes*	(U.K.)
	Mittelholzer:	*Eltonsbrody*	(U.K.)
	Palmer:	*A Broken Vessel*	(J)
	Reid:	*Sixty-Five*	(U.K.)
	Salkey:	*Escape to an Autumn Pavement*	(U.K.)
1961	Carew:	*The Last Barbarian*	(U.K.)
	Drayton:	*Zohara*	(U.K.)
	Harris:	*The Far Journey of Oudin*	(U.K.)
	Hearne:	*The Land of the Living*	(U.K.)
	Hercules:	*Where the Humming Bird Flies*	(U.S.)
	Khan:	*The Jumbie Bird*	(U.K.)
	Mittelholzer:	*Thunder Returning*	(U.K.)
	Mittelholzer:	*The Piling of Clouds*	(U.K.)
	Naipaul:	*A House for Mr. Biswas*	(U.K.)
	Nicole:	*Shadows in the Jungle*	(U.K.)
	Roy:	*Black Albino*	(U.K.)
1962	Frazer:	*Wounds in the Flesh*	(U.K.)
	Harris:	*The Whole Armour*	(U.K.)
	Mittelholzer:	*The Wounded and the Worried*	(U.K.)
	Nicole:	*Ratoon*	(U.K.)
	Palmer:	*The Adventures of Jimmy Maxwell*	(J)
	Wynter:	*The Hills of Hebron*	(U.K.)
1963	Anthony:	*The Games Were Coming*	(U.K.)
	Dathorne:	*Dumplings in the Soup*	(U.K.)
	Donaldson:	*Heart's Triumph*	(T)
	Harris:	*The Secret Ladder*	(U.K.)
	Mittelholzer:	*Uncle Paul*	(U.K.)
	Naipaul:	*Mr. Stone and the Knights Companion*	(U.K.)
	Nicole:	*Dark Noon*	(U.K.)
	Palmer:	*A Taste of Danger*	(J)
	Selvon:	*I Hear Thunder*	(U.K.)
	Williams:	*Other Leopards*	(U.K.)

1964	Bennett:	*God the Stonebreaker*	(U.K.)
	Clarke:	*The Survivors of the Crossing*	(U.K.)
	Dathorne:	*The Scholar Man*	(U.K.)
	Harris:	*Heartland*	(U.K.)
	Khan:	*The Obeah Man*	(U.K.)
	Nicole:	*Amyot's Cay*	(U.K.)
	Nicole:	*Blood Amyot*	(U.K.)
	Patterson:	*The Children of Sisyphus*	(U.K.)
	Salkey:	*Hurricane*	(U.K.)
	St. Omer:	*Syrop*	(U.K.)
1965	Anthony:	*The Year in San Fernando*	(U.K.)
	Braithwaite:	*A Choice of Straws*	(U.K.)
	Clarke:	*Amongst Thistles and Thorns*	(U.K.)
	Harris:	*The Eye of the Scarecrow*	(U.K.)
	Kempadoo:	*Old Thom's Harvest*	(U.K.)
	Lovelace:	*While Gods are Falling*	(U.K.)
	Mittelholzer:	*The Aloneness of Mrs. Chatham*	(U.K.)
	Mittelholzer:	*The Jilkington Drama*	(U.K.)
	Nicole:	*The Amyot Crime*	(U.K.)
	Salkey:	*Earthquake*	(U.K.)
	Selvon:	*The Housing Lark*	(U.K.)
1966	Emtage:	*Brown Sugar*	(U.K.)
	Nicole:	*White Boy*	(U.K.)
	Palmer:	*The Cloud with the Silver Lining*	(U.K.)
	Rhys:	*Wide Sargasso Sea*	(U.K.)
	Salkey:	*Drought*	(U.K.)
	Salkey:	*The Shark Hunters*	(U.K.)
1967	Anthony:	*Green Days by the River*	(U.K.)
	Barrett:	*Song for Mumu*	(U.K.)
	Clarke:	*The Meeting Point*	(U.K.)
	Harris:	*The Waiting Room*	(U.K.)
	Hercules:	*I Want a Black Doll*	(U.K.)
	Naipaul:	*The Mimic Men*	(U.K.)
	Naipaul:	*A Flag on the Island*	(U.K.)
	Patterson:	*An Absence of Ruins*	(U.K.)
	Salkey:	*Riot*	(U.K.)

Secondary Bibliography

(Place of publication is London unless otherwise indicated)

i. *Books and Pamphlets*

Augier, Gordon, Hall and Reckord, *The Making of the West Indies*, 1960.

Bailey, Beryl L., *Jamaican Creole Syntax*, 1966.

Bennett, Louise, *Jamaica Labrish*, 1967.

Bone, Robert, *The Negro Novel in America*, New Haven, Yale University Press, 1958.

Bronz, Stephen H., *Roots of Negro Racial Consciousness*.

Cameron, N. E., *The Evolution of the Negro*, Printed by the Argosy Company Limited, Georgetown, Demerara, Vol. I 1929, Vol. II 1934.

Cassidy, F. G., *Jamaica Talk*, 1961.

Coulthard, G. R., *Race and Colour in Caribbean Literature*, 1962.

Cronon, E. D., *Black Moses*, University of Wisconsin Press, Madison, 1955.

Curtin, Philip, *Two Jamaicas*, Harvard University Press, 1955.

Daly, P. H., *West Indian Freedom and West Indian Literature*, The Daily Chronicle Press Ltd., Georgetown, 1951.

Davies, John, *The History of the Caribby Islands*, 1666.

Edwards, Bryan, *The History, Civil and Commercial, of the British West Indies*, 1798.

Fanon, Frantz, *The Wretched of the Earth*, 1965.

Froude, James Anthony, *The English in the West Indies*, 1887.

Gordon, Shirley C., *A Century of West Indian Education*, 1963.

Harris, Wilson, *Tradition, the Writer and Society*, 1967.

Jahn, Jahnheinz, *Muntu*, 1961.

    A Bibliography of Neo-African Literature, 1965.

James, C. L. R., *Party Politics in the West Indies*, Vedic Enterprises, San Juan, Trinidad, 1962.

    Beyond a Boundary, 1962.

Jones, Eldred, *Othello's Countrymen*, 1965.

Jones, Joseph, *Terranglia*, Twayne Publishers, New York, 1965.

Lamming, George, *The Pleasures of Exile*, 1960.

Legum, Colin, *Pan Africanism*, 1962.

Leslie, C., *A New and Exact Account of Jamaica*, 1740.

Long, Edward, *The History of Jamaica*, 1774.

McCullough, N. Verrle, *The Negro in English Literature*, 1962.

McKay, Claude, *A Long Way from Home*, Lee Furman Inc., New York, 1937.

    Harlem: Negro Metropolis, E. P. Dutton Inc., New York, 1940.

McLeod, A. L. (ed.), *The Commonwealth Pen*, Cornell University Press, New York, 1961.

Naipaul, V. S., *The Middle Passage*, 1962.

    An Area of Darkness, 1964.

Nugent, Lady Maria, *Lady Nugent's Journal*, 1839.

Padmore, George, *Pan Africanism or Communism?*, 1956.

Patterson, Orlando H., *The Sociology of Slavery*, 1967.

Press, John (ed.), *Commonwealth Literature*, 1965.

Ramsaran, J. A., *New Approaches to African Literature*, Ibadan University Press, 1965.

Roberts, W. Adolphe, *Six Great Jamaicans*, Pioneer Press, Kingston, Jamaica, 1952.

Rogers, Joel Augustus, *From Superman to Man*, A. Donohue and Co., Printers, 1917.

Russell, Thomas, *The Etymology of Jamaican Grammar*, 1868.

Salkey, Andrew (ed.), *West Indian Stories*, 1960.

    Caribbean Stories, 1965.

Smith, Raymond T., *British Guiana*, 1962.

Sypher, Wylie, *Guinea's Captive Kings*, University of North Carolina Press, 1942.

Secondary Bibliography

Thomas, J. J., *The Theory and Practice of Creole Grammar*, Port of Spain, 1869.
  Froudacity, 1889.
Trollope, Anthony, *The West Indies and the Spanish Main*, 1859.

ii. *Current West Indian Periodicals*

Bim, c/o The Editors, Woodville, Chelsea Rd., St. Michael, Barbados.
Caribbean Quarterly, Department of Extra Mural Studies, University of the West Indies, Mona, Jamaica.
Caribbean Studies, Institute of Caribbean Studies, University of Puerto Rico, Rio Pedras.
Jamaica Journal, Journal of the Institute of Jamaica, 12–15 East Street, Kingston, Jamaica.
New World Quarterly, New World Group Ltd., P.O. Box 221, Kingston 7, Jamaica.
Voices, The Bookshop, 2A Marli Street, Port of Spain, Trinidad.

iii. *Defunct Periodicals and Special Issues*

Focus, Kingston, Jamaica. Issues in 1943, 1948, 1956 and 1960.
Kyk-Over-Al, Georgetown, Guyana (1945–61).
Life and Letters, London. Especially, issues for February, March, April and November of 1948.
The Beacon, Port of Spain, Trinidad (1931–3).
The Tamarack Review, Toronto. Issue XIV, Winter 1961.

Index

Index

Index

Negro, The
Exotic writing in English about, 3 and 3 n. 1
In the nineteenth century
alienated middle class prefigured, 30
colonial office views on education of, 20
educated Negroes, 26
insecurity of the educated, 31
isolation of the educated, 30
secondary education of, 26–31
unable to offer lead, 30
Novel in America, The, 240
Racial Consciousness, Roots of, 244 n. 1, 250 n. 1
Pan-Negro movements in 20th century, 132–5
See also Africa, Négritude
Nicole, Christopher
Off White, 44, 45
Shadows in the Jungle, 164 n. 2
Nugent, Lady Maria
Lady Nugent's Journal, 86–7, 120

Ogden, C. K., 244
Ogilvie, W. G.
Cactus Village, 118, 119
Okara, Gabriel, 78, 81
The Voice, 78–80

Padmore, George
Pan-Africanism or Communism, 132 n. 5
Pankhurst, Sylvia, 244
Patterson, H. Orlando, 118, 127
The Children of Sisyphus, 129–31
The Sociology of Slavery, 118 n. 1
Periodicals
Beacon, The, 63–5
Bim, 72, 72 n. 2, 3, 208, 212
Cambridge Magazine, The, 244, 244 n. 3
Caribbean Quarterly, 73
Focus, 71–2
Jamaica Quarterly Journal, 35
Kyk-over-al, 71, 72 n. 3
Liberator, The, 243, 245, 246
Life and Letters, 73
Pearson's Magazine, 243
Transition, 80
Trinidad, 64
Worker's Dreadnought, 244, 244 n. 2

Ramsaran, J. A., 153

New Approaches to African Literature, 153 n. 1
Reading
attitudes to, illustrated, 25, 26
in nineteenth-century schools, 23, 24
Redcam, Tom [Thomas H. MacDermot], 3, 44, 51–55, 52 n. 1, 239, 241
Becka's Buckra Baby, 54
One Brown Girl And—, 44, 52–4
Reeves, William Conrad, 26 n. 1
Reid, V. S.
New Day, 99, 100, 101
The Leopard, 154–9
Report on the Rastafari Movement in Kingston, Jamaica, 127 n. 3
Rhys, Jean
Wide Sargasso Sea, 224, 230–6
Richards, I. A., 244
Roberts, W. Adolphe, 73
Six Great Jamaicans, 51, 56 n. 1
Rogers, J. A.
From Superman to Man, 240
Roy, Namba
Black Albino, 149–54, 172 n. 2
Russell, Thomas
The Etymology of Jamaican Grammar, 86, 91

Salkey, Andrew
A Quality of Violence, 129
West Indian Stories, 101 n. 1
Scott, Michael
Tom Cringle's Log, 87–8, 97
Selvon, Samuel, 73
A Brighter Sun, 61, 73, 98, 99, 105, 119
'Brackley and the Bed', 102
Ways of Sunlight, 102 n. 1
Senghor, Leopold Sedhar
and negritude, 133–4, 256
Seymour, A. J., 72
Slinger, Francisco [Sparrow], 114
Smith, M. G.
'West Indian Culture', 119 n. 1
Smith, Raymond T., 190 n. 1
British Guiana, 190 n. 1
Snod, E. [E. A. Dodd]
Maroon Medicine, 54
Spencer, John, 82

Thomas, J. J., 31
Froudacity, 26
Theory and Practice of Creole Grammar, 26

Index